CONTENTS

Boxes

Tables

Figures

The following symbols have been used throughout this volume:

. . . to indicate that data are not available;

— to indicate that the figure is zero or less than half the final digit shown, or that the item does not exist;

– between years or months (for example, 1997–99 or January–June) to indicate the years or months covered, including the beginning and ending years or months;

/ between years (for example, 1998/99) to indicate a fiscal or financial year.

"Billion" means a thousand million; "trillion" means a thousand billion.

"Basis points" refer to hundredths of 1 percentage point (for example, 25 basis points are equivalent to ¼ of 1 percentage point).

"n.a." means not applicable.

Minor discrepancies between constituent figures and totals are due to rounding.

As used in this volume the term "country" does not in all cases refer to a territorial entity that is a state as understood by international law and practice. As used here, the term also covers some territorial entities that are not states but for which statistical data are maintained on a separate and independent basis.

PREFACE

The *Global Financial Stability Report* (GFSR) assesses global financial market developments with a view to identifying systemic vulnerabilities. By calling attention to potential fault lines in the global financial system, the report seeks to play a role in preventing crises, thereby contributing to global financial stability and to sustained economic growth of the IMF's member countries.

The analysis in this report has been coordinated in the Monetary and Capital Markets Department (MCM) under the general direction of Jaime Caruana, Counsellor and Director. The project has been directed by Hung Q. Tran, Deputy Director; Peter Dattels and Laura Kodres, Division Chiefs; and L. Effie Psalida, Deputy Division Chief, all of MCM. The report benefited from comments and suggestions from Christopher Towe, Deputy Director, and Mahmood Pradhan, Assistant Director, both of MCM.

Primary contributors to this report also include Brian Bell, Sean Craig, Udaibir S. Das, John Kiff, Ulrich Klueh, Rebecca McCaughrin, Paul Mills, Christopher Morris, Shinobu Nakagawa, Mustafa Saiyid, Olaf Unteroberdoerster, and Christopher Walker. Other contributors include Roberto Benelli, Turgut Kisinbay, Annamaria Kokenyne, Gillian Nkhata, Seiichi Shimizu, Tao Sun, Leslie Teo, and Judit Vadasz. Professors Jon Danielsson and Badi Baltagi provided consultancy support. Martin Edmonds, Oksana Khadarina, Yoon Sook Kim, Ned Rumpeltin, and Kalin Tintchev provided analytical support. Shannon Bui, Norma Cayo, and Christy Gray were responsible for word processing. David Einhorn of the External Relations Department edited the manuscript and coordinated production of the publication.

This particular issue draws, in part, on a series of discussions with banks, securities firms, asset management companies, hedge funds, pension funds, credit rating agencies, financial consultants, and academic researchers, as well as regulatory and other public authorities in major financial centers and countries. The report reflects information available up to September 4, 2007.

The report benefited from comments and suggestions from staff in other IMF departments, as well as from Executive Directors following their discussion of the *Global Financial Stability Report* on September 14, 2007. However, the analysis and policy considerations are those of the contributing staff and should not be attributed to the Executive Directors, their national authorities, or the IMF.

EXECUTIVE SUMMARY

Since the April 2007 *Global Financial Stability Report* (GFSR), global financial stability has endured an important test. Credit and market risks have risen and markets have become more volatile. Markets are recognizing the extent to which credit discipline has deteriorated in recent years—most notably in the U.S. nonprime mortgage and leveraged loan markets, but also in other related credit markets. This has prompted a retrenchment from some risky assets and deleveraging, causing a widening of credit spreads in riskier asset classes and more volatile bond and equity markets. The absence of prices and secondary markets for some structured credit products, and concerns about the location and size of potential losses, has led to disruptions in some money markets and funding difficulties for a number of financial institutions, as some counterparties have been reluctant to extend credit to those thought to hold lower quality, illiquid assets. The resulting disruption has required extraordinary liquidity injections by a number of central banks to facilitate the orderly functioning of these markets.

The potential consequences of this episode should not be underestimated and the adjustment process is likely to be protracted. Credit conditions may not normalize soon, and some of the practices that have developed in the structured credit markets will have to change. At the same time, the global economy entered this turbulent period exhibiting solid growth, especially in emerging market countries. Systemically important financial institutions began this episode with adequate capital to manage the likely level of credit losses. So far, despite the significant ongoing correction in financial markets, global growth remains solid, though some slowdown could be expected. Downside risks have increased significantly and, even if those risks fail to materialize, the implications of this period of turbulence will be significant and far

reaching. Eventually, lessons for both the private sector and the regulatory and supervisory arenas will have to be drawn in order to strengthen the financial system against future strains.

The threat to financial stability increased as the uncertainty became manifest in the money markets that provide short-term financing (especially commercial paper markets). At the center of the turmoil is a funding mismatch whereby medium-term, illiquid, and hard-to-value assets, such as structured credit securities, were being funded by very short-term money market securities—often asset-backed commercial paper. The market illiquidity and the difficulty in valuing the complex, structured products held as assets has compounded the risks of the funding mismatch. Thus, while potentially helping protect the financial system from concentrations of credit risk in banks, the dispersal of structured credit products has substantially increased uncertainty about the extent of the risks and where they are ultimately held.

This funding mismatch was undertaken by a significant number of conduits and special purpose vehicles that had assumed they could hold their illiquid assets to maturity. Many have been associated with regulated banks, and to a large extent their funding strategies were backed by contingent liquidity lines from those banks. When doubts about the quality of some of the underlying assets emerged and the high ratings were perceived as less reliable, prices of the assets fell, the rollover of associated asset-backed commercial paper became very difficult, and funding began to be squeezed. As a consequence, what had been contingent, off-balance-sheet liabilities for regulated banks threatened to move "on balance sheet." The funding difficulties were first felt in Europe and, subsequently, in a number of other places. The rapid transmission of disturbances in one part of the financial system to other parts, sometimes through opaque and intertwined channels, has surprised both market participants and the official sector. The uncertainty about where off-balance-sheet bank exposures will materialize next has led to a tiering of interbank lending rates. Banks that are believed to either have structured credit product losses, or that need to satisfy contingent credit lines to their conduits or special purpose vehicles, face higher interbank rates. In some cases, the flows in the interbank market are stymied by some large banks' desire to hold onto liquidity in case they need to finance other activities, such as the large pipeline of leveraged buyouts scheduled for the remainder of the year. Overall, there has been a sharp rise in perceived counterparty risk, and a desire to keep the additional liquidity on hand, at least for now.

The April 2007 GFSR flagged the underlying causes of the current correction. The weakening of credit discipline and the potential complacency, which were highlighted in that edition, led to a buildup of credit risks in the U.S. mortgage market, leveraged buyout market, and some lending to emerging markets. The benign economic and financial conditions of recent years weakened incentives to conduct due diligence on borrowers and counterparties. Moreover the "originate and distribute" model used for credit products by many financial institutions meant that many such institutions could choose not to hold the credit risk they originated, reducing their incentives to monitor borrowers. Investors in the distributed securities may have relaxed their due diligence in assessing liquidity and leverage risks or chosen to rely excessively on ratings agencies to analyze risks in complex financial instruments. Stress in the U.S. housing market then weakened mortgage-backed securities, an important component of the global financial system. The resulting multiple credit downgrades of these securities by ratings agencies led to downward pressure on their prices and started to deepen the repricing episode that began some time ago.

Leverage has played a key role in amplifying the disturbances. The ease with which some

banks and other investment vehicles, including hedge funds, were able to borrow against difficult-to-price collateral traded in illiquid markets severely aggravated conditions when market liquidity evaporated, resulting in a process of forced deleveraging at "fire sale" prices and the failure of some funds. Institutions that have suffered the most have had strategies that were based on high levels of leverage and had assumed continued liquidity in secondary markets.

A long period of abnormally low market volatility likely exacerbated the episode. Risk premia in many markets had fallen to historically low levels as more and more investors bet on a continuation of the benign, low-volatility environment. Returns became more correlated. As markets fell, risk premia expanded quickly. Similar risk management techniques, common investors, and similar positions may have exacerbated the situation. Losses were magnified as many market participants tried to exit similar positions simultaneously.

Chapter 1 of this report summarizes the overall assessment of stability using the global financial stability map introduced in the April 2007 GFSR. Extending the work in the last GFSR, the chapter focuses on the fallout from weakening credit discipline in the U.S. nonprime mortgage market and the leveraged buyout market (including the market turbulence of August 2007, which resulted in a drying up of term lending in money markets), and details linkages across markets. The chapter explains how volatility has been amplified by high leverage and how risks are transmitted between institutions. It gathers evidence on where the risks now reside, and what might be the impact on banks, corporations, and households as losses surface.

The chapter also examines the global aspects of the lack of credit discipline. Overall, emerging market risks remain finely balanced, with many countries benefiting from improved macroeconomic fundamentals and better policymaking frameworks. External sovereign debt has been reduced and debt structures are better managed. Nonetheless, offsetting these positive aspects, credit growth has been rapid in a number of emerging markets, with some banks (both domestic and foreign) borrowing abroad in foreign currency to lend domestically, taking on indirect credit risks through their foreign-currency-denominated loans. In addition, the low yields in mature markets and high risk appetite have allowed emerging market corporates easy access to foreign capital, including through synthetic and structured products to generate higher yields.

Chapter 1 also looks at some of the routes taken by foreign investors to gain access to certain emerging markets where there are capital account restrictions. The chapter cautions that some emerging markets are vulnerable to a pullback in the availability of capital, and that this pullback could continue even after the mature market funding difficulties subside. To understand in greater depth the stability implications of foreign participation in local emerging markets, the chapter provides empirical work on foreign equity flows into several different emerging markets in order to distinguish between institutional investors and others. Lastly, the chapter reviews the growth in the activities of hedge funds in emerging markets.

Chapter 1 also includes an annex exploring some aspects of sovereign wealth funds (SWFs). The growth of these entities can be seen as the result of the strong accumulation of foreign assets by the official sector—in part, due to high natural resources prices or prompted by large balance of payments surpluses and capital inflows. SWFs are becoming an important investor group, and questions have been raised about the impact of their cross-border asset allocations. The annex attempts to clarify some of the discussion surrounding their structures and goals by providing a taxonomy of sovereign wealth funds and their asset allocation frameworks.

Although the recent episode of turbulence is ongoing, and it is too early to make definitive conclusions, it is already clear from the analysis in Chapter 1 that several areas will require increased attention. The first is the important role of uncertainty and lack of information. Accurate and timely information about underly-

ing risks are critical components in the market's ability to differentiate and properly price risk. This would include both qualitative and quantitative information about how risks are managed, valued, and accounted for, especially in areas of risk transfer. Greater transparency is also needed on links between systemically important financial institutions and some of their off-balance-sheet vehicles. Only by disclosing fully their interrelationships with asset managers, conduits, and special purpose entities will investors be able to assess the true creditworthiness of the institutions with which they deal. However, given the volume and complexity of the information that could potentially be provided, and the cost of providing it, it will be important to carefully consider the appropriate amount and type of disclosure needed to alleviate the problems evident in this episode.

Second, while securitization, and financial innovation more generally, through enhanced risk distribution have made markets more efficient, there is a need to understand how they may have contributed to the current situation. In particular, it is important to consider the extent to which the incentive structure, in the context of very benign times, may have diluted the incentives for originating lenders to monitor risk. In the U.S. mortgage market, the public sector costs associated with the lack of supervisory oversight of some mortgage originators will need to be balanced against the improved access to credit that some households received. Generally, the relationship between checks and balances throughout the supply chain of structured products may require some rethinking.

Third, there is a need to examine risk analysis of credit derivatives and structured products and the role of ratings agencies. Ratings and ratings agencies will continue to be a fundamental component in the functioning of financial markets. However, there is some concern about the rating methodology of complex products, particularly when securities, with very different structures, assumptions, and liquidity characteristics, receive the same ratings. Ratings of complex structured products may have become too connected to facilitating origination. In periods of turbulence, the rapid downgrades then raise questions about the reliability of these ratings and their usefulness for the investors. We repeat the call from the April 2006 GFSR for a more differentiated scale of ratings for structured products. Investors also have an obligation and responsibility to understand the dynamics and liquidity risks associated with the products they buy—they wrongly assumed that a low probability of default meant a low likelihood of losses from market movements. In the case of complex structured credit products, investors need to look behind the ratings—they should not assume that the simple letter ratings provided by ratings agencies show equivalent risks as those for other asset classes. Differentiation and transparency in the underlying assumptions and construction of the various structures would facilitate appropriate due diligence by investors.

Fourth, the valuation of complex products in the context of a market where liquidity is insufficient to provide reliable market prices requires more consideration. When purchasing complex products, investors will need to consider the associated liquidity aspects and include an appropriate liquidity risk "premium" as part of the price. Financial institutions holding such securities as collateral will need to assign a "haircut" that factors in liquidity characteristics. Importantly, financial institutions need to make sure that they have robust funding strategies appropriately suited for their business model and that such funding strategies can accommodate stressful conditions. More generally, the rapid growth of some illiquid instruments raises questions about whether originators of such securities should be expected to provide secondary markets to contribute to the valuation process.

Fifth, the relevant perimeter of risk consolidation for banks has proved to be larger than the usual accounting or legal perimeters. There are two notable examples: (1) reputational risk may force banks to internalize losses of legally independent entities; and (2) new instruments or structures may mask off-balance-sheet or contingent liabilities. The result is that risks that appear to have been distributed may yet return in various forms to the banks that distributed them. The relevant perimeter is not only an issue for supervisors, but also for the financial institutions themselves—their risk management systems, audit processes and internal oversight and governance structures.

Policymakers now face a delicate balancing act. They must establish frameworks that encourage investors to maintain high credit standards and strengthen risk management systems in good times as well as bad. Actions should only be undertaken if the public policy benefits outweigh the costs, taking care to thoroughly examine possible unintended consequences. In general, the current regulatory systems have proven resilient to date, and regulators must be continually mindful that households and firms have benefited greatly from the financial innovation and solid growth and financial stability of recent years.

* * *

Chapters 2 and 3 examine two respective issues that are the outcome of the lengthy period of low mature market yields and unusually low financial market volatility over the last several years. Chapter 2 examines the extent to which market risk management methods may have encouraged more risk-taking during this relatively benign period, perhaps resulting in a more rapid withdrawal from risky assets than would otherwise be the case as conditions change. In light of rapid capital flows to emerging market countries, Chapter 3 investigates how countries can best deal with capital flow volatility in the medium term by improving the depth, liquidity, and institutional quality of their domestic financial markets.

Chapter 2 specifically examines market risk management techniques to see whether their common usage, while seemingly prudent for individual institutions, could exacerbate market volatility during periods of stressful market conditions. The question is examined in two ways. The first is by using a stylized version of the most common market risk model, value-at-risk (VaR), which is the estimated loss a firm is unlikely to exceed at a given degree of confidence. For instance, a firm's one-day estimated VaR of $10 million at a confidence level of 95 percent implies that the firm would expect to lose more than $10 million on its portfolio only five days out of 100. A stylized model is used to demonstrate how VaR declines during a lower volatility environment, but rises when higher volatility returns. The stylized portfolios are then "stressed" by examining how VaR would respond with data from previous episodes of financial market turbulence. Lastly, simulations are conducted in which several firms are hypothesized to use the same, or slightly different, VaR models, also during periods of stress. Results suggest that such firms, acting according to their own models to contain risks, could collectively make markets more volatile, especially if risk aversion is low. The simulations also show, however, that a greater diversity of models would help to reduce such potential instability.

Chapter 2 also examines risk management procedures of investment banks and hedge funds to see whether they conform to the preconditions necessary to amplify market volatility in practice. While all firms maintain that they would not rigidly follow their VaR models in stressful circumstances, there are a number of ways in which VaR metrics, or related risk limits, could act to amplify market volatility. In fact, recent turbulence suggests some of these techniques may be contributing to the current turbulent conditions to some degree. Overall, VaR and other risk management techniques will encourage financial institutions to respond more rapidly to changes in risk. Normally, this will facilitate early detection and prompt correction of risks deemed excessive by the institution. However, the use of similar techniques across institutions during periods of stress can lead to larger price movements than would occur if different techniques were used. It is thus worthwhile for regulators and supervisors to acknowledge the benefits of discretion when implementing risk management systems (including new ways to incorporate credit and liquidity risks) and to promote the use of "stress testing"—encouraging all firms to consider their interactive effects during periods of stress, as some do already. A diversity of investment positions and types of participants is even more important to help stabilize markets. Regulators and supervisors would also do well to consider more concretely than they do now how they would respond to the amplifying effects when individual firms naturally attempt to protect their firm's franchise value.

Chapter 3 empirically analyzes a common view—whether, in addition to strong macroeconomic fundamentals, a well-functioning domestic financial market encourages capital inflows and reduces their volatility over the medium term. A panel estimation technique is used to examine the factors that determine the volume and volatility of annual capital inflows for a sample of developed and emerging market economies from 1977 to 2006. The factors include financial variables such as equity market depth and liquidity and financial openness, and a shorter sample also includes institutional quality variables such as corporate governance quality and accounting standards. The results of the empirical work show that the liquidity of equity markets and financial openness positively influence the level of capital inflows. Moreover, the panel estimations show that more financial openness reduces the volatility of inflows. Separately, the chapter shows that improvements in a broad set of institutional quality variables are correlated with lower volatility.

Chapter 3 also examines how five emerging market countries have coped with the recent rise in capital inflows and discusses some of their policy options. These five country examples reveal the difficulty of finding a common set of financial policies that help deal with capital inflows. Generally, policies that encourage financial market development over the medium term—including a well-regulated system, better transparency and broader institutional quality, and improved risk management for financial institutions—will likely cushion the financial system from the potentially destabilizing effects of abrupt capital outflows better than will short-term fixes.

CHAPTER 1

ASSESSING RISKS TO GLOBAL FINANCIAL STABILITY

Financial risks have increased and underlying conditions have worsened since the April 2007 Global Financial Stability Report (GFSR). The period ahead may be difficult, as bouts of turbulence are likely to recur and the adjustment process will take some time. Uncertainty about the final size of losses, and when and where they will be revealed, will likely continue to keep market sentiment and conditions unsettled in the near term. This chapter outlines a number of the causes and consequences of the recent episode of turmoil and offers some initial thoughts on possible responses that the private and public sectors might consider to help improve global financial resilience.

Following an extended period of exceptionally favorable financial market conditions, international markets have entered a difficult period. The current episode of turbulence represents the first significant test of several categories of innovative financial instruments used to distribute credit risks broadly. Although the dislocations, especially to short-term funding markets, have been large and in some cases unexpected, the event hit during a period of above-average global growth. Credit repricing and the constriction of liquidity experienced to date will likely slow the global expansion. Systemically important financial institutions began this episode with more than adequate capital to absorb the likely level of credit losses. Corporations have, for the most part, been able to secure the financing they need to maintain their operations. However, the adjustment period is continuing, and if the intermediation process stalls and financial conditions deteriorate further, the global financial sector and real economy could experience more serious negative repercussions.

This chapter first summarizes our overall assessment of global financial stability using

the global financial stability map introduced in the April 2007 GFSR (IMF, 2007a). Although the stability map treats the various risk factors and underlying conditions as separate so as to facilitate their formal analysis, the latest episode highlights their interrelatedness in practice—with liquidity risks, both market and funding liquidity, at the forefront of the current episode of turbulence. What began as a deterioration in credit quality altered the market liquidity of a number of structured credit products. Market illiquidity, in turn, produced uncertainty about those products' valuations, which translated into a disruption in the underlying funding markets. Thus, monetary and financial conditions, as well as the risk appetite of market participants, have been adversely affected.

This chapter delves into some of the relevant areas in more detail, examining how weakening credit discipline in the U.S. mortgage market—especially the subprime market—and the overly rapid expansion of the leveraged buyout market have extended to the broader structured finance sector. The ensuing disruptions in the short-term funding markets are then examined. Global linkages are addressed with particular attention to the impact that investment flows to emerging markets have on financial stability. Lastly, the chapter highlights a number of conclusions that emerge from the analysis.

Note: This chapter was written by a team led by Peter Dattels and comprising Brian Bell, Sean Craig, John Kiff, Rebecca McCaughrin, Christopher Morris, Mustafa Saiyid, Olaf Unteroberdoerster, and Christopher Walker.

Global Financial Stability Map

The global financial stability map (Figure 1.1) presents an overall assessment of how changes in underlying conditions and risk factors are expected to bear on global financial stability in the period ahead.[1]

Credit risks have increased significantly.

The largest increase in risks is represented by an increase in our assessment of *credit risks*.[2] The April 2007 GFSR highlighted rising credit risk in U.S. mortgage-related instruments, a loosening of credit standards across a range of markets, and risks of spillovers to other credit markets. Since then, these credit risks have materialized and intensified, with ratings agencies downgrading significant amounts of mortgage-related securities, and spreads on mortgage-related securities widening (Figure 1.2). These risks have been exacerbated by signs of similar credit indiscipline in the leveraged buyout (LBO) sector. Through mid-2007, there had been a marked rise in covenant-lite loans, less creditworthy deals, leverage, and price multiples on acquisitions. Moreover, now that ratings agencies are revising their model assumptions for structured products collateralized by mortgages, uncertainty has risen about the ratings of the broader structured credit market, including collateralized loan obligations (CLOs) that distribute leveraged loan financing to institutions. Reflecting the broader repricing of credit risk, spreads on high-yield corporate debt have widened from the tight levels reached earlier in the year (Figure 1.3). Although aggregate corporate leverage remains relatively low, its increase over the past year, particularly for those entities that

Figure 1.1. Global Financial Stability Map

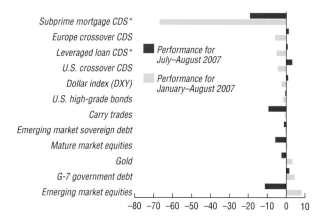

Risks

—— April 2007 GFSR

—— Current (October 2007)

Emerging market risks

Credit risks

Macroeconomic risks

Market and liquidity risks

Monetary and financial

Risk appetite

Conditions

Source: IMF staff estimates.
Note: Closer to center signifies less risk or tighter conditions.

Figure 1.2. Selected Asset Class Returns
(In percent)

Subprime mortgage CDS*
Europe crossover CDS
Leveraged loan CDS*
U.S. crossover CDS
Dollar index (DXY)
U.S. high-grade bonds
Carry trades
Emerging market sovereign debt
Mature market equities
Gold
G-7 government debt
Emerging market equities

■ Performance for July–August 2007

■ Performance for January–August 2007

−80 −70 −60 −50 −40 −30 −20 −10 0 10

Sources: Bloomberg L.P.; JPMorgan Chase & Co.; Merrill Lynch; and IMF staff estimates.
Note: DXY is a weighted average of the dollar exchange rate vis-à-vis six major world currencies. CDS = credit default swaps; crossover CDS indices consist of mostly speculative grade and some higher yielding investment grade entities.
*From inception date of index.

---

[1]Annex 1.1 details how indicators that compose the rays of the map are measured and interpreted. The map provides a schematic presentation that incorporates a degree of judgment, serving as a starting point for further analysis. See the April 2007 GFSR for a fuller discussion of indicators and their placement in the map.

[2]Credit risks measure changes in credit quality that have the potential for creating losses resulting in stress in systemically important financial institutions.

have been the subject of buyouts, has heightened vulnerabilities, especially as financial, and possibly economic, conditions turn less benign.

Meanwhile, mature market financial system default risk, as reflected in credit derivatives referencing large complex financial institutions (LCFIs), has risen sharply (Figure 1.4).[3] The rise was driven mainly by large U.S. investment banks that are especially exposed to the nonprime mortgage and leveraged loan markets. The widening in interest rate swaps and credit default swaps (CDS) referencing some investment banks illustrates market concerns of deeper stress for financial institutions. While potential losses appear to be manageable and banks appear well capitalized to weather more severe stress, there is at present considerable uncertainty regarding the magnitude and distribution of losses stemming from the correction in credit markets, and their possible impact on broader financial stability.

Uncertainty regarding overall losses and exposure has raised market and liquidity risks, with potentially broader implications for financial institutions.

Reflecting the potential rise in market losses, we have raised our assessment of *market and liquidity risks*.[4] Uncertainty regarding ultimate losses has increased market risks associated with a wide range of assets, beyond structured credit products. In the face of this uncertainty and higher volatility, lenders have raised margins, even for highly rated borrowers, and lowered the mark-to-market value of collateral. Other indicators also suggest that market risks have risen. For instance, the correlation of returns

Figure 1.3. U.S. High-Yield Corporate Bond Spreads Index

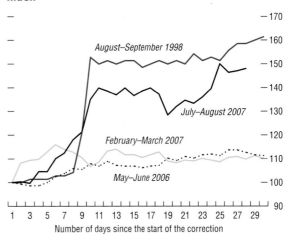

Sources: Merrill Lynch; and IMF staff estimates.
Note: Spreads are normalized to 100 at the beginning of the crisis.

[3]This issue of the GFSR continues to use credit derivatives-based credit risk indicators to review the evolution of market perceptions of default risk in mature market financial systems. The mature market credit risk indicators measure the probability of multiple defaults within three groups of 11 financial institutions, implied from the prices of credit default swaps (IMF, 2005, Chapter II). The three groups are LCFIs, commercial banks, and insurance companies.

[4]Market and liquidity indicators measure the potential for instability in pricing risks that could result in broader spillovers and/or mark-to-market losses.

Figure 1.4. Probability of Multiple Defaults in Select Portfolios
(In percent)

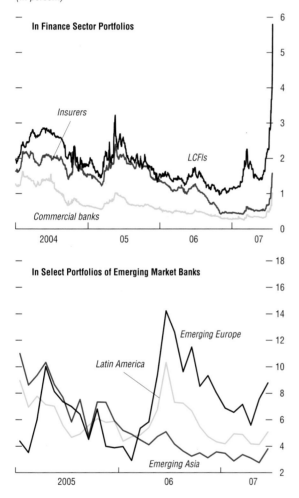

Sources: Bloomberg L.P.; and IMF staff estimates.
Note: LCFIs = large complex financial institutions.

across asset classes has continued to rise, eroding the benefits of portfolio diversification, while speculative positioning in futures markets has become increasingly concentrated. At the same time, the reduction in market liquidity is evident in a range of indicators, including wider bid-ask spreads, reduced turnover volume, and higher financing rates across a range of typically liquid markets.

The overall deterioration in market and liquidity risks has been partially mitigated by the recent increase in risk premia. Realized and implied volatility has risen across fixed income and equities. There has been an upward shift in the entire swaption volatility curve, suggesting that the rise in risk premia may last longer.

Risk appetite generally declined, albeit from a high level.

As investors have become more generally discriminating across the credit spectrum, they have also become more risk averse. From the elevated levels at the time of the April 2007 GFSR, we have reduced our indicator of *risk appetite*, bringing the overall level of risk appetite to neutral. Although recent turbulence has been associated with increased market volatility and an unwinding of positions predicated on a low volatility environment, some broad global indicators still signal a willingness to establish or extend positions in risky assets. We expect continued prospects for global expansion to underpin investor attitudes toward risk.

Emerging market risks are balanced.

Our overall assessment of *emerging market risks* represents a delicate balance between slightly lower sovereign risks amid a positive economic background, and rising risks in some economies experiencing rapid credit growth and increasing reliance on flows from international capital markets, with the offsetting pressures canceling each other out in the overall assessment. Reflecting a weakening in credit discipline that has emerged along with the growth in credit, private sector borrowers in certain emerging markets are adopting relatively risky strategies to raise financing, often embedding exchange rate risk or options and thus increasing their exposure to volatility. Most noticeably, in some countries in Eastern Europe and Central Asia, banks are increasingly using capital market financing to help finance credit growth. Nevertheless, generally benign emerging market banking system default risk indicators continue to reflect market perceptions of healthy capitalization and profitability, as well as diverse earnings sources and sound asset quality (Figure 1.4).[5] These trends warrant increased surveillance, as circumstances vary considerably across countries. Authorities in some emerging markets need to ensure that vulnerabilities do not build to more systemic levels. Across all emerging market countries, policies that support continued resilience should help, as global market conditions are likely to remain volatile.

Financial and monetary conditions have tightened...

Since the April 2007 GFSR, policy rates have risen further across a number of countries, while the ongoing repricing in credit markets has tightened financing conditions for some segments—specifically, for less creditworthy U.S. households seeking mortgage credit and for highly leveraged corporate borrowers. Reflecting these developments and their likely continuation, we have shifted our assessment of *monetary and financial conditions* to signify slightly tighter conditions.

...posing potential downside risks to the macroeconomy.

Tighter monetary and credit conditions could reduce economic activity through a few channels. First, a tightening of the supply of credit to

weaker household borrowers could exacerbate the downturn in the U.S. housing market. Second, falling equity prices could reduce spending through the wealth effect and a weakening of consumer sentiment. Third, capital spending could be curtailed owing to a higher cost of capital for the corporate sector. Last, and perhaps most importantly, the dislocations in credit and funding markets during the period of market turbulence could restrict the overall provision and channeling of credit.

The chances of a more severe tightening of credit conditions cannot be dismissed. Such a tightening could have significant global macroeconomic consequences, with the incidence of such tightening falling most heavily on more marginally creditworthy borrowers. For this reason, the United States may experience a more significant impact given the importance, for instance, of U.S. high-yield corporates as recipients of credit. By August, debt issuance by high-yield corporates and issuance of asset-backed securities (ABS) and collateralized loan obligations had slowed sharply (Figure 1.5). By contrast, high-grade issuance in the month of August rebounded. To some extent, the economic impact of any reduction in borrowing on U.S. capital investment spending may be muted, given that recent borrowing has been focused more on increasing leverage in the capital structure (through share buybacks and LBOs) than on business investment. In Europe, where there is greater reliance on bank lending, debt issuance has been less affected than in the United States. The LBO boom was less advanced in continental Europe than in the United States, so any slowing of buyout activity will have a more modest impact. However, European banks appear to have greater contingent exposures to asset-backed commercial paper (ABCP), suggesting one channel whereby European banks may have to tighten credit conditions more than their U.S. counterparts. Given all these considerations, it is unclear at this point what are the prospects for tightening credit conditions, and the consequent impact, in the United States versus Europe.

[5]This issue of the GFSR introduces a set of equity market-based credit risk indicators to review the evolution of market perceptions of default risk in emerging market financial systems. The emerging market credit risk indicators measure the probability of multiple defaults within three groups of five banks, implied by Moody's KMV Expected Default Frequencies (EDFs™). EDFs™ are constructed using balance sheet and equity price data using a Merton-type structural model for estimating the probability of default (Kealhofer, 2003). The three geographic groupings are emerging Asia, emerging Europe, and Latin America.

With respect to the impact of tighter U.S. mortgage credit, although mortgage financing flows to the nonprime segment have slowed and tighter lending standards are likely to restrain housing activity further, strong household income growth, a high ratio of net worth to disposable income, and low unemployment should help households absorb some of the impact of the declines in house prices.[6]

Despite the continued strength of emerging market economies, global macroeconomic risks have generally increased.

This view is broadly consistent with the current baseline scenario in the October 2007 *World Economic Outlook,* which continues to forecast solid global growth with mostly limited inflationary pressures (IMF, 2007b). The downside risks to the baseline scenario are mainly related to the knock-on effects of potentially weaker U.S. domestic demand due to the changes in financial risks and market conditions discussed above, and secondarily, to a potential spike in global inflation, which would be lessened under a scenario of slower global growth. A disorderly unwinding of global imbalances is also still a risk, particularly if foreign investors' preferences for U.S. assets were to diminish as a result of the turmoil in financial markets. Alternatively, slower U.S. growth and a depreciation of the dollar would help to lower the U.S. current account deficit, reducing the amount of financing needed. These risks have increased since earlier in the year, prompting a slight increase

Figure 1.5. Gross Debt Issuance by Sector
(In billions of U.S. dollars)

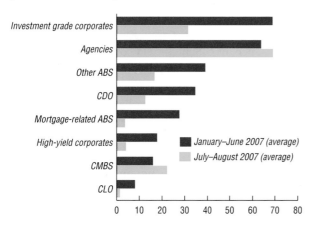

Sources: Bloomberg L.P.; Citigroup; and JPMorgan Chase & Co.
Note: ABS = asset-backed security; CDO = collateralized debt obligation; CMBS = commercial mortgage-backed security; CLO = collateralized loan obligation.

[6]Partly as a result of rising house prices, the ratio of net worth to disposable income rose to around 5¾ times by end-2006. A 10 percent fall in house prices, if that were to occur, would reduce household assets by around 3 percent and lower the ratio of net worth to disposable income to about 5½ times—roughly where it was in 2004. Although household leverage would increase further, in aggregate, declines on this scale appear manageable. However, the minority of borrowers who are overextended and lack home equity accumulation would undoubtedly face financial pain. Mortgage debt as a proportion of total assets, as well as the debt service burden, have both been on a steady upward path in recent years as households extracted equity from their homes, and their "leverage" rose (net worth to assets fell).

in our assessment of *macroeconomic risks.* By contrast, the continued strong performance of emerging market economies provides the potential for further upward surprises to growth.

Credit Indiscipline in Mature Markets

The U.S. nonprime mortgage market has experienced significant stress, with further deterioration likely.[7]

Since the April 2007 GFSR, the U.S. nonprime mortgage market has continued to suffer from rising delinquencies on principal and interest payments.[8] As detailed in that report, the deterioration reflects a combination of lax underwriting standards, "risk layering," and adverse trends in employment and income in certain regions.[9] Delinquencies on the 2006 vintage of subprime loans have climbed above 13 percent of the original balance, while alt-A loan delinquencies have also risen (Figure 1.6). Subprime delinquencies on the 2006 vintage have exceeded delinquencies on loans originated in 2000 at comparable seasoning (loan age)—the worst performing vintage in the recent past—and are expected to rise further if the historical pattern holds.[10] Loans originated in 2007 do not have sufficient

---

[7]Nonprime refers primarily to subprime and alternative-A (alt-A) mortgages. Subprime loans are typically made to borrowers with one or more of the following characteristics: weak credit histories that include payment delinquencies and bankruptcies; reduced repayment capacity as measured by credit scores or debt-to-income ratios; or incomplete credit histories. Alt-A mortgages, though of higher quality than subprime mortgages, are considered lower credit quality than prime mortgages due to one or more nonstandard features related to the borrower, property, or loan.

[8]Other measures of mortgage credit show a similar deterioration, including early payment defaults (mortgage loans that are more than 30 days delinquent within six months of the start of the mortgage) and foreclosures.

[9]"Risk layering" refers to the practice whereby mortgage lenders combine nontraditional mortgages with weaker credit controls, for instance, by accepting high combined loan-to-value ratios, reduced documentation, and little or no downpayment.

[10]Delinquencies tend to peak roughly at 24 to 30 months after origination. Some market participants estimate that subprime delinquencies on the 2006 vintage will peak at 20 to 25 percent of the original balance during 2008.

Figure 1.6. Nonprime 60-Day Delinquencies by Mortgage Vintage Year
(In percent of original balance)

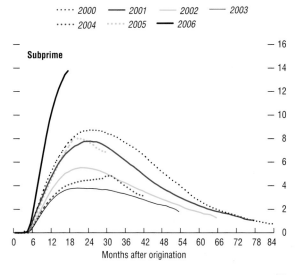

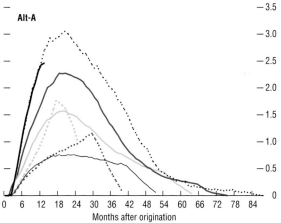

Sources: Merrill Lynch; and Intex.

Figure 1.7. Monthly Mortgage Rate Resets
(First reset in billions of U.S. dollars)

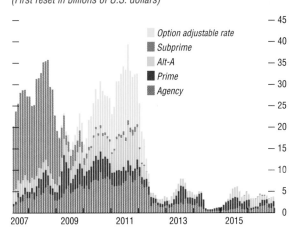

Source: Credit Suisse.

Figure 1.8. Rising Number of Downgrades of Mortgage-Related Products

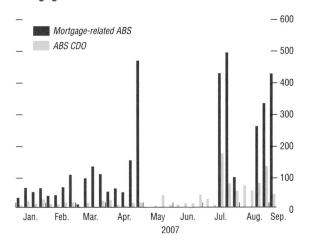

Sources: Bloomberg L.P.; and IMF staff estimates.
Note: ABS = asset-backed security; CDO = collateralized debt obligation.

seasoning to gauge overall performance, but the loan attributes are similar to those issued on loans in 2006. Thus, some of the same risk layering characteristics endemic to the 2006 vintage appear to have persisted at least through the first half of 2007, despite reportedly tighter underwriting standards.[11]

Regardless of whether collateral quality improves, the effects of previous excesses are likely to continue at least through 2008, as low introductory "teaser" rates on adjustable-rate mortgages (ARMs) reset to higher rates, and as mortgages start to amortize (Figure 1.7).[12] Unlike previous years, borrowers experiencing payment difficulties are expected to have fewer refinancing options, since falling house prices reduce the amount of homeowner equity, while tighter lending standards limit the range of mortgages available to nonprime borrowers.

A broad reevaluation by ratings agencies triggered a wave of downgrades in mid-2007.

Following the deterioration in certain subprime and alt-A loans, ratings agencies downgraded an unprecedented amount of ABS collateralized by subprime mortgages, resulting in subsequent downgrades in collateralized debt obligations (CDOs) that use lower-rated ABS tranches as collateral (Figure 1.8).[13] The majority of securities were downgraded three to four notches, mostly from BBB to BB–. Some

[11]For instance, the combined loan-to-value ratios and credit scores on nonprime mortgages originated during the first half of 2007 were little changed relative to loans originated in 2006, and the percentage of loans with second liens actually increased. However, the average credit support required by ratings agencies on the securitized loans also increased, to account for the underlying poorer collateral quality. Reflecting more restrictive lending activity, the Federal Reserve Board's Senior Loan Officer Survey shows that the percentage of banks reporting tighter lending standards for residential mortgages rose during the first half of 2007 to the highest level observed since the first half of 1991 (Federal Reserve Board, 2007).

[12]Interest-only ARMs often include negative amortization options that expose borrowers to potentially large upward adjustments in loan payments, typically two to three years after origination.

[13]See the April 2007 GFSR for a discussion on subprime mortgage securitization (IMF, 2007a).

AAA-rated tranches were downgraded multiple notches as well. Market participants expect further downgrades as the underlying loans continue to age, resets take effect, and delinquencies convert to foreclosures.

The ratings agencies cited various factors that contributed to the weaker-than-expected performance of mortgage loans, especially those issued in recent years, and noted, in particular, the impact of risk layering and poor data quality. These problems may have been compounded by a high incidence of fraud, resulting at least in part from limited borrower income documentation, and aggressive lending practices, such as offering short-term, below-market interest rates so as to qualify borrowers.

In response, the ratings agencies revised their methodologies to include higher loss severity assumptions, more severe stress tests, and increased monitoring of fraud prevention by lenders, thus effectively increasing the default risk of ABS and ABS CDOs. The agencies now estimate that home prices will fall more significantly than previously anticipated. Higher estimates of the magnitude of home price declines suggest lower recovery and higher losses from foreclosures. The agencies are also increasing loss estimates on loans that are not yet delinquent and are assuming lower prepayments from underlying mortgage loans, and therefore lower protection for subordinated securities.

Even with these changes, there remain broader problems with the structured credit product rating methodologies and processes.

First, structured credit products are likely to suffer more severe, multiple-notch downgrades relative to the typically smoother downgrade paths of corporate bonds, which calls into question the use of corporate bond rating scales.[14]

Second, the assumptions regarding the default correlations on mortgages in the ABS and CDO collateral pools can significantly affect their value.[15] The higher the correlation, the more likely defaults are to impact senior tranches, so if the correlation assumption is too low, the AAA and AA tranches could be overrated. While ratings agencies typically assume higher correlations for subprime mortgages than for other typical CDO assets (e.g., corporate bonds and loans), some analysts question whether they are high enough. Little empirical work has been done on this issue, largely because the market is too young to provide sufficient data.

Third, in the case of ABS CDOs, the ratings agencies assess credit risk based on default probabilities and loss severities associated with the rated ABS rather than the underlying mortgages. Thus, the CDO rating reaction to deteriorating underlying mortgage performance may be delayed by the need to await the downgrades of the component ABS and an analysis of the CDOs' often complex cash flow dynamics.

Finally, credit ratings evaluate only default risk, and not market or liquidity risks, and this seems to have been underappreciated by many investors.

Loss estimates are highly uncertain.

Even before the series of ratings downgrades occurred, market participants began to increase their expectations for nonprime mortgage-related losses. This was reflected in a pronounced widening in cash and CDS spreads on ABS and CDOs backed by recently originated subprime mortgages, beginning in early 2007. Spreads have since widened across the capital structure, especially on lower-rated ABS and ABS CDO tranches, but also on AAA-rated senior tranches (Figure 1.9). Implied losses based on these spreads total roughly $200 billion, exceeding the high end of estimated realized losses by roughly $30 billion—an indication that market uncertainty and liquidity concerns may have pushed down prices further than warranted by fundamentals (Box 1.1). While many structured

---

[14]See Violi (2004) for an analysis of structured credit product credit rating migration risk, and Fender and Mitchell (2005) for a discussion of how CDO structural risk increases the potential for multi-notch downgrades.

[15]Default correlation measures the extent to which defaults are expected to occur in clusters.

credit products were bought under the assumption that they would be held to maturity, those market participants who mark their securities to market have been (and will continue to be) forced to recognize much higher losses than those who do not mark their portfolios to market. So far, actual cash flow losses have been relatively small, suggesting that many highly rated structured credit products may have limited losses if held to maturity.

Losses across the mortgage supply chain—who holds the risk?

Mark-to-market losses and uncertainty about future cash flow losses have started to impact various segments of the mortgage supply chain. The peripheries of the supply chain have been most visibly affected, including, in particular, a number of poorly capitalized specialty finance companies.[16] While there has been limited impact on mortgage servicers thus far, their ability to manage losses is likely to be tested as delinquencies continue to rise.

Financial intermediaries active in the mortgage market have complex webs of exposure, but the largest such institutions—the core commercial and investment banking groups—are viewed by IMF staff and private sector analysts as sufficiently capitalized, diversified, and profitable to absorb direct losses (Figure 1.10).[17] While total exposures are difficult to gauge,

---

[16]Originators that have either consolidated or exited the industry through bankruptcy represent roughly 40 percent of the subprime market.

[17]The large capital buffers built up in recent years are expected to help insulate core U.S. commercial and investment banks. By way of illustration, if losses from nonprime mortgages rise to $200 billion and these banks were exposed to one-quarter of that amount, then losses would represent less than one-twentieth of their capital and the ratio of their regulatory capital to risk-weighted assets (CRAR) would drop to 12.5 percent from the current 13 percent. If, in addition, banks were forced to provision for an average 5 percent markdown on all the roughly $300 billion of leveraged loans in the pipeline, their CRARs would edge down to 12.4 percent, still higher than it was in 2000, and well above its longer term average level. The impact on European and Asian banks would likely be less due to their lower exposures to ABS and ABS CDOs.

Figure 1.9. Representative Spreads of Mortgage-Backed ABS and ABS CDOs
(In basis points)

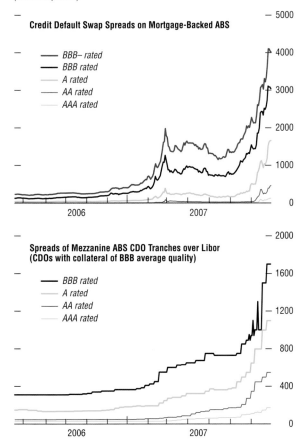

Source: JPMorgan Chase & Co.
Note: ABS = asset-backed security; CDO = collateralized debt obligation.

Figure 1.10. Mortgage Market Flows and Risk Exposures

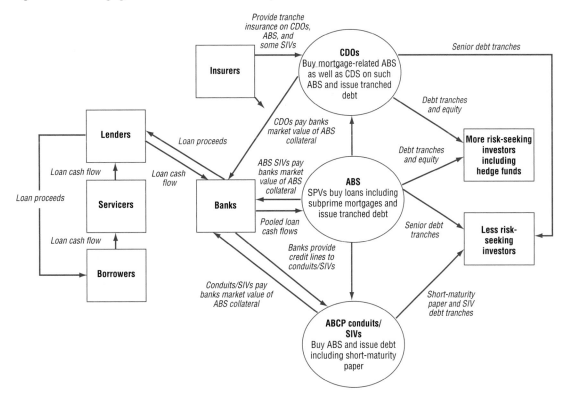

Source: IMF staff estimates.
Note: ABS = asset-backed security; ABCP = asset-backed commercial paper; CDO = collateralized debt obligation; CDS = credit default swap; SIV = structured investment vehicle; SPV = special purpose vehicle.

aggregate real estate–related losses on commercial banks' loan books have been minor thus far, with net chargeoffs on residential loans totaling a mere 0.04 percent of Tier 1 capital. Going forward, analysts expect a number of banks to incur revaluation losses from wider spreads; credit losses from their securities holdings; reduced revenues from trading, securitizing, and structuring mortgages; and additions to their balance sheets from conduits drawing on contingent credit lines, raising associated regulatory capital. The negative impact is expected to be manageable for the industry as a whole. Smaller, less diversified institutions are viewed as more vulnerable.

Among nonbank investors, hedge funds have the greatest risk exposure to ABS CDOs (Fig-

ure 1.11).[18] A few specialized mortgage hedge funds have already closed or are under redemption pressures stemming from losses in trading mortgage-related securities. However, thus far, these losses have been limited relative to total outstanding assets under management, and in fact some funds with ample liquidity are actively seeking to acquire distressed assets.

Some financial guarantors—especially monoline insurers that provide credit enhancement to senior ABS and CDO tranches and insurance to securitizations of mortgage originators and ser-

[18]In some cases banks have reportedly encouraged hedge funds to buy the equity tranche of CDOs they have structured by offering attractive terms that enable hedge funds to leverage up their investments.

Box 1.1. Estimates of Nonprime Mortgage Losses

This box presents the loss estimates on U.S. subprime and alt-A mortgages based on two approaches. The first estimates losses over the lifetimes of the mortgages, and the second estimates mark-to-market losses.

Loss estimates on mortgages vary considerably, in part due to the different assumptions about inputs and differences in valuation methods. The top panel of the table estimates lifetime losses based on a scenario in which house prices decline by 5 percent over the first year and then stabilize.[1] In this scenario, 25 percent of the subprime mortgages and 7 percent of the alt-A mortgages are assumed to eventually default, and average loss severities (amounts ultimately not received) are assumed to be, respectively, 45 and 35 percent. Of the resulting $170 billion of estimated losses, about 25 percent would be directly absorbed by the banking system, and the other $130 billion by ABS and ABS CDOs.

The lower panel estimates the mark-to-market losses since February 2007 on all outstanding nonprime mortgage-related securities. Admittedly, they might represent worst-case devaluations, because they assume that all ABS and ABS CDOs issued in 2004 through 2006 remain outstanding, ignoring the impact of prepayments and defaults. Also, the securities are priced off ABX indices (for the ABS) and TABX tranches (for the ABS CDOs), which may represent worst-case prices.[2] On the other hand, the estimates do not include potential losses on nonprime mortgage-backed synthetic CDOs, which are difficult to estimate given the opacity of these markets. However, keeping all of this in mind, the table estimates mark-to-market losses of about $200 billion.

In addition to differences in input assumptions and valuation methods, other factors increase the uncertainty of the magnitude and timing of estimated losses. The magnitude of losses is uncertain because delinquencies on recently originated nonprime loans significantly exceed the prior trend, making historical relationships of limited use. The proliferation of various derivations of mortgage securities, including ABS CDOs, CDOs of CDOs, CDS on CDOs, etc., each with unique cash flow distribution rules, further complicates the process of calculating the impact of collateral losses on securities.[3] The timing of cash flow losses is similarly uncertain, since structured securities tend to delay the transmission of losses from the underlying collateral, and cash flow distribution

Note: This box was authored by John Kiff and Mustafa Saiyid.

[1]Potential losses on nonprime mortgages tend to be highly correlated with the path of future house prices, so assumptions on house prices are a key input to forecasted losses.

[2]The ABX is an index of credit default swaps linked to 20 underlying subprime mortgages. The TABX is an index that tranches synthetic CDOs based on the BBB- and BBB ABX indices. The TABX is fairly illiquid, and does not reflect the impact of collateral management on the cash ABS and ABS CDOs being priced in the table. In fact, analysis has shown that ABS CDO collateral managers have minimized exposure to the worst-performing 2006 vintages.

[3]For instance, the impact of loan losses on cash flows to these securities is reduced by credit enhancement mechanisms, such as subordination of securities, excess servicing, over-collateralization, and credit insurance.

vicers—are also exposed to the downturn in the mortgage market. While the net par exposure of the industry as a whole to mortgage originators' and servicers' assets appears to be limited, and capital sufficient, financial guarantor exposure could have important implications for broader structured credit markets and the market for municipal bonds.[19]

[19]See Fitch Ratings (2007a) and Standard & Poor's (2007a). There is a high concentration of financial guarantors referenced in synthetic corporate CDOs. Financial guarantors also play a key role in U.S. municipal bond markets through the provision of default insurance.

Loss Estimates for ABS and ABS CDOs Since February 2007

	Outstanding (Billions of U.S. dollars)	Percent of Total Mortgage Debt	Assumed Default (Percent of Origination)	Assumed Loss Severity (In percent)	Estimated Cash Flow Loss (Billions of U.S. dollars)	Estimated Mark-to-Market Loss (Billions of U.S. dollars)
Subprime total	1,300	15	25	45	~145	
Alt-A total	1,000	11	7	35	~25	
Nonprime Total	2,300				~170	
ABS						~65–70
ABS CDOs						~120–130
Total ABS and ABS CDOs						~200
	AAA	AA/A		BBB/BBB–		Not Rated
Mortgage ABS Issuance (Billions of U.S. dollars)						
2004	258	41		9		13
2005	283	57		13		11
2006	281	54		14		28
Estimated ABX Implied Mark-to-Market Losses of Mortgage ABS Tranches (Percent of outstanding par)						
2004	2–3	5–10		8–10		n.a.
2005	4–5	10–20		20–22		n.a.
2006	7–8	20–40		48–50		n.a.
ABS CDO Issuance (Billions of U.S. dollars)						
2004	35	3		1		6
2005	61	8		3		23
2006	135	15		5		11
Estimated Tranched ABX (TABX) Implied Mark-to-Market Losses of CDO Tranches (Percent of outstanding par)						
2004–06	40–70	40–60		40–45		n.a.

Sources: Lehman Brothers; Merrill Lynch; and IMF staff estimates.
Note: Estimated mark-to-market losses are issuance times estimated tranche losses. Aggregate loss numbers for ABS, ABS CDOs, and the overall total shown above are computed using five different tranches (AAA, AA, A, BBB, and BBB–); for the sake of simplicity and to highlight the wide range of pricing, the table has combined tranches rated AA and A, BBB, and BBB–. ABS = asset-backed security; ABX = synthetic asset-backed security; CDO = collateralized debt obligation; TABX = tranched asset-backed security.

rules may change in the event of a rating downgrade. Uncertainty regarding the extent of loan modifications, or the process of renegotiating terms on delinquent loans, further complicates the timing and magnitude of foreclosures and losses.

Losses extend beyond U.S. borders, highlighting the benefits of spreading risk, but also the global reach of the credit deterioration.

Direct exposure extends beyond the United States, with European and Asian investors active in the ABS and related markets (Figure 1.11). A handful of European institutions have already reported difficulties or closed owing to their exposure to U.S. mortgage markets and the withdrawal of their short-term funding, and still more are believed to be exposed to indirect mark-to-market losses stemming from their credit lines to conduits and structured investment vehicles.[20] Within the Asia Pacific region,

[20]European banks have been significant providers of funding to third-party vehicles, and a reduction in that funding could potentially threaten such vehicles' business models.

Table 1.1. Weakening Discipline in Subprime Lending Mirrored in Leveraged Buyouts

Subprime	Leveraged Buyouts
Higher loan-to-value ratios	Higher debt/EBITDA
Interest-only, negative amortizing loans	Covenant-lite and pay-in-kind toggle notes
Cash-out refinancing	Dividend re-cap
Zero percent down	Lenders providing equity bridges
Home price appreciation	Purchase multiple expansion

Source: IMF staff estimates.
Note: EBITDA = earnings before interest, taxes, depreciation, and amortization.

various market analyses suggest that exposure to mortgage-related products is concentrated in Japan, Australia, Taiwan Province of China, and Korea, but their overall exposure has been characterized as manageable and that region appears to be insulated from default risk.[21]

There has been a parallel weakening of credit discipline in the corporate segment...

There are similarities between the credit weakening in the nonprime mortgage market and that in the leveraged loan market (Table 1.1). This weakening, by extension, affects the market for CLOs, structured finance vehicles managed to invest primarily in senior leveraged loans (Figure 1.12).[22] The current leveraged buyout boom entered a new, more aggressive phase in 2006 that intensified in early 2007.

Underwriters and debt markets continued to increase leverage. Leverage levels rose to eight to 10 times EBITDA and purchase price-to-earnings ratios were in excess of 10.[23]

Analogous to the innovation in the nonprime mortgage market, financing innovations—such as covenant-lite loans and incurrence covenants[24]—allowed more marginal firms to be considered as targets, and encouraged deal sponsors to buy companies at higher earnings multiples. By the second quarter of 2007, more than a third of the companies that were the subject of buyout deals were rated split-B or below (rated B or lower by two ratings agencies), and around 30 percent of leveraged loans were covenant-lite (Figure 1.13).

...exposing banks to increased underwriting, marketing, and syndication risks, as short-term risks and uncertainty have increased and the pipeline of LBO deals has swelled.

As credit market strains emerged over the summer of 2007, lenders began to demand better terms, and spreads on leveraged loans, high-yield bonds, and related derivative indices widened sharply, prompting the postponement of several pending deals. Secondary market trading of leveraged loans weakened, with many deals trading at a significant discount to their issue prices (Figure 1.14). An estimated $300 billion of leveraged loans was planned

---

[21]See Standard & Poor's (2007b); and Moody's (2007).

[22]A leveraged loan is typically defined as any loan that has a debt rating below Baa3/BBB– from Moody's and Standard & Poor's, respectively, has a debt-to-EBITDA ratio of 3.0 times or greater, and tends to be priced at least 125 basis points over LIBOR at issue. (EBITDA stands for earnings before interest, taxes, depreciation, and amortization.) As detailed in the April 2007 GFSR, the expansion in the leveraged loan market has been in part driven by the maturation of the CLO market. Instead of retaining leveraged loans to fund buyouts on its balance sheet, a bank can sell such loans into the CLO market, thus freeing up capital to extend new loans to other private equity firms.

[23]Previously, leverage levels averaged about 4.5 times and average purchase price multiples were about 7.5 times. By late 2005, many observers thought such levels had gone as high as they safely could.

[24]Unlike traditional covenants (called "maintenance covenants"), incurrence-only loans are similar to those in high-yield bonds in that the company is only in default if it breaches the set threshold *and* takes some deliberate corporate action that exacerbates the situation. For example, a company could have fallen below the minimum cash set out in its cash interest cover ratio covenant, but, were it an incurrence covenant, would only be in breach if it subsequently issued a dividend, or raised additional borrowing.

to come to the market in the second half of this year, equivalent to around one-third of the total shareholder equity of the top 10 banks most involved in financing leveraged buyouts. But overall demand for the loans from CLOs and other market participants is now uncertain. The shift in credit conditions is helping to impose greater discipline on the buyout market—as evidenced in higher bid premia for private equity deals and increased repo terms. However, in the near term, financial institutions are exposed to potential syndication risks, with unsold bridge commitments contributing to an overhang in the market. Mitigating this to some extent, banks sometimes have clauses in their financing agreements with deal sponsors that allow them to turn all or part of the deal back to the sponsor if financing conditions become difficult, thus limiting their downside risks. In addition, banks can attempt to manage some of the shock from potential hung bridges by temporarily expanding their balance sheets, increasing their loan loss reserves, opting to pay a break-up fee, or selling their residual equity or loans directly to hedge funds, though it is unclear whether such funds will fully absorb the outstanding loans and mortgage positions.

The sensitivity of recent LBO targets to business and economic shocks has also increased...

At higher leverage and price multiples, LBO targets are subject to greater business and economic risks. To illustrate this, Table 1.2 shows how a stylized private equity deal reacts to a number of possible scenarios. The example shows that deals are most sensitive to stagflation.[25]

Events have shown that, as LBO deals push toward extremes, rising interest rates present

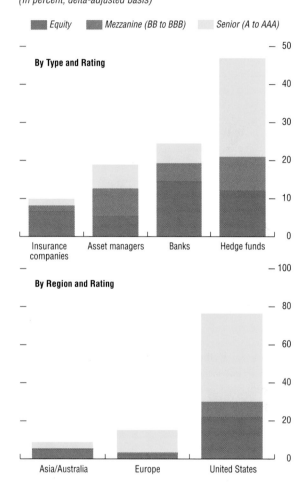

Figure 1.11. Buyers of ABS CDOs
(In percent, delta-adjusted basis)

Source: Citigroup.
Note: ABS = asset-backed security; CDO = collateralized debt obligation. Delta adjustment multiplies the holdings by the delta (i.e., leverage) of the tranche. Hence, it magnifies more junior tranches (i.e., equity) and thus gives a better picture of risk appetite.

[25]This assumes an initial debt multiple of annual cash flows of seven, and a price multiple of cash flows of 10—both broadly in line with the current overall market average, but low compared with more aggressive deals. An initial debt multiple of nine times leads to losses for the deal sponsor under all states of the world.

Figure 1.12. U.S. CDO Outstanding Volume
($900 billion through July 2007)

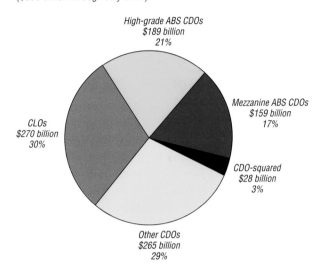

Source: Credit Suisse.
Note: CDO = collateralized debt obligation; ABS = asset-backed security; CLO = collateralized loan obligation. CDOs are defined as high-grade or mezzanine on the basis of the average rating of the underlying collateral. The collateral of high-grade CDOs is usually rated AA/A while that of mezzanine CDOs is BBB. CDO-squared entities are those CDOs whose collateral includes tranches of other CDOs.

Figure 1.14. Average Bid Price for U.S. and European Leveraged Loans

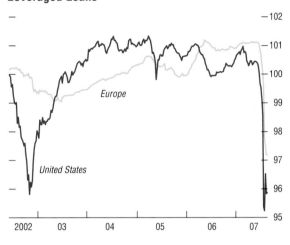

Sources: Markit Loans; and Standard & Poor's Leveraged Commentary & Data.
Note: Pricing for commonly traded loans.

Figure 1.13. Number of Covenant-Lite Loans to Total Number of Institutional Term Loans
(In percent)

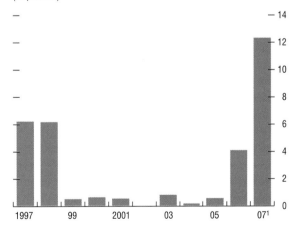

Source: Standard & Poor's Leveraged Commentary & Data.
¹First half of 2007.

Figure 1.15. Interest Coverage Statistics on Private Equity
(U.S. deals with cash flows [EBITDA] greater than $50 million)

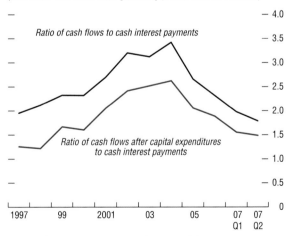

Source: Standard & Poor's Leveraged Commentary & Data.
Note: EBITDA = earnings before interest, tax, depreciation, and amortization.

Table 1.2. Private Equity Deal Scenarios

	Positive Conditions	Slow Growth	Higher Inflation	Higher Yields	Slow Growth and Higher Yields
Assumptions					
Sales growth (percent)	10	0	10	10	0
Profit margin to sales (percent)	15	10	10	15	5
Debt service cost (percent)	8	8	10	12	12
Results (at end of year seven)					
Enterprise value (US$ millions)	441.0	80.8	229.0	390.0	−62.4
Return on firm equity at time of exit (percent)	33.0	6.0	15.1	22.6	−3.6
Capital gain on private equity (percent)	1,135.0	126.0	543.0	992.0	−274.8
Capital gain on public company (US$ millions)	341.0	−19.2	129.0	290.0	−162.4

Source: IMF staff estimates.

Note: Example based on a public company with enterprise value of $100 million, gross profit of 10 percent, and debt service cost of 7 percent. Firm is assumed to be sold at end of year seven.

a challenging environment. This can be seen in the interest coverage ratios (that is, cash flows relative to cash interest payments) in recent deals—which rose steadily through 2004, but which have since dropped sharply to levels last observed at the start of the decade (Figure 1.15). Any subsequent rises in interest rates, cash dividends, or unplanned expenditures will squeeze this ratio further. Gains to private equity holders on LBO targets are increasingly reliant on earnings growth, as valuation multiples and leverage rise, and as leveraged loan rates have increased. It appears that private equity has picked most of the "low hanging fruit," potentially straining the viability of targets in the period ahead.

…raising questions about LBO refinancing risks in the medium term.

Even if the LBO market weathers this initial storm, medium-term prospects appear challenging. The most recent deals will likely face refinancing difficulties. The analogy with resets in the mortgage market suggests some firms may struggle to secure financing on attractive terms, and may therefore have to carry a more demanding debt service burden than anticipated. Defaults are therefore likely to rise—though, barring a significant economic downturn, they appear unlikely to reach previous cyclical peaks.

Near-term contagion—the proximate source being uncertainty of losses and repricing of credit—has been transmitted to broader markets through several channels.

While the shift in financial conditions is helping to restore credit discipline, the correction has also magnified vulnerabilities that extend beyond the mortgage and leveraged loan sectors. Tangentially related markets are being affected through second- and third-order effects, as concerns in structured finance markets trigger a broad-based increase in risk premia and induce a reluctance to lend, a reduced distinction across investments, and other changes in market psychology. These effects are difficult to gauge, and will depend on the duration and extent of the market correction. As additional information is released, the market will likely be able to distinguish among risks with greater accuracy, helping to contain the effects of contagion.

Negative knock-on effects, though, have already been felt by other entities, including hedge funds, structured investment vehicles (SIVs), and other ABCP conduits—where investors are demanding wider spreads to compensate for the uncertainty about how risks are allocated and managed (Box 1.2). In some cases, ABCP programs' inability to roll over maturing paper has forced banks to provide funding support, which, in turn, has increased market-wide

Box 1.2. Concerns in the Asset-Backed Commercial Paper Market

The deterioration in the mortgage market has magnified funding difficulties in the short-term credit market. This box discusses the key entities that issue asset-backed commercial paper and the vehicles most vulnerable to the reduction in liquidity in that market.

Similar to asset-backed securities (ABS), asset-backed commercial paper (ABCP) programs repackage pools of assets into special purpose vehicles that are funded by issuing short-maturity debt. These vehicles use the proceeds from the debt to fund purchases of financial assets. The three most common vehicles are traditional conduits, which generally use the debt to finance receivables, leases, and loans; structured investment vehicles (SIVs), which buy mainly longer-maturity corporate bonds and lower-rated structured credit products; and security arbitrage conduits (SACs), which use the debt proceeds to invest in highly rated structured credit. Unlike conduits, SIVs and SACs are tranched: any losses are first absorbed by equity holders, and only subsequently by holders of medium-term notes and commercial paper.

As of early September 2007, the size of the U.S. dollar–denominated ABCP market was around $1 trillion, representing more than one-half of the outstanding commercial paper market, though outstandings dropped in the weeks that followed. ABCP-funded conduits and SIVs have been especially popular among banks in North America and Europe, in part due to the potential reduction in required regulatory capital on highly rated instruments.[1]

Most ABCP programs have well-diversified assets, but some have significant mortgage-related exposure. Conduits have about an 11 percent exposure to mortgage loans and a further 11 percent exposure to ABS securities, some of which are mortgage-related securities.

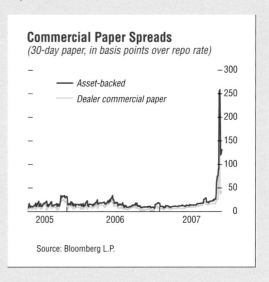

Commercial Paper Spreads
(30-day paper, in basis points over repo rate)

— Asset-backed
— Dealer commercial paper

Source: Bloomberg L.P.

SIVs and SACs have about a 20 to 25 percent exposure to residential mortgage-related securities and an 11 percent exposure to collateralized debt obligations (CDOs), some of which may be mortgage-related CDOs. A subset of SIVs—SIV lites—are almost entirely invested in mortgage-related securities. The mortgage-related exposure is diversified globally, including the United States, United Kingdom, Germany, Australia, and the Netherlands.

ABCP programs face important liquidity risks.[2] If an ABCP program cannot roll over or extend commercial paper coming due, it must achieve some sort of short-term financing or else dissolve itself and sell the underlying assets. In some cases, this risk is mitigated by having backstop funding arrangements. The availability of a liquidity provider does not prevent the assets from being sold, but it gives time to achieve an orderly liquidation.

A loss of market liquidity in the market for U.S. mortgage-related credit was largely to blame for difficulties in rolling maturing ABCP, prompting a sharp widening in spreads. Downgrades and lower mark-to-market valuations of the underlying collateral further compounded

Note: This box was authored by John Kiff and Mustafa Saiyid.

[1]Vaguely defined clauses governing funding arrangements for some ABCP vehicles were partly responsible for recent rollover failures in Canada. At issue was the definition of a "general market disruption" that resulted in bank funding requests of some Canadian ABCP issuers being denied.

[2]The maturity of such short-term debt averages 45 days but can be as long as 364 days (or more in the case of "extendible" commercial paper).

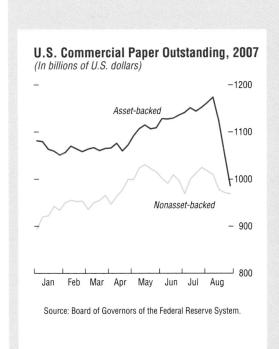

U.S. Commercial Paper Outstanding, 2007
(In billions of U.S. dollars)

Asset-backed

Nonasset-backed

Jan Feb Mar Apr May Jun Jul Aug

Source: Board of Governors of the Federal Reserve System.

Key Types of Asset-Backed Commercial Paper Vehicles

Asset-Backed Commercial Paper
~$1,400 billion[1]

Cash Flow Structures

Conduits
~$1,100 billion

Mark-to-Market Structures

SIVs
~$100 billion

SIV Lite
~$10–15 billion

Security Arbitrage Conduits
$200 billion

Sources: Bank for International Settlements; JPMorgan Chase & Co.; and IMF staff estimates.
Note: Outstanding par of global asset-backed commercial paper. SIVs (structured investment vehicles) are short-term liabilities only.
[1]Approximately, United States, $1,000 billion; Europe, $300 billion; and Canada, $100 billion.

difficulties. SIVs and SACs tend to be more vulnerable to losses resulting from forced liquidation of assets than conduits. First, any losses from forced liquidation of underlying assets are magnified to holders of equity in SIVs and SACs as a result of leverage.[3] In this respect, they are similar to CDOs, though with lower leverage. Second, SIVs and SACs are more heavily exposed to mortgage-related collateral—the key source of market concern—compared with other types of vehicles.

[3]Any losses from liquidation are first absorbed by equity holders of the SIV and subsequently by subordinated notes before they reach the commercial paper, the most senior liability.

Difficulties in the ABCP market have the potential to impact capital markets broadly, as has been amply demonstrated by recent bank liquidity problems. Bank exposure to some CDOs may have been transferred to off-balance-sheet conduits, but bank credit lines to those conduits will likely put risk back onto bank balance sheets. As a result of short-term illiquidity, some banks could become insolvent, requiring bailouts. In addition, market uncertainty about the size of potential losses for holders of commercial paper could lead to redemptions from money market funds that hold mostly commercial paper. The market for super-senior tranches of corporate CDOs could be affected, as these securities are typically purchased by conduits.

funding pressures, calling for a broadening of allowable collateral and extraordinary liquidity injections from central banks (Figure 1.16). To some extent, these legal structures have transformed credit risk into counterparty and funding risk. For example, some of the risk that is transferred out of the banking system to

hedge funds could return to the system as prime broker counterparty risks. Similarly, risks transferred to SIVs and other conduits are returning to the banking system via funding support facilities.

In addition, concerns regarding "ratings migration" have channeled uncertainty to a broad range of rated products. The ratings agencies acknowledged significant failures in their ABS and ABS CDO models, assumptions, and methodologies, and this sparked concern that such failures may extend to the broader structured finance market, introducing uncertainty regarding the validity of other ratings.

The forced unwinding of leverage in an environment of reduced market liquidity represents another means through which volatility is transmitted across markets (see Chapter 2). A modest decline in value can have a dramatic impact on a portfolio that layers leverage on top of products that already have embedded leverage. For instance, in the simple hypothetical example in Table 1.3, a small loss in value can force funds to sell large amounts of assets as liquidations to meet margin calls and, simultaneously, their redemptions, increase.[26] Such "fire sales" could lead to vicious circles of forced sales, as the widening of spreads forces hedge funds and others who mark portfolios to market to post losses, possibly sparking investor withdrawals and further forced sales. Already, the liquidations of several hedge funds with high concentrations of exposure to mortgage credit have increased the risk of further margin calls, in turn sparking a spiral of widening spreads across other markets.[27] Such episodes highlight the reliance of funds holding illiquid structured products on

Figure 1.16. U.S. Money Market Interest Rates, 2007
(*90-day rates, in percent*)

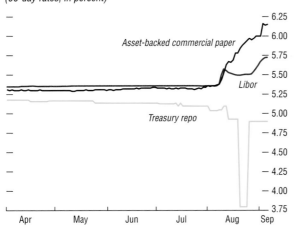

Source: Bloomberg L.P.

[26]The initial drop in value reduces equity in the fund, which automatically pushes up leverage. The broker (or repo desk) makes a margin call that forces the fund to sell assets to bring leverage back to its initial level. However, in addition, the prime broker (or repo desk) now imposes a higher margin (or "haircut") to reflect the fact that the assets are now riskier. This requires the fund to reduce borrowing further. Last, redemptions require further asset sales. This example is liberal in that it assumes the maximum use of available leverage, but it is conservative in that it considers only first-round effects, not second-round declines in value from the sale of the collateral.

[27]Similar scenarios apply to other investor types. For instance, downgrades of ABS CDO tranches could force some investors (e.g., pension funds, insurance companies) that face credit ratings-based constraints to sell the downgraded securities.

Table 1.3. Stylized Example of a Forced Unwind of Leverage

	Asset Value	Equity	Borrowing	Leverage	Margin (%)
At start	100.0	15.0	85.0	5.7	15.0
After loss of value	95.0	10.0	85.0	8.5	10.5
After margin call	66.7	10.0	56.7	5.7	15.0
After increase in margin	40.0	10.0	30.0	3.0	25.0
After sales to meet redemptions	36.0	9.0	27.0	3.0	25.0

Initial margin	15%
Loss in value	5%
New margin at lower value	25%
Redemptions	10%

Modest loss of value and higher haircuts generate large forced sales

Source: IMF staff estimates.

their ability to obtain continuous liquidity for funding their leveraged positions.[28]

In a similar vein, uncertainty has led to concerns regarding a further reduction in market liquidity through "haircut contagion," increasing funding rates in a broader range of markets beyond structured credit products.[29] This could create a cycle of declining asset values, withdrawal of market liquidity, forced sales, and further valuation declines in unrelated markets until some market participants with ample cash and a willingness to buy step in to provide a floor (Table 1.4). Participants such as pension funds, insurance companies, and sovereign wealth funds with longer investment horizons and little if any leverage could be expected to help put a lower bound on price declines (see Annex 1.2 on characteristics of sovereign wealth funds.)

Strains in the mortgage market have also revealed the importance of reputational risk

as a transmission mechanism. Firms may feel obligated to support legally separated entities financially in order to maintain their reputation as viable firms. Thus, risk can be transmitted from a peripheral unit to, perhaps, a systemically important institution. Given the large number of separate asset management companies, special purpose vehicles, and conduits, this is an important consideration, particularly for the boards of directors of the sponsoring institutions, where oversight of these entities needs to be based on accurate and relevant information about their risks and returns.[30]

The rapid deterioration in the U.S. nonprime mortgage sector has also led to concerns about dislocations in non-U.S. mortgage markets, especially in the U.K. nonconforming mortgage sector and, to a lesser extent, the Australian subprime sector. A number of other countries have overvalued housing markets and are vulnerable to a downturn in house prices but have small nonconforming mortgage sectors.[31] The U.K. nonconforming mortgage market is significantly smaller than the U.S.

[28]For instance, when liquidity dried up, Bear Stearns provided a back-up facility for its asset management arm, and the other affected funds were pushed into forced liquidations and deleveraging. The Bear Stearns-managed funds quickly lost value within a few weeks.

[29]A "haircut" refers to the deduction from the market value to account for the risk that the asset will be worth less if it needs to be sold when the investor pledging the security has difficulties. The size of a haircut changes depending on the class of a security, its market risk, and the time to maturity. For instance, haircuts fluctuate from 0 to 30 percent (on equities) to 100 percent (for securities with past-due delivery). A higher haircut lowers the value of the asset being financed.

[30]For instance, Bear Stearns Cos Inc. had only very small direct stakes in the hedge funds that collapsed under Bear Stearns Asset Management. Even so, when the funds were on the point of collapse, Bear Stearns Cos Inc. provided back-up financing to the funds that carried its name.

[31]See Box 1.2 in the October 2007 *World Economic Outlook* (IMF, 2007b).

Table 1.4. Typical Haircuts: Bond, Leveraged Loan, and ABS and CDO
(In percent)

Rating	January–May 2007	July–Aug 2007
	Bond	
Investment grade	0–3	3–7
High-yield	0–5	10+
	Leveraged Loan	
Senior	10–12	15–20
2nd lien	15–20	20–30
Mezzanine	18–25	30+
	ABS and CDO	
AAA	2–4	8–10
AA	4–7	20
A	8–15	30
BBB	10–20	50
Equity	50	100

Source: Citigroup.
Note: ABS = asset-backed security; CDO = collateralized debt obligation.

subprime market and there is limited evidence to suggest that U.K. loans shared the same combination of risk layering, poor underwriting standards, and declining home prices as in the United States. Nonetheless, these concerns (together with higher domestic interest rates) have pushed U.K. mortgage rates higher on more recent vintages and reportedly led lenders to withdraw their more risky mortgage products.[32]

[32]For instance, the average combined loan-to-value ratios on U.K. nonconforming loans in 2006 (76 percent) is significantly lower than those for U.S. 2006 subprime loans (85 percent), and there is minimal adverse credit lending in the U.K. market, reflecting tighter underwriting standards. Expectations of loss severity in the United Kingdom are around one-third of those in the United States, mainly due to lower foreclosure costs. Meanwhile, in contrast to the U.S. market, the underlying performance of recently-originated U.K. nonconforming loans has been stronger compared with prior vintages. The Australian subprime market is small, and Australian real estate loans give the lender greater structural protection than U.S. lenders enjoy.

Weaker Credit and Market Discipline Warrants Increased Surveillance in Emerging Markets

Overall, emerging market risks remain low relative to historical experience, with many countries benefiting from improved macroeconomic fundamentals and strong external balances. Nonetheless, developments in mature markets raise concerns that vulnerabilities may be growing in emerging markets related to a weakening of credit and market discipline in global markets, with some emerging market countries more exposed than others. This section highlights five such concerns.

First, it considers the growing market of privately placed syndicated loans to emerging markets, which shares similar evidence of credit indiscipline as in the leveraged loan segment.

Second, in some regions, emerging market banks—both domestic and foreign banks acting on behalf of subsidiaries—are relying increasingly on international borrowing to finance rapid domestic credit growth. This development—flagged in the April 2007 GFSR—is a growing vulnerability.

Third, emerging market corporates appear increasingly engaged in carry-trade-style external borrowing that could pose losses if carry trades rapidly unwind.

Fourth, emerging market financial institutions in some countries are increasingly using structured and synthetic instruments to increase returns, potentially exposing them to losses as volatility rises.

Finally, the section explores whether foreign investors in emerging market equities increase the risks for volatility or the mispricing of emerging market equities.

Emerging market corporations have enjoyed easy access to international markets for some time, and credit discipline appears to be weakening.

The private placement loan market has experienced rapid growth in emerging Europe, the Middle East, and Africa (EMEA) and, to a lesser extent in Asia, partly at the expense of public bond and equity markets (Figure 1.17).[33] In some cases, private placements may allow issuers to avoid the more extensive disclosures required by public listings, since such placements are not subject to the same contractual protection as in public markets. Weaker credits and more first-time issuers—some of which may be inadequately covered by analysts and ratings agencies—are becoming involved in the high-yield debt market. On the demand side, many hedge funds are attracted to the high yield offered by some borrowers, as well as the lack of mark-to-market accounting on such loans, as these private placements have fitted well into the broader trend of hedge funds seeking credit exposure. While such loans have found strong primary market demand, their secondary market liquidity is likely to be very limited in the event of a downturn or when credit difficulties arise.

In some countries in emerging Europe and central Asia, external funding is supporting rapid domestic credit growth...

To date, abundant global liquidity has funded rapid credit growth in emerging Europe and central Asia—credit in these regions now absorbs nearly half of all international bank and bond financing. In many cases, banks' growing use of external financing has provided a large proportion of funding for overall credit growth (Figure 1.18). Private sector credit growth has been correlated with foreign funding of local banking systems over the last few years as foreign financing has enabled

---

[33]In contrast, corporate borrowing in Latin America has been growing strongly in traditional local equity and debt markets. Large pools of domestic savings, primarily a result of the development of private pension funds, and often with restrictions on foreign asset holdings, encourage corporate issuers to tap the domestic market. At the same time, international investors are reportedly buying up to 80 percent of new initial public offerings in Brazil. International debt issuance tends to be by large multinational corporations, and is both in U.S. dollars and increasingly in domestic currency. There appears to be no significant Latin American corporate borrowing in the low-yielding currencies.

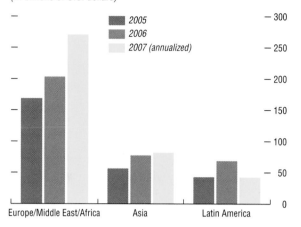

Figure 1.17. Emerging Market Private Loan Placements
(In billions of U.S. dollars)

Source: Thomson Financial.

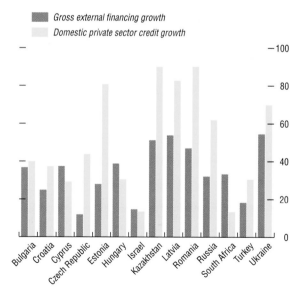

Figure 1.18. Growth in External Funding of Banks and Private Sector Credit in 2006
(In percent)

Sources: Bank for International Settlements; and IMF staff estimates.
Note: Private sector credit growth converted into U.S. dollars before computing growth rates.

Figure 1.19. Correlation of Credit Growth with Growth in Foreign Financing of Banks, 2004–06
(In percent)

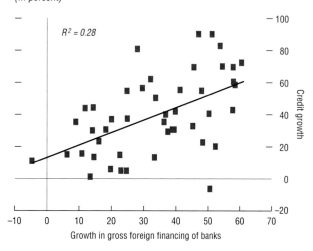

Sources: Bank for International Settlements; and IMF staff estimates.

banks to increase liabilities more rapidly than the expansion of local deposits would allow (Figure 1.19).

...but lower-rated banks are at risk if appetite from international investors suddenly declines, potentially raising the systemic risks for some banking systems.

Bond financing has increasingly gone to banks with low credit ratings and countries where credit is expanding rapidly (Table 1.5), suggesting an adverse selection problem. International banks are often unwilling to lend to such banks through the interbank market owing to the difficulty of assessing their true financial condition, but these same banks can still issue international bonds, though the risk is reflected in wider spreads. Banks that rely predominantly on bond financing are more vulnerable to a sudden drop in demand for bonds—either due to a rise in domestic loan defaults or an increase in global risk aversion—triggering funding difficulties for the banks. The drop-off in capital inflows could, in turn, pose challenges for countries reliant on these inflows to finance large current account deficits. Less at risk are the stronger banking systems in emerging Europe that rely more on relatively stable foreign interbank financing, reflecting better transparency and the funding of foreign bank subsidiaries by their parent.

Emerging market firms—particularly in Asia—appear to be increasingly engaged in carry-trade-style external borrowing, warranting increased surveillance of such exposures.

Firms in Asia increasingly have established or extended positions that offer long exposure to foreign currencies (Figure 1.20). Although many countries restrict foreign borrowing by domestic institutions, in some cases firms use loopholes to borrow directly in low-yielding funding currencies or to swap liabilities using cross-currency swaps. For instance, in India, firms with a multinational presence borrow directly in yen, or use cross-currency swaps (as can national firms) to convert foreign exchange exposure. External borrowing by Indian corporations—both nonfinancial and financial—is increasingly in yen and left largely

Table 1.5. Structure of External Financing and Banking System Soundness and Ownership
(In percent)

Country	Share of Bonds in External Bank Financing	Fitch Stand-Alone Bank Soundness Rating	Private Credit Dollarized Growth in 2006
Kazakhstan	62	D	90
Russia	53	D	62
South Africa	47	B	13
Bulgaria	33	D	40
Poland	30	D	. . .
Hungary	27	D	30
Ukraine	26	D	70
Cyprus	23	D	29
Turkey	22	D	30
Estonia	19	D	81
Czech Republic	16	B	44
Croatia	6	B	37
Slovak Republic	6	D	. . .
Romania	5	D	90
Latvia	4	C	83

Sources: Bank for International Settlements; Fitch; and IMF staff estimates.
Note: Lowest Fitch rating is E; Highest Fitch rating is A.

unhedged.[34] Nevertheless, debt-to-equity ratios are not particularly high, so even though Indian firms may be taking on greater foreign exchange exposure, they remain at low leverage levels. In Korea, yen-linked loans have also reportedly become more common, particularly among small and medium-sized importers (Figure 1.21). The extent of this yen exposure appearing on domestic bank balance sheets is now about $15 billion—still moderate when scaled to the size of the domestic banking sector.[35] In addition, some borrowing occurs off-balance sheet or through derivatives markets. On balance, it appears that there has been a significant uptick in foreign currency-denominated borrowing in India and Korea, much of which reflects firms seeking nominally cheaper sources of funding than is available in local currency. The authorities in both countries have recently introduced measures to limit such foreign currency exposure and to slow the buildup in (short-term) external borrowing.[36]

The search for yield and duration has spurred issuance of synthetic and structured credit products.

In addition to currency risk, emerging markets have also grown more vulnerable to a rise in volatility. Amid low domestic interest rates, tight credit spreads, and underdeveloped bond markets, some investors are increasingly turning to structured products and hybrid derivatives markets for yield enhancement and duration extension.[37] Losses emanating from such volatility-based strategies will likely be revealed as the environment becomes less benign. The structured products market in Asia totals more than $100 billion by some estimates, reportedly with Korea and Taiwan Province of

---

[34]Market intelligence estimates that Indian firms hedge only 50 percent of their exchange rate risk, and that positions are especially exposed to tail risk.

[35]The total gross liabilities of Korean commercial banks amounted to $888 billion as of March 31, 2007.

[36]See Chapter 3 for a discussion of various approaches to limit the effects of rapid capital inflows.

[37]About 60 percent of structured products involve a view on rates, 30 percent are equity-linked, and the remainder are foreign exchange-linked products.

Figure 1.20. Emerging Asia: Short-Term Foreign-Currency-Denominated Borrowing
(In billions of U.S. dollars)

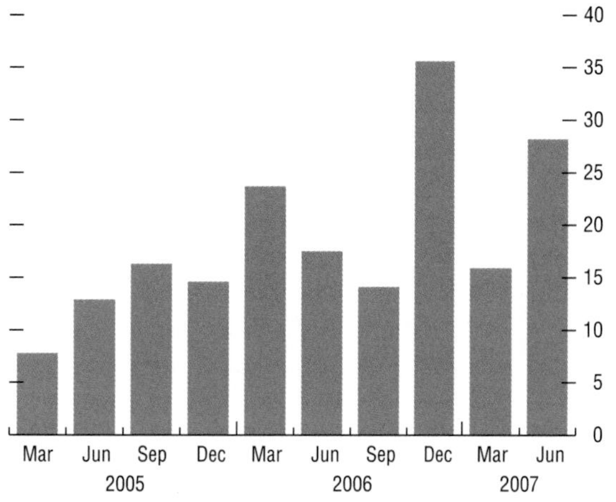

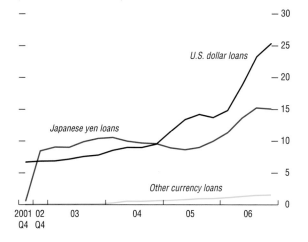

Sources: Bloomberg L.P.; and IMF staff estimates.
Note: Includes borrowing in Japanese yen, U.S. dollars, euros, or British pounds, with maturities up to 12 months.

Figure 1.21. Korea: Foreign-Currency-Denominated Loans of Commercial, Special, and Foreign Banks
(In billions of U.S. dollars)

Source: Bank of Korea.
Note: Includes loans of commercial, special, and foreign banks. Data for 2007 are not publicly available.

China having the largest markets.[38] A range of investors—including retail investors—are involved in the market, but Taiwanese insurance companies and, to a lesser extent, Korean companies appear particularly exposed to such structures.[39] Taiwanese insurance companies are subject to asset allocation limits of 5 percent on structured products and 45 percent on foreign currency products, though some market participants have suggested that these requirements can be circumvented. The Taiwanese Financial Supervisory Commission recently increased the ceiling on foreign investment for insurance companies and is considering further liberalization, including lifting allowable overseas investments to 50 percent of total assets and allowing insurers to raise debt as well as more actively manage investment-linked accounts.[40]

In Korea, life insurance companies, banks, pension funds, and retail investors are the largest consumers of structured products, generally demanding yields of 7 percent with a preference for local currency-denominated structures and an average maturity of 10 years. In practice, many of these instruments are callable by the issuing banks, and this limits their yield-enhancing potential. The most popular trades include power spread notes and various types of range accrual

[38]Taiwan Province of China was among the first markets in the region to authorize investment in ABS, including residential mortgage-backed securities, commercial mortgage-backed securities, and collateralized fixed-income products. More recently, Taiwanese investors have turned to more exotic products and are applying greater leverage.

[39]Range accrual instruments are especially popular among Taiwanese life insurance companies that are experiencing a mismatch in duration and depressed profitability. With such products, an enhanced payoff is received if an asset remains within a predetermined range during the life of the note. If the rate moves outside the range, no payout is received through maturity. Such products originated in dollar-denominated markets, but have started to migrate into local currency markets.

[40]There are no official statistics on Taiwanese life insurers' structured product holdings, but the average CDO exposure of two of the top three insurers is reported to be around 2 percent of funds invested.

notes.[41] Domestic insurers and pension funds requiring duration have also sought structures, such as 20-year synthetic bonds.[42] Korean insurance companies have also invested in credit-linked notes based on a basket of Korean credits rather than on single names, as a way to generate a slightly higher yield than single names. Korean investors also tend to buy AAA/AA-rated CDOs (mostly collateralized with U.S. and European debt) with a tenor of seven years or higher. Almost all are managed deals, with most purchases treated as buy-and-hold positions. These investments offer leveraged returns and tend to involve the selling of options to increase yield. Investors in these products are thus exposed to a rise in volatility. In fact, losses may already have occurred, but the lack of mark-to-market accounting may have camouflaged the impact on balance sheets. To the extent that Asian investors are invested in CDOs, they are also exposed to the volatility from ratings downgrades.

Investment Inflows into Emerging Markets—Do They Destabilize Local Markets?

After two years of stellar performance, the average price-to-earnings ratio of emerging market equities is comparable to mature markets, at about 14 (Figure 1.22).[43] Driven in part by carry traders engaging in interest rate arbitrage, emerg-

---

[41]Power spread structures exploit the arbitrage offered by the abnormal circumstance in which the government yield is higher than the interest rate swap rate. The issuing bank borrows dollars in the offshore market (since there are limits on onshore funding), swaps dollars to won, and uses the won to buy government securities. Such structures average $50 million to $100 million per transaction, but are leveraged as much as eight times. Since power spreads involve large purchases of government securities, such products have the effect of flattening the government yield curve (since most structures are 10-year tenors), while dollar borrowing in the offshore market appears to have increased short-term bank borrowing.

[42]The longest duration available on local currency Korean debt is 20 years, but demand tends to outstrip supply, as reflected in frequently oversubscribed auctions.

[43]It has been argued that the greater volatility of some such markets may imply a lower long-term price-to-earnings ratio, as prices are lower to compensate for increased risk.

Figure 1.22. Price/Earnings Ratios
(12-months forward)

Source: I/B/E/S.

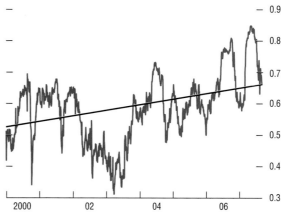

Figure 1.23. Correlation of Emerging and Mature Market Equities
(90-day rolling window)

Sources: Morgan Stanley Capital International; and IMF staff estimates.

ing market bond yields have also converged with mature market levels. Not surprisingly, over the same period, correlations between the returns on emerging market assets and other assets have increased (Figure 1.23). The confluence of higher correlation with lower expected returns suggests that some global investors may be inclined to reassess the diversification benefits available from emerging market investments. The corollary is that emerging markets may become more sensitive to global developments as the "cushion" of excess returns is reduced.

Against this backdrop and strong inflows from global investors over the last several years, this section presents preliminary work on the potential for the behavior of foreign institutional and hedge fund investors to destabilize emerging market equities.

A study of high-frequency data on equity flows into emerging markets supplied by the Bank of New York (BONY) points to some useful conclusions about the nature and short-term impact of emerging market inflows.[44] The data largely reflect the activities of institutional investors such as pension funds, mutual funds, and insurance companies, and can therefore be used to study the behavior of some types of foreign flows on prices. This section examines the impact of these foreign flows on local equity price levels, as well as coincident changes in local equity prices and their relation to "herding" across countries within a region by foreign institutional investors. The positions of institutional investors versus leveraged investors during a market correction are then compared.

Surprisingly, institutional inflows appear to have little impact on equity prices...

Contrary to what might be expected from reports of foreign investors crowding into small local markets, the measurable effect of foreign inflows on domestic equity price levels is not

readily apparent (Box 1.3). Reinforcing the finding, tests performed on markets grouped by region show little or no indication of the net effect of inflows on prices. One explanation is that local markets may have become deeper and better able to absorb flows over time as domestic investors have increased their trading activity and their role in price determination (see Chapter 3).

...but there are indications of "imported" volatility.

At the same time, there is support for the widely held perception that foreign investors are sometimes inclined to herd into individual markets, in some cases switching from one country to another within a specific region. Foreign investors' position changes are also correlated with higher volatility, a potentially undesirable characteristic for an asset market. Even so, as suggested above, the evidence suggests that foreigners are not feeding local equity bubbles, since they have no appreciable effect on price levels.

Foreign institutional investors appear to behave differently from hedge funds in times of stress.

During recent periods of market turbulence in May–June 2006 and February–March 2007, evidence suggests that sales by some foreign investors did have a strong effect on the prices of several types of assets, including equities. The activities of hedge funds, which are sometimes seen as market bellwethers, appear to fall into this category. Leveraged investors, such as hedge funds and bank proprietary desks, often need to operate positions with stops to limit excessive capital losses as a result of the leverage that they employ (see Chapter 2). This tends to force liquidations when prices move sharply down. Indirect evidence of this is found by comparing the behavior of institutional and foreign investors during the May–June 2006 correction. Institutional investors were less likely on average to exit equity market positions than foreign investors were as a whole (Figure 1.24).[45] This

---

[44]With the proliferation of markets open to foreign inflows and new financial products for investing in those markets, it is difficult to make universal claims about the nature of other inflows.

[45]Figure 1.24 uses data for those emerging market countries that have both BONY and official foreign equity

Box 1.3. Equity Inflows and Emerging Markets

This box makes use of high-frequency data supplied by the Bank of New York (BONY) on equity flows into 16 major emerging markets over a period of more than five years in order to provide insights into these flows and their effects.[1]

The findings here suggest that the effect of foreign inflows on domestic equity price levels is not statistically apparent. Impulse response functions calculated from panel vector autoregressions employing scaled equity inflows and percentage changes in equity prices as the two endogenous variables show either an insignificantly positive or a zero net cumulative response of prices to inflows for the full panel of 16 emerging markets (see figure).[2] Reinforcing the finding, there is no significant regional variation in the results, with impulse response functions calculated for each of the three main emerging market regions (Asia; Latin America; and Europe, the Middle East, and Africa) also indicating little or no net effect of inflows on prices. That stands in contrast to the findings of the study by Froot, O'Connell, and Seasholes (2001), pointing to a change in investor behavior between the earlier 1990s and the most recent five-year period.

Persistence—a possible sign of herding behavior—is one prominent and readily observable feature of the BONY flows. Variance ratio tests, which are widely used in analysis of financial time series, show clear autocorrela-

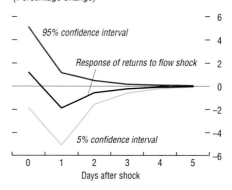

Impulse Response of Returns to a One Standard Deviation Increase in Foreign Inflows
(Percentage change)

95% confidence interval

Response of returns to flow shock

5% confidence interval

Days after shock

Source: IMF staff estimates.
Note: Panel vector autoregressions are run over 16 emerging market countries (a total of 9,779 observations).

tion in flows at both short and long lags (see table).[3] Moreover, the substantially higher rates of autocorrelation at the longer lags indicate that herding of investors into a given market is a process that takes place over several days, weeks, or even months. This is notably the case for Latin American markets, for which the 20-day variance ratio exceeds seven. Previous studies of flows into emerging markets also identified clear persistence of approximately the same degree as that reported here (Froot, O'Connell, and Seasholes, 2001).

Investors also show some inclination to chase returns. Making use of the same panel vector

Note: The main author of this box is Chris Walker.

[1]Daily data over a period of five years for 16 countries, yielding about 22,000 individual observations. In many cases, the BONY data provide more detail on flows into a given market than is available from public or national sources. Where aggregate daily data on overall foreign net flows into a given market are available, the pattern of the BONY flows broadly matches that of the aggregate foreign inflows, accounting, on average, for about 1 to 5 percent of the flows into the given market. Correlation coefficients are all positive, ranging from 0.05 in the case of Indonesia to 0.38 for Korea. Correlation coefficients range from –1 (full negative correlation) to +1 (full positive correlation).

[2]In the orthogonalization of error terms, the time t shock to flows is assumed to precede the time t price shock.

[3]In the simplest, single-period lag case the variance ratio statistic VR(2) is equivalent to VR(2) = $\text{Var}(r_t + r_{t+1})/2\text{Var}(r_t) = (2\text{Var}(r_t) + 2\text{Cov}(r_t, r_{t+1}))/2\text{Var}(r_t)$ = $1 + \rho$, where $\rho = \sigma_{xy}/\sigma_x^2$ is the coefficient in a first-order autoregression of r. Note that a VR(2) statistic greater than 1 indicates persistence/autocorrelation at a single lag. At longer lags (e.g., VR (5)), the statistic is equivalent to summing across autocorrelations at the intermediate lag intervals, and will yield higher values than the VR(2) statistic if the true underlying process is autoregressive (AR(n)) at an order higher than 1.

Box 1.3 *(continued)*

autoregressions used to assess the impact of flows on prices, impulse response functions were calculated to measure the impact of price changes on flows. This impact turned out to be significant and persistent over a period of several days, implying that an unexpected positive movement in equity prices leads to higher-than-average foreign inflows over a period of several days. These results are also similar to those obtained by Froot, O'Connell, and Seasholes (2001).

Volatility tests provide some support for occasional claims by policymakers of a connection between volatile foreign inflows and volatility in domestic markets. The tests performed here, however, using the popular generalized autoregressive conditional heteroscedasticity (GARCH) model, cannot assign a direction of causation. That is, they show a strong, statistically significant, positive correlation between the contemporaneous volatility of flows and that of returns. But they do not, on their own, provide a way of determining where the volatility shock originates, or, indeed, if it originates with a third omitted variable. However, assuming that prices respond more quickly to shocks than do flows (i.e., quantities), an observer might infer that it is volatility in foreign flows that leads to asset price volatility, rather than the converse.

Market reports of investment flows sometimes cite a tendency of foreign investors to shift focus from one emerging market to a neighboring market, as assets become fully valued or economic policies are adjusted. Examples include a shift away from Korean equities in the latter part of 2005, following strong inflows into that market over the previous two years, even as capital

inflows to other Asian nations remained robust. There are also accounts of switching among European, Middle Eastern, and African markets as specific problems arise in individual markets. To test for such activity, variance ratio statistics for entire regions were computed by summing across flows into each of the markets within that region. The results provide some modest evidence of switching behavior within regions, notably in Latin America, where the persistence of flows to the region as a whole exceeds that of flows to the constituent economies. Significantly, the exercise also showed persistence of flows to emerging markets overall as being greater than that of flows to the separate regions.[4]

Contrary to an earlier study, it does not appear that foreign inflows have regularly driven up equity prices in recent years (Froot, O'Connell, and Seasholes, 2001). However, the tests here suggest that equity flows into emerging markets are consistent with a herding pattern, with periods of above-normal inflows persisting for many days at a time. There is also evidence that foreign investors chase returns and switch between markets. In addition, the study finds some evidence of "volatility contagion," with volatility of inflows reflected in contemporaneous equity price volatility.

A key point is that foreign flows do not necessarily represent a shift in foreign demand in and of itself. For example, an increase in domestic demand could result in foreign outflows (as foreigners sell shares to domestic investors), together with a domestically driven increase in equity prices—the opposite combination to what would be expected if the flows only result from an increase in foreign demand for domestic equities. If, as suggested in Chapter 3, equity

Relationship of Flow Variance to the Variance of Returns
(GARCH model)

Coefficient	Coefficient Value	Standard Error	T-Statistic
β_2 (flow variance)	6.12	2.0	3.06
α	0.06	0.02	3.25
β_1	0.90	0.03	26.94

Model: $\sigma^2_{msci,t} = w + \alpha\varepsilon^2_{t-1} + \beta_1\sigma^2_{msci,t-1} + \beta_2\,\sigma^2_{flow,t}$

[4]In the two-market case, switching should arise only if there is a positive correlation between flows into market 1 at time t and flows into market 2 at time $t+1$ that is not fully explained by contemporaneous time t correlations between the two flow series, after controlling for the autocorrelations of each series. In other words, there must be some tendency of investors to move funds from one market to another within the group.

Box 1.3 *(concluded)*

markets have become deeper and more liquid in recent years, that could explain why the estimated impact from foreign flows to prices has declined or disappeared. Importantly, the Chapter 3 analysis does not apply to short-term equity

price volatility. Regardless of whether foreign or domestic demand becomes more volatile, the model suggests that this volatility is transmitted directly to equity prices, and that this impact is likely to be detectable.

Persistence in Daily Bank of New York Portfolio Flows: Variance Ratio (VR) Tests, January 2002 to May 2007

	VR(2)		VR(5)		VR(20)	
	Ratio	Standard error	Ratio	Standard error	Ratio	Standard error
Asia	**1.26**	**0.004**	**3.75**	**0.011**	**5.88**	**0.032**
India	1.20	0.010	3.70	0.024	7.72	0.060
Indonesia	1.32	0.005	3.86	0.013	5.28	0.039
Hong Kong SAR	1.24	0.004	3.60	0.010	5.96	0.029
Korea	1.16	0.005	3.21	0.013	4.18	0.034
Malaysia	1.28	0.004	3.87	0.012	6.76	0.043
Philippines	1.32	0.012	4.13	0.028	6.71	0.059
Singapore	1.20	0.011	3.41	0.023	5.57	0.050
Thailand	1.30	0.022	3.71	0.047	5.70	0.076
Taiwan Province of China	1.23	0.004	3.32	0.010	5.21	0.029
Latin America	**1.39**	**0.021**	**4.09**	**0.049**	**7.16**	**0.094**
Brazil	1.37	0.025	3.92	0.055	6.61	0.106
Mexico	1.22	0.009	3.16	0.021	4.99	0.049
Europe, Middle East and Africa	**1.38**	**0.011**	**4.07**	**0.025**	**6.19**	**0.061**
Turkey	1.38	0.035	4.12	0.075	5.30	0.119
Poland	1.30	0.008	3.63	0.019	5.65	0.051
Hungary	1.15	0.097	2.84	0.189	3.60	0.260
Czech Republic	1.25	0.011	3.54	0.024	5.10	0.066
South Africa	1.32	0.009	4.07	0.022	7.45	0.048
Emerging Markets Total	**1.39**	**0.005**	**4.29**	**0.012**	**7.71**	**0.038**

Source: IMF staff estimates.
Note: Variance ratio test using 1, 4, and 19 lags for VR(2), VR(5), VR(20), respectively. Regional flows are based on the sum of country flows in that region.

is consistent with the often-reported view that institutional investor flows tend to be more sticky than hedge fund flows.

However, the line between hedge funds and institutional investors is becoming more blurred.

On the one hand, institutional investors are increasingly allowed to invest in derivatives,

such as CDS, and many now have some flexibility within their mandate to sell short. In addition, some institutional investors can also now leverage their positions through structures, such as so-called 130/30 funds.[46] On the other hand, hedge funds have increasingly refocused their investment strategies in emerging markets away from traditional fixed-income investments,

---

flow data that appear broadly consistent, and where there was a significant outflow of foreign money in the equity market during the May–June 2006 correction.

[46]130/30 funds allow a maximum 30 percent short position, the proceeds of which can be used to fund up to a 130 percent long exposure.

Figure 1.24. Net Flows into Emerging Market Equities, May–June 2006
(In percent of prior 4-year cumulative flow)

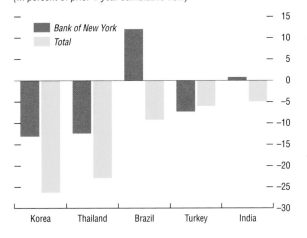

Sources: Bank of New York; CEIC database; and IMF staff estimates.

Figure 1.25. Emerging Market Hedge Fund Allocations
(In billions of U.S. dollars of assets under management)

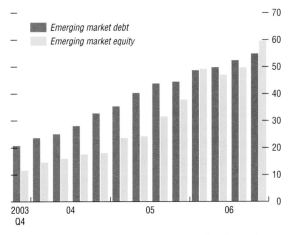

Source: Hedgefund.net/II News 2006–2007 Hedge Fund Asset Flows and Trends Report.

seeking other higher-yielding assets—both in equity markets and in structured products. The shift toward emerging market equity from debt is shown in Figure 1.25. Some hedge funds are also seeking seemingly uncorrelated risk by moving into illiquid products, such as more exotic equity markets (e.g., Vietnam, Sri Lanka) and real assets (e.g., private equity, real estate) and are becoming active in providing financing via structured products to local firms that have difficulty in accessing credit markets.[47] Other examples of structured trades include the direct purchase of nonperforming loan portfolios from commercial banks in Latin America. Some hedge funds are operating with much wider tolerance for losses than would be the case with more traditional liquid instruments such as external bonds. These hedge funds have attempted to increase lock-in periods in an effort to reduce redemption risk on investments with longer maturation periods, better matching their asset and liability maturities and mimicking more institutional investor commitments. The commonly used distinction between hedge funds and other leveraged investors, such as proprietary trading desks, and institutional investors is breaking down as a consequence.

Hedge funds are increasingly setting up in emerging market countries, raising important regulatory questions.

Onshore hedge funds have grown rapidly in a number of emerging markets, forcing policymakers to confront new financial stability issues. In Brazil, there has been a rapid rise in the assets under management of local hedge funds in the last few years. These funds are regulated both by the securities regulator and by the central bank as "multi-market" mutual funds. Individual investor protection is likely to be a key focus for regulators, as it has been in mature markets that have an established hedge fund sector. At the same time, authorities in a number

---

[47]Such financing is usually structured to provide some protection to more senior tranches, with the hedge funds purchasing more mezzanine and equity tranches.

of countries are actively planning to change the regulatory structure that onshore hedge funds face as part of plans to develop the financial sector. Asia, in particular, has seen a rapid expansion of the local hedge fund industry (Box 1.4). In response to this expansion, Hong Kong SAR has simplified licensing procedures to encourage hedge funds to set up or relocate to their jurisdiction, while Korea has recently unveiled a road map that envisages allowing onshore hedge funds as of 2012 as part of its plan to transform the country into a financial hub.

Policy Challenges

Policymakers need to better detect and understand how risks develop within the modern financial system...

The turbulence in global credit markets has been rooted in the weakening of credit discipline, a buildup of leverage in segments of the financial system, and investor complacency that had developed during the period of ample liquidity and benign financial conditions. Features of the modern financial landscape make it difficult to detect the location of these risks. When losses materialized, leverage and a lack of transparency in some segments made the impact worse. Structured products have spread those losses, but some market participants were ill equipped to handle the risks they assumed.

Overseers of financial stability need to strengthen their tools to identify such situations and prevent them from recurring. Stronger systems for monitoring and analyzing both the direct and embedded leverage that systemically important financial institutions are using or granting would help to anticipate challenges to financial stability.[48] Also, to reduce the financial transmission of disturbances, it is particularly important to have a degree of diversity in terms of investor bases, markets, strategies, investment horizons, risk management systems, counterparties, and returns among market participants. Long periods of stability should sensitize regulators and private institutions to the dangers of complacency. The trend toward transferring risks should be a focus, and regulators and those responsible for financial stability could probe further how credit risk transfer techniques may have reshaped stability risks.

In all of this analysis, regulators and supervisors should look at both on- and off-balance-sheet exposures of the institutions they are regulating and evaluate the array of risks that might eventually migrate to these institutions during a time of market strain. If these linkages were known, market discipline could function better, counterparty risk assessments could be improved, and policymakers and central banks would be better prepared.

...and help sustain market discipline by ensuring that financial intermediaries have adequate risk management capabilities to assess risks associated with complex structured products.

Many investment products are much more complex than in the past, especially in credit markets. Regulators need to renew efforts to test the capacity of their regulated institutions to manage the risks they are assuming. Regulated financial institutions should thoroughly explore the dynamics and sensitivities of the assets they hold and use as collateral, particularly if they are hard to value and have illiquid secondary markets, being aware of various "tail-risk" scenarios. Supervisors can better audit the risk management systems employed by such institutions to verify that they are appropriately tailored to their individual risks (see Chapter 2).

Supervisors will want to check that counterparty risk is being given high priority. In particular, the relationship between prime brokers and the hedge funds they service should remain in focus. The financial system relies heavily on that relationship working properly to ensure that hedge funds do not borrow to assume

---

[48]Metrics should include mortgage loan-to-value ratios, buyout debt levels and price multiples, prime brokerage margins and repo haircuts, and embedded leverage and over-collateralization levels in credit derivatives and funding vehicles.

Box 1.4. The Role of Hedge Funds in Emerging Asia

This box discusses the expansion and key character-istics of hedge funds with investment mandates in emerging Asia.

Growth in Asia-focused hedge funds has outpaced the rapid expansion of the global hedge fund industry in recent years (see first figure). Assets under management (AUM) of Asian hedge funds—broadly defined as hedge funds with a predominant investment mandate in Asia and/or managers located in Asia—have increased almost sevenfold, from $22 billion in 2001 to $146 billion at the end of the first quarter of 2007, compared with a sixfold increase of the global industry to about $1.5 trillion.[1] Within Asia, the main impetus for growth has come from emerging markets, in part reflecting reinvestments of relatively high returns, while the size of Japan-focused hedge funds has remained broadly stable since 2005. With AUM of some $100 billion at end-2006, emerging Asia

hedge funds accounted for nearly 60 percent of emerging market funds worldwide.[2]

Yet, the United States and the United Kingdom remain the centers for Asian hedge funds, with Hong Kong SAR the leader inside the region (see second figure). A favorable regulatory environment, ease of cross-border capital transactions, a large human talent pool, and a deep trading infrastructure are all factors helping to explain the locational preferences of hedge funds in Asia.[3]

Assets Under Management of Asian and Global Hedge Funds
(In billions of U.S. dollars)

Source: Alternative Investment Management Association.

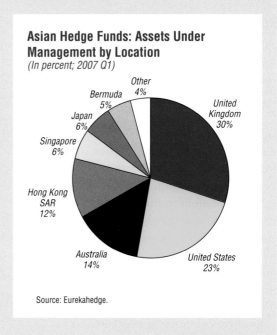

Asian Hedge Funds: Assets Under Management by Location
(In percent; 2007 Q1)

Source: Eurekahedge.

Equities are the focus of most Asian hedge fund strategies and investment allocations (see third figure)—some 60 percent of hedge funds employ long-short equity strategies, a share that has declined only slightly in recent years. This, in part, reflects the dominance of equity trading in Asian capital markets, while bond markets remain fragmented and underdevel-

Note: This box was authored by Olaf Unteroberdoerster.

[1]Following Ryback (2007), hedge funds are understood to be privately organized investment vehicles managed by professionals for a performance-based fee. Hedge funds operate under a flexible mandate in pursuit of alternative investment strategies.

[2] Laurelli (2007) estimates that emerging market hedge funds totaled $174.5 billion at end-2006.

[3]According to Baddepudi (2007), somewhat surprisingly, hedge funds based in Asia do not necessarily perform better than those focused on Asia, but based elsewhere.

oped. Regarding leverage, 40 percent of the self-described hedge funds in Hong Kong SAR do not use any leverage, while the majority (85 percent) of other funds report leverage of less than 200 percent of the reported net asset value.[4] AUM of Asian-focused hedge funds only represent a very small fraction of asset markets in Asia, often less than 1 percent in selected markets. Relative to debt securities in emerging Asia, the ratio increases to over 2½ percent, reflecting the slower development of bond markets in the region.

However, one factor that is not easily captured by available data is the capacity of hedge funds to take leveraged positions and employ derivatives. Their active trading also implies a much higher share in market turnover than is suggested by their size alone. In 2006, hedge funds globally were estimated to account for nearly 60 percent of trading volume in credit derivatives, and nearly half of the trading volumes in distressed debt and emerging market debt (Fitch Ratings, 2007b).

In line with global trends, the hedge fund industry is moving away from its traditional role in identifying pricing anomalies and exploiting arbitrage opportunities. Hedge funds are becoming increasingly like merchant banks, offering syndicated loans (Irvine, 2007), asset-backed finance and structured products (such as collateralized debt obligations), or entering "specialty situations" as co-investors with

[4]According to the Hong Kong SAR Securities and Futures Commission, various calculations of leverage were reported, with the more common definition applied being: (long market value + short market value)/net asset value. Still, these figures do not account for the leverage embedded in assets bought by hedge funds.

Distribution of Investment Strategies
(In percent of number of hedge funds)

Sources: Eurekahedge; and Hong Kong SAR, Securities and Futures Commission.

traditional private equity firms. Asia, Australia, Japan, Singapore, and Hong Kong SAR are the only jurisdictions that offer a legal framework for structured products and hence growth in this area. Amid the abundance of capital flowing into the region, funds' financial strength continues to grow and their lock-in periods are becoming longer, thereby facilitating the trend into credit derivatives and less liquid markets. Increasingly hedge funds have been able to negotiate directly as capital providers building on their own structuring capability, and thus bypass investment banks. At the same time, mutual funds and other institutional investors are beginning to emulate hedge fund strategies by setting up funds with limited leverage and with performance-based fees.

more risk than is prudent. Parties lending against hard-to-price collateral should verify that adequate mechanisms are in place for limiting the buildup of leverage. The hedge fund deleveraging seen in July and August 2007 brings into question the adequacy of repo collateral requirements. Lenders that applied unusually small haircuts for repo financing in an effort to win business suffered greater losses than those that imposed more traditional levels of haircuts.

Some of the risk is thereby transferred to prime brokers from hedge funds.

Greater transparency is needed with regard to the links between on- and off-balance-sheet entities.

Off-balance-sheet entities play a key role in modern finance. They can be a useful tool for managing risks and for ensuring that risk capital is used efficiently. However, the firms themselves and their investors need to be able to see the full range of links between the parent institution and the other entities with which it is involved. Regulators will need to consider the issue of providing greater clarity than at present as regards the links between various investment entities and institutions that sponsor them, benefit from them, provide services to them, or stand to offer support to them under certain circumstances. Banks and regulators alike need to assess the contingent draws on funding channels that can occur and assess the risks that such funding might result ultimately in credit exposure where collateral is hard to price. Consideration might also need to be given to whether capital charges on such standby credit lines are sufficient. The relevant perimeter of risk consolidation for banks may need to be reconsidered, as the usual accounting and legal perimeters appeared to be insufficient to guarantee adequate risk controls.

Although the collapse of a major hedge fund is not likely to pose a systemic threat (unless the failure impairs systemically important institutions), recent developments have shown that confidence can easily be shaken in a situation where losses are unknown and conduits and off-balance-sheet commitments are not transparent. One lesson of this experience, therefore, is the need for greater disclosure of relationships and potential exposures of major banks with SIVs and other conduits to funding difficulties.

It is especially important to examine short-term funding markets for potential risks from liquidity mismatches.

The short-term money markets used for wholesale funding, including, in particular, commercial paper and asset-backed commercial paper, play a vital role in the global finan-

cial system, but are often overlooked. Signs of market strains often show up in these markets before they materialize elsewhere, and it is frequently the loss of access to funding that moves an institution from illiquidity to insolvency. The authorities should therefore continue to intensely monitor the functioning of the repo and money markets for any signs of distress and be ready to raise a warning flag when signs of strain emerge. They will also want to verify that systemically important entities operating in the wholesale funding business have adequate controls and practices for assessing collateral.

One dimension of the recent episode of turbulence was the degree to which funding markets have been linked globally, as problems were transmitted and amplified because of, for instance, the extent to which banks in one country/continent required access to short-term offshore markets. This was evident when some banks had difficulty accessing foreign currency swaps to channel liquidity in the currency where liquidity demands had increased. As well, the broad mismatch of liquidity of ABCP conduits and SIVs should be assessed as a source of systemic concern where confidence in such structures became challenged, and where in some cases credit lines served as false insurance (to the vehicle) or as a channel of credit contagion. It was also clear that investors in money market funds were surprised to find the degree to which they were subject to losses on portfolios promising higher returns.

The need for a differentiated scale of credit ratings has again been made apparent.

The fallout in the mortgage market has drawn attention to the role of credit ratings agencies in structured credit markets. Less sophisticated investors, who were content to delegate the risk assessment of their positions to the credit ratings agencies, were negatively surprised by the intensity of downgrades. Previous GFSRs have pointed out that structured credit products are likely to suffer more severe, multiple-notch downgrades relative to the typically smoother downgrade paths of corporate bonds (IMF, 2006). The experience of the past year has underscored the need for further efforts to inform investors of these risks, but better still would be the introduction by ratings agencies of a more differentiated scale for structured credit products. For example, a special rating scale for structured credits could be introduced to highlight to investors that they should expect a higher speed of migration between ratings than on a traditional corporate bond.

On a related point, in the case of structured credit products that reference other structured credit products (e.g., ABS CDOs, ABCP, and "CDO-squareds"), investors should be mindful of the compounding effect of downgrades. Moreover, when ratings agencies are slow to recognize the deterioration of the performance of assets that underlie some structured credit products, investors should be aware that downgrades could be delayed and more severe.

Institutional investors, as buyers of structured credit products, must ensure that their investment mandates do not lead to an over-reliance on agency letter ratings, and that they do not (implicitly) delegate the job of examining complex assets to ratings agencies. Due to their embedded leverage, the prices of CDOs tend to be more volatile than similarly rated corporate bonds, which is reflected in higher spreads on the former. Hence, investors and brokers should delve beneath the published credit ratings to understand the price dynamics of the instruments. They should seek to understand the likely speed and intensity by which the value of the asset can change. Where possible, they should undertake their own analysis to verify their understanding of the main drivers of the value to the asset, and its sensitivity to changes in those variables, including scenario tests for extreme values. Investors should also seek to understand the liquidity of the market for the asset, both in good times and bad, and the likely ease or difficulty they might have in exiting the position. Ideally, investors should use real-time price quotations of the underlying collateral to mark the assets to market.

At the same time, regulators should seek to strike a balance between protecting consumers and facilitating innovation.

Although new origination and funding technology appears to have made the financial system more stable for the United States, it has exposed holes in the U.S. consumer protection regulatory framework—and other countries could usefully take note. Policymakers need to tighten lending standards and restrictions on aggressive lending, while preserving a model that successfully disperses exposure to higher-risk mortgages away from the banking system. For example, supervisory agencies have tightened their guidance on appropriate subprime lending practices and how to better oversee mortgage originators that are not under the usual bank supervision umbrella. However, some proposals suggest that banks involved in securitization, and even the holders of mortgage-related securities, should be liable for any "predatory" loans they handle or hold. If potential liability were uncapped, there is a danger that few, if any, subprime loans would be originated or securitized.

Emerging markets need to ensure that policies support continued resilience should global market conditions remain volatile.

Policies should take into account that emerging markets with current account deficits financed with short-term capital flows could be particularly vulnerable to rapid shifts in global risk appetite. In addition, those countries that have either engaged in, or been a destination for, carry-trade-related activities may be impacted by adjustments in exchange rates resulting from an unwinding of global carry trades. This would include, for example, countries in emerging Europe where household mortgages have been denominated in Swiss francs. More generally, the repricing of credit will raise the cost of capital to emerging market corporates borrowing externally, creating a drag on growth.

Emerging markets need to step up surveillance of risks of credit indiscipline and related vulnerabilities.

The vulnerabilities that may be building as a result of the weakening of credit and market discipline represent an area for attention. In some cases, private sector borrowers in emerging markets are adopting relatively risky strategies to raise financing, often taking exchange rate risk, and thus increasing their exposure to volatility. Capital market financing has supported rapid credit growth, but investors may not be willing in the event of continued turbulence to lend to weaker banks. As well, emerging markets are facing other challenges related to surging capital inflows. Thus, even as the funding liquidity disruptions in mature markets work themselves out, deleveraging and a pullback from risky assets is likely to continue. While these developments may be offset to some degree by high GDP growth and improved macroeconomic policies, authorities in some emerging markets could intensify monitoring and strengthen policies to ensure that risks remain manageable.

Greater external borrowing by emerging market corporations and exposure to foreign currency risk require increased surveillance, as does the exposure of domestic financial institutions to synthetic and structured products.

Many emerging market central banks collect information on foreign borrowing by local corporations. However, the growth of cross-currency swap markets and the availability of various means of transforming currency exposure mean that monitoring systems need to be strengthened. Regulators should be proactive in gathering market intelligence that can reveal the underlying scale and motivations for capital flows. In addition, financial engineering that takes credit exposures offshore through various entities may not be fully captured by official data. Financial institutions in countries where local markets are underdeveloped or have low yields have found structured and synthetic instruments alluring. While these instruments have their rightful place under sound asset and liability management practices, users of them need to be aware of risks

should volatility disrupt pricing and returns. Regulators could try to ensure that exposures to interest rate and currency derivatives that embed features that enhance yield are well understood by local investors and borrowers, and that exposures are seen as manageable.

With numerous two-way channels open to international markets, and the growth of derivative-related transactions, capital controls may be offering less insulation.

Expectations of exchange rate appreciation can increase short-term debt-related flows into emerging markets. These can complicate policymaking, leading to imbalances in domestic markets and increasing external financing risks. This makes it more difficult for policymakers to set independent paths for interest rates and/or exchange rates. Official restrictions on offshore-onshore trading offer some protection against speculative flows. However, persistent imbalances between onshore and offshore rates tend to encourage circumvention, as has been the case in a number of Asian and Latin American markets. Efforts to strictly enforce barriers have had mixed results (see Chapter 3).

Addressing structural weaknesses and fragilities in local markets and strengthening the framework for monetary operations are a critical focus.

Capital inflows can pose significant challenges for policymakers, at times overwhelming foreign exchange and money markets. Market volatility in the short term—some of which is attributable to rapid inflows—can hamper banks' efforts to manage their assets and liabilities, as hedging becomes more difficult. Policymakers need to develop flexible monetary operation frameworks and remove remaining rigidities in money markets to avoid inadvertently inviting speculative inflows.

In sum, recent events have suggested a number of areas requiring the attention of both the public and private sectors. Some initial lessons and possible policy responses are provided above, but there is still much to learn, since events are still unfolding. It will be important for policymakers to weigh the benefits of rapid responses against the longer-term costs (perhaps unintended) that they may entail.

Annex 1.1. The Global Financial Stability Map

This annex outlines the indicators selected for each of the broad risks and conditions in the global financial stability map. To complete the map, these indicators are supplemented by market intelligence and judgment that cannot be adequately represented with available indicators.

To begin construction of the stability map, we determine the percentile rank of the current level of each indicator relative to its history to guide our assessment of current conditions, relative both to the April 2007 GFSR and over a longer horizon. Where possible, we have therefore favored indicators with a reasonable time series history. However, the final choice of positioning on the map is not mechanical and represents the best judgment of IMF staff. The stability map remains a work in progress and will be developed further in future GFSRs. As the concepts underlying the risks and conditions are refined, alternative indicators that represent them more effectively could replace some of those discussed below.[49]

Table 1.6 shows how each indicator has changed since the April 2007 GFSR and our overall assessment of the movement in each risk and condition.

Monetary and Financial Conditions

The availability and cost of funding linked to global monetary and financial conditions (Figure 1.26). To capture movements in general monetary conditions in mature markets, we begin by examining the cost of central bank liquidity, measured as the average level of real short rates across the G-7. From there, we take a broad measure of excess liquidity, defined as the difference between broad money growth and estimates for money demand. Realizing that the channels through which the setting of monetary policy is transmitted to financial

[49]Bell and Dattels (forthcoming) provides a fuller discussion of the concepts and construction of the global financial stability map.

Table 1.6. Changes in Risks and Conditions Since the April 2007 *Global Financial Stability Report*

Conditions and Risks	Change since April 2007 GFSR
Monetary and Financial Conditions	↓
• G-7 average real short rate	↓
• G-3 excess liquidity	↑
• Financial conditions index	↓
• Growth in official reserves	↑
Risk Appetite	↓↓
• Investor survey of risk appetite	↓
• State Street investor confidence	↑
• Flows into emerging market bond and equity funds	↓
• Risk aversion index	↓
Macroeconomic Risks	↑
• *World Economic Outlook* global growth risks	↑
• G-3 confidence indices	↔
• Economic surprise index	↓
Emerging Market Risks	↔
• Fundamental EMBIG spread	↔
• Sovereign ratings upgrades/ downgrades	↔
• Private sector credit growth	↑
• Inflation volatility	↔
Credit Risks	↑↑↑
• Global high-yield index spread	↑
• Credit quality composition of high-yield index	↑
• Speculative default rate forecast	↑
• LCFI portfolio default probability	↑
Market and Liquidity Risks	↑↑
• Hedge fund estimated leverage	↓
• Speculative positions in futures markets	↑
• Common component of asset returns	↑
• World implied equity risk premia	↔
• Composite volatility measure	↑
• Financial market liquidity index	↑

Note: Changes are defined for each risk/condition such that ↑ signifies more risk or easier conditions and ↓ signifies the converse. ↔ indicates no appreciable change. EMBIG = Emerging Markets Bond Index Global; LCFI = large complex financial institutions.

markets are complex, some researchers have found that including capital market measures more fully captures the effect of financial prices and wealth on the economy. We therefore also use a financial conditions index that incorporates movements in exchange rates, interest rates, credit spreads, and asset market returns.

Rapid increases in official reserves held by the central bank create central bank liquidity in the domestic currency and in global markets. In recent years, the investment of a large share of these reserves into U.S. treasuries and agencies has contributed to the low yields in global fixed-income markets. To measure this, we look at the growth of official international reserves held at the Federal Reserve.

Risk Appetite

The willingness of investors to take on additional risk by increasing exposure to riskier asset classes, and the consequent potential for increased losses (Figure 1.27). We aim to measure the extent to which investors are actively taking on more risk. A direct approach to this exploits survey data that explicitly seek to determine the risk-taking behavior of major institutional investors. The Merrill Lynch Investor Survey asks more than 300 fund managers what level of risk they are currently taking relative to their benchmark. We then track the net percentage of investors reporting higher-than-benchmark risk-taking. An alternative approach is to examine institutional holdings and flows into risky assets, on the basis that an increase in such positions signals an increased willingness of institutional investors, relative to individual domestic investors, to take on risk. The State Street Investor Confidence Index uses changes in investor holdings of equities relative to safer assets to measure risk appetite, covering portfolios with around 15 percent of the world's tradable assets. In addition, we take account of flows into emerging market equity and bond funds as these represent another risky asset class. Risk appetite may also be inferred indirectly by examining price or return data. As an example of this approach, the Goldman Sachs Risk Aversion Index measures investors' willingness to invest in risky assets as opposed to risk-free securities, building on the premises of the Capital Asset Pricing Model. By comparing returns between treasury bills and equities, the model allows the level of risk aversion to move over time. Taken together, these

measures cover various aspects of risk-taking and provide a broad indicator of risk appetite.

Macroeconomic Risks

Macroeconomic shocks with the potential to trigger a sharp market correction, given existing conditions in capital markets (Figure 1.28). Our principal assessment of the macroeconomic risks is based on the analysis contained in the *World Economic Outlook* and is consistent with the overall conclusion reached in that report on the outlook for, and risks associated with, global growth. We complement that analysis by examining measures that focus on movements in confidence about the overall economic outlook. First, we look at the GDP-weighted sum of confidence indices across the major mature markets to determine whether business and consumers are optimistic or pessimistic about the economic outlook. Second, we examine an index of economic activity surprises. This index shows whether data releases are consistently surprising financial markets on the upside or downside to capture the extent to which informed participants are likely to have to revise their outlook for economic growth in light of realized outcomes.

Emerging Market Risks

Underlying fundamentals in emerging markets and vulnerabilities to external risks (Figure 1.29). These risks are conceptually separate, though closely linked to macroeconomic risks, as they focus on emerging markets only as opposed to the global environment. Using the model of emerging market sovereign spreads presented in previous GFSRs, we can identify the movement in Emerging Markets Bond Index Global (EMBIG) spreads accounted for by changes in the fundamentals of emerging market countries as opposed to the spread changes resulting from external factors. These fundamental factors account for changes in economic, political, and financial risks within the country. This is then complemented by examining the trend in sovereign rating actions of Standard & Poor's and

Moody's. Such a measure attempts to capture improvements in both the macroeconomic environment facing such economies and progress in reducing vulnerabilities arising from external financing needs. We also want to measure fundamental conditions in emerging market countries that are separate from those related to sovereign debt, particularly given the reduced need for such financing across many emerging market countries. Consequently, we examine the growth in private sector credit across emerging market countries. Rapid rates of credit growth have the potential to lead to financial sector and household vulnerabilities and upward inflationary pressures. Finally, we examine the volatility of inflation rates across emerging markets to capture the extent to which domestic monetary policies are successfully controlling inflation.

Credit Risks

Changes in and perceptions of credit quality that have the potential to create losses resulting in stress in systemically important financial institutions (Figure 1.30). Spreads on a global high-yield index provide a market price-based measure of investors' assessments of corporate credit risk. We recognize, however, that such an assessment forms only part of the pricing of such assets, and that prices can deviate from fundamental valuation over extended periods of time. Consequently, we also focus on more direct measures of credit quality. To do this, we examine the credit quality composition of the high-yield index to identify whether it is increasingly made up of higher or lower quality issues. To be precise, we report the percentage of the index comprised of CCC or lower rated issues. This captures two distinct effects: first, a change in the ratings of corporate issues already in the index, and second, differences in the quality of new issues that are entering the index compared with the current constituents. Both are important in measuring the overall level of credit quality. We also examine forecasts of the global speculative default rate produced by Moody's. While forecast default rates depend

on the robustness of the underlying econometric model, they at least conceptually present a forward-looking measure of defaults as opposed to the traditional trailing-realized default rates. Finally, we use the credit risk indicator for LCFIs to highlight market perceptions of systemic default risk in the financial sector, given our remit of focusing on financial stability.

Market and Liquidity Risks

The potential for instability in pricing risks that could result in broader spillovers and/or mark-to-market losses (Figure 1.31). An indicator attempting to capture the extent of market sensitivity of hedge fund returns provides a market risk indicator for this important trading group. We also produce a speculative positions index, constructed from the noncommercial average absolute net positions relative to open interest across a range of futures contracts covering most asset classes as reported to the Commodity Futures Trading Commission. This measure will rise when speculators are taking large positional bets on futures markets relative to commercial traders. Next, we estimate the proportion of return variance across a range of asset classes that can be explained by a common factor. Higher correlations across asset classes tend to increase the risks of a more disorderly correction of market prices in the face of a shock. We also look at an estimate of equity risk premia in mature markets using a three-stage dividend discount model. Low ex ante equity risk premia may suggest that investors are underestimating the risk attached to equity returns and so increase potential market risks. We also look at a measure of implied volatility across a range of assets to assess the extent of market concern over risk, though it may also indicate the extent to which markets are too complacent about those risks. Finally, we attempt to capture funding, secondary market trading, and perceptions of counterparty risks in core markets. To measure this aspect, we examine the spread between major mature market government securities yields and interbank rates, bid-ask spreads on major mature market currencies, and daily return-to-volume ratios of equity markets.

Figure 1.26. Global Financial Stability Map: Monetary and Financial Conditions

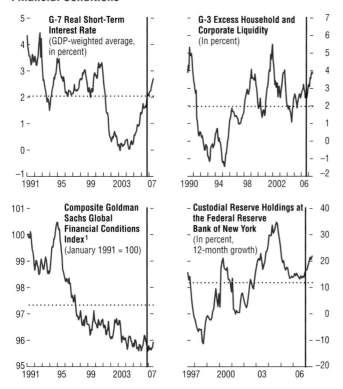

Sources: Bloomberg L.P.; Goldman Sachs; OECD; and IMF staff estimates.

Note: Dashed lines are period averages. Vertical lines represent data as of the April 2007 GFSR.

[1]A GDP-weighted average of China, the euro area, Japan, and United States. Each country index represents a weighted average of 3-month LIBOR (35% weight), the 10-year swap rate plus the 10-year credit default swap or CDX (55%), the Goldman Sachs nominal trade-weighted dollar index (5%), and the S&P 500 stock price index (5%). Prior to October 2003, the Moody's A-rated corporate bond index is used for corporate bond yields.

Figure 1.27. Global Financial Stability Map: Risk Appetite

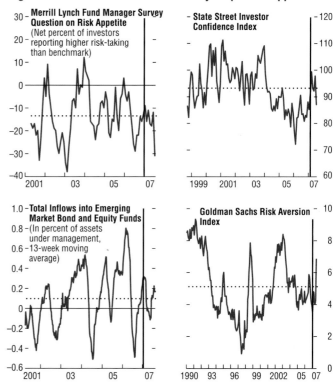

Sources: Emerging Portfolio Fund Research, Inc.; Goldman Sachs; Merrill Lynch; State Street Global Markets; and IMF staff estimates.

Note: Dashed lines are period averages. Vertical lines represent data as of the April 2007 GFSR.

Figure 1.28. Global Financial Stability Map: Macroeconomic Risks

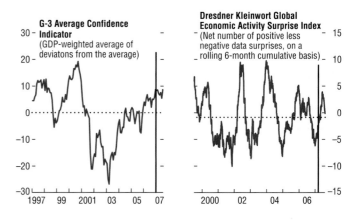

Sources: Bloomberg L.P.; Dresdner Kleinwort; and IMF staff estimates.

Note: Dashed lines are period averages. Vertical lines represent data as of the April 2007 GFSR.

Figure 1.29. Global Financial Stability Map: Emerging Market Risks

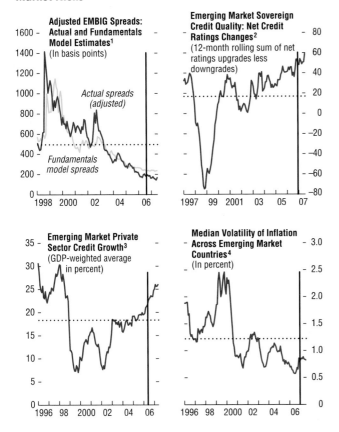

Figure 1.30. Global Financial Stability Map: Credit Risks

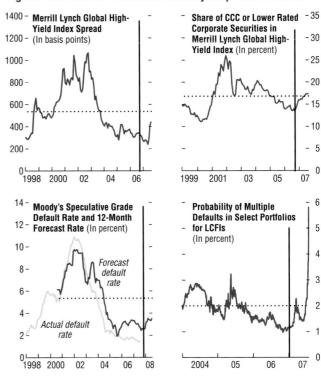

Sources: Bloomberg L.P.; Merrill Lynch; Moody's; and IMF staff estimates.
Note: Dashed lines are period averages. Vertical lines represent data as of the April 2007 GFSR. LCFIs = large complex financial institutions.

Sources: Bloomberg L.P.; IMF, *International Financial Statistics*; JPMorgan Chase & Co.; The PRS Group; and IMF staff estimates.
Note: Dashed lines are period averages. Vertical lines represent data as of the April 2007 GFSR.
[1]EMBIG = Emerging Markets Bond Index Global. The model and its output exclude Argentina because of breaks in the data series related to debt restructuring. Owing to short data series, the model also excludes Indonesia and several smaller countries. The analysis thus includes 32 countries.
[2]Net actions of upgrades (+1 for each notch), downgrades (−1 for each notch), changes in outlooks (+/− 0.25), reviews and creditwatches (+/− 0.5).
[3]Using data of 44 countries.
[4]Average of 12-month rolling standard deviations of consumer price changes in 25 emerging markets.

Figure 1.31. Global Financial Stability Map: Market and Liquidity Risks

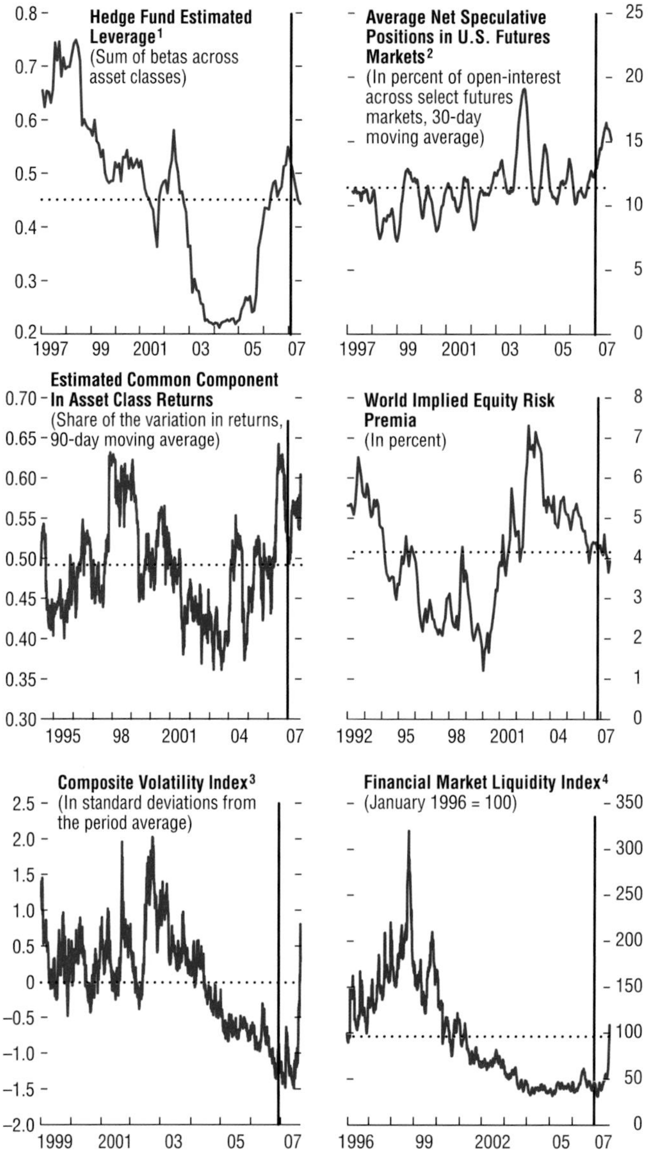

Sources: Bloomberg L.P.; JPMorgan Chase & Co.; Credit Suisse Tremont Index LLC; I/B/E/S; Morgan Stanley Capital International; and IMF staff estimates.

Note: Dashed lines are period averages. Vertical lines represent data as of the April 2007 GFSR.

[1]36-month rolling regressions of hedge fund performance versus real asset returns.

[2]Data represent the absolute value of the net positions taken by noncommercial traders in 17 select U.S. futures markets. High values are indicative of heavy speculative positioning across markets, either net-long or net-short.

[3]Data represent an average z-score of the implied volatility derived from options from stock market indices, interest, and exchange rates. A value of 0 indicates the average implied volatility across asset classes is in line with the period average (from 12/31/98 where data are available). Values of +/−1 indicate average implied volatility is one standard deviation above or below the period average.

[4]The index is calculated combining the spread between government securities yields and interbank rates, currency bid-ask spreads, and daily return-to-volume ratios of equity markets. A higher value indicates tighter market liquidity conditions.

Annex 1.2. Sovereign Wealth Funds

Note: This annex was prepared by a Monetary and Capital Markets Department staff team led by Udaibir S. Das, with inputs from the Fiscal Affairs and Statistics Departments.

Tentative estimates of foreign assets held by sovereigns include $5.6 trillion of international reserves and between $1.9 trillion and $2.9 trillion in types of sovereign wealth fund (SWF) arrangements. These amount to about 10 times less than the assets under management of mature market institutional investors ($53 trillion) and modestly higher than those managed by hedge funds ($1 trillion to $1.5 trillion) (Financial Stability Forum, 2007). Current IMF projections are that sovereigns (predominantly emerging markets) will continue to accumulate international assets at the rate of $800 billion to $900 billion per year, which could bring the aggregate foreign assets under sovereign management to about $12 trillion by 2012. Against the backdrop of this expected growth, this annex provides a taxonomy of SWFs, discusses their asset allocation frameworks, and highlights some operational issues.

Overview

The growth of SWF-type institutional arrangements can be seen as a policy response to the strong accumulation of foreign assets by the official sector. However, SWFs are not new, especially in countries rich in natural resources (e.g., oil). SWFs have recently gained prominence in several (non-oil) emerging markets and commodity-based developing countries, reflecting large balance of payments surpluses.

Large current account surpluses and capital inflows have prompted an ongoing debate on sovereigns' underlying policies and possible adjustments, such as the appropriate level of exchange rate flexibility, the "optimal" level of reserves, and the potential allocation of foreign assets to SWFs.

The growth in sovereign assets is turning the official sector into an active investor group.[50] Sovereigns' cross-border asset allocation choices are assuming importance in the context of prudent management of public financial assets. The recent literature on SWFs has focused on (1) issues of transparency in the external and government accounts; (2) different objectives of the funds, and approaches toward risk and longer-term investment horizons; and (3) the emphasis on "return" rather than "liquidity" for balance of payment needs. In particular, questions remain as to the potential impact of countries' asset allocations and strategic investments on international capital movements and asset prices.

Sovereign Wealth Funds: One Type or Several?

The reporting of sovereign financial assets has focused thus far on the appropriate methodological treatment of reserve assets (Box 1.5). Although there is no universally agreed-upon definition, SWFs can generally be defined as special investment funds created or owned by governments to hold foreign assets for long-term purposes. SWFs can be classified according to at least two criteria: (1) the sources of sovereign wealth, and (2) their policy objectives (Table 1.7).

Sources of Sovereign Wealth Funds

The funding of SWFs comes from different sources, which can be combined. Some funds are byproducts of fiscal budget surpluses accumulated due to a combination of revenues from exports and spending restraint. Fiscal surpluses and public savings generated domestically, such as privatization receipts, can also be sources for SWFs, as can large balance of payment surpluses, with or without a corresponding budget surplus.[51]

---

[50]See Chapter 2 of the April 2007 GFSR (IMF, 2007a).
[51]SWFs from public savings and privatization are more akin to nonrenewable resource funds, as they represent an increase in net financial wealth.

Box 1.5. Sovereign Wealth Funds: A Statistical Perspective

Statistical and data issues raised by the use of sovereign wealth funds (SWFs) are currently being studied by the International Monetary Fund. This box provides some information about these issues.

The draft sixth edition of the *Balance of Payments and International Investment Position Manual (BPM6)* includes a methodology for determining whether foreign assets held in SWFs should be included in reserve assets. To be included in reserves, the foreign assets of the SWF need to be readily available to the monetary authorities and be a liquid claim in foreign currency on nonresidents.

A specific issue for SWFs is whether there is some legal or administrative guidance that results in the assets being encumbered in a way that precludes their ready availability to the monetary authorities. If the SWF's external assets are on the books of the central bank or an agency of the central government that exercises control over the disposition of funds, then the presumption is that the assets are international reserves, provided all other criteria for being a reserve asset are met, particularly liquidity *(BPM6)*. If, however, the funds are held in a long-term fund separately incorporated, the presumption is that they should not be included in reserves. But any final determination of whether an asset can be classified as a reserve asset depends upon close examination of the circumstances.

Assets held in a resident SWF that are claims on nonresidents but do not meet the criteria to be classified as reserve assets are classified in the financial accounts (transactions) and international investment position under the appropriate instrument and functional category.

A Taxonomy Based on Policy Objectives

The following types of funds can be distinguished, based on their dominant objectives:
- *Stabilization funds* are set up by countries rich in natural resources to insulate the budget and economy from volatile commodity prices (usually oil). The funds build up assets during the years of ample fiscal revenues to prepare for leaner years.
- *Savings funds* are intended to share wealth across generations. For countries rich in natural resources, savings funds transfer non-renewable assets into a diversified portfolio of international financial assets to provide for future generations, or other long-term objectives (IMF, 2007c).[52]
- *Reserve investment corporations* are funds established as a separate entity either to reduce the negative cost-of-carry of holding reserves or to pursue investment policies with higher returns. Often, the assets in such arrangements are still counted as reserves.
- *Development funds* allocate resources for funding priority socioeconomic projects, such as infrastructure.
- *Pension reserve funds* have identified pension and/or contingent-type liabilities on the government's balance sheet.[53]

Additional objectives include enhancing transparency in the management of revenues from (commodity) exports and fiscal policy. In practice, SWFs typically have multiple or gradually changing objectives. For example, some countries set up funds for both stabilization and savings objectives. As circumstances change, the objectives of the funds may also change. This is especially true for countries that export natural resources. Initially, a stabilization fund is established to smooth fiscal revenue or sterilize foreign currency inflows. As the assets

---

[52]See IMF (2007c). While newer oil funds predominantly focus on stabilization objectives, the recent increase in oil prices has added emphasis to savings objectives, and in some cases, enhanced asset management.

[53]To some extent, development funds and even pension reserve funds can be considered as subsets of SWFs that are (explicitly or implicitly) linked to long-term fiscal commitments.

in the fund continue to grow beyond the level needed for the purpose of stabilization, country authorities may revisit the objectives and redesign the structure of the fund to broaden the objective. This often leads to assets being split into several tranches for different objectives, or to the creation of separate funds with different objectives.[54]

Sovereign Wealth Funds and Strategic Asset Management

Two major considerations usually guide the allocation and distribution of SWF assets. The first is the accumulation and withdrawal rules regarding the fund's future cash flows where applicable. The second is the fund's objectives. Together, these considerations drive the strategic asset allocation (SAA), which reflects the return objective, risk tolerance, and identified constraints (such as liquidity and financing needs, investment horizon, and legal and regulatory requirements).

SWFs may hold assets with negative correlation to the country's major exports (e.g., oil) or offset the price risk of future imports (depending on the country's risk profile) via its SAA decisions. Funds without identified liabilities allow for a more exclusive focus on a return objective and acceptable level of risk. However, for some SWFs, sterilization instruments used to mop up excess liquidity may need to be considered as liabilities, especially from an integrated asset and liability management perspective.[55] The objectives of SWFs could be undermined

by the accumulation of liabilities elsewhere in the public sector.[56] Some funds, such as pension reserve funds, may have identified liabilities to be matched within the SAA framework to allow for a clear operational framework and transparent objectives.

SWFs' allocations of sovereign reserve assets to domestic investments have macroeconomic implications, especially for developing and emerging market economies. To invest domestically, SWFs would typically need to convert part of their accumulated assets back into domestic currency, possibly reversing the economic policies that led to reserve accumulation. Investing domestically could stimulate domestic demand with inflationary consequences. Issues of fiscal accounting, transparency, and risk could also emerge if those investments are actually government spending operations that should take place within the budget. Therefore, domestic investments are generally seen to be ruled out in SWFs.

Different types of SWFs could have markedly different SAAs reflective of their different objectives and constraints. Stabilization funds, for instance, are generally conservative in their SAA, using shorter investment horizons and low risk-return profiles, or other instruments (perhaps longer-term) that vary inversely with the risk the fund is meant to cover. Typically, such funds are designed to insulate the budget from terms-of-trade shocks and to meet contingent financing requirements. In this regard, they are akin to reserves, which are managed for safety and liquidity, and it is only after such considerations are satisfied that higher risk/return objectives are set.

SWFs with long-term objectives, such as savings funds, may be better able to accommodate short-term volatility in asset returns. Nonetheless, savings funds and pension reserve

---

[54]The institutional arrangements for managing these different types of arrangements are broadly of three categories. The first two pertain to those managed by the central bank and/or an independent agency. A third category of SWFs consist of those funds already established that acquire the modality of "tiers of accounts," that is, separate funds for different purposes. In some instances, the central bank transfers funds to the SWF, while in other cases funds are transferred to the central bank for management purposes.

[55]Returns on the SWFs are therefore net of interest payments to the holders of the sterilization instruments. At the same time, the currency mismatch, often resulting from issuing domestic currency liabilities, would need

to be taken into consideration when setting the SWF's investment strategy.

[56]Accumulating assets in an SWF may not affect the net wealth of the public sector if, for instance, the fund is being financed by issuance of public debt.

Table 1.7. Size and Structure of Major Sovereign Wealth Funds

Country	Fund Name	Assets	Source of Funds	Ownership and Investment Management	Investment Strategy and Strategic Asset Allocation (SAA)
United Arab Emirates	Abu Dhabi Investment Authority (ADIA)/ Abu Dhabi Investment Council (ADIC)	$250 billion to $875 billion[1]	Oil	Owned by the emirate of Abu Dhabi, ADIA has been the primary conduit for investing oil surpluses in overseas assets since 1976. Recently a separate legal entity, the ADIC, was established to encourage competition with the ADIA. Abu Dhabi's surpluses will now be allocated to both the ADIA and ADIC.	Major global investor. Investment strategy and asset allocation is unknown.
Norway	Government Pension Fund—Global	$308 billion (as of March 31, 2007)	Oil	Owned by the government and managed by Norges Bank Investment Management.	Global asset allocation with 40 percent in equities and 60 percent in global fixed income.
Saudi Arabia	No designated name	$250+ billion[2]	Oil	Saudi Arabia Monetary Agency manages the foreign assets: $225 billion is held on its own balance sheet, a portion of which is designated as reserves, and $51 billion is managed on behalf of various government agencies.	Major global investor. Although the size of assets is known, the investment strategy and SAA is not known beyond broad indications.
Kuwait	Kuwait Investment Authority (KIA) General Reserve Fund (GRF) and Future Generations Fund (FGF)	$160 billion to $250 billion[1]	Oil	The KIA is an autonomous government body responsible for the management of the GRF and FGF, as well as any other funds entrusted to it on behalf of the government of Kuwait.	The GRF is invested in the local, Arab, and international financial markets. The FGF has a global asset allocation based on investment guidelines approved by the FGF board.
Singapore	Government Investment Corporation (GIC)	$100+ billion	Other	Separate investment corporation established in 1981, fully owned by the government.	Global asset allocation (not made public). Invests in all major asset classes.
	Temasek Holdings	$100+ billion	Other	Temasek Holdings is a private company, set up in 1974 to hold and manage investment previously held by the principal shareholder, the Ministry of Finance.	SAA weights unknown. Geographical distribution as of March 2006 was 38 percent Singapore assets, 40 percent in rest of Asia, 20 percent in the Organization for Economic Cooperation and Development, and 2 percent in "other" countries.
China	State Foreign Exchange Investment Corporation[3]	$200 billion	Other	To be determined.	To be determined.
Russia	Oil Stabilization Fund[4]	$127 billion (as of August 1, 2007)	Oil	Owned by the government and managed by the Russian Central Bank.	Invests largely in fixed-income assets, with 44 percent in U.S. dollars, 46 percent in euros, and 10 percent in pound sterling.

Table 1.7 *(concluded)*

Australia	Australian Future Fund	$42 billion (as of May 1, 2007)	Other	Established in 2006. Owned by the government and managed by the Future Fund Management Agency. The aim is to underwrite the government's future superannuation liabilities.	Australia
United States (Alaska)	Alaska Permanent Reserve Fund	$35 billion (as of June 30, 2007)	Oil and minerals	Owned by the state of Alaska, established in 1976, and managed by the state-owned Alaska Permanent Fund Corporation.	SAA consists of 53 percent equities, 29 percent fixed income, 10 percent real estate, and 8 percent alternative assets.
Brunei	Brunei Investment Authority General Reserve Fund[1]	$30 billion	Oil	Owned by the government and managed by the Brunei Investment Agency.	Invests in a large global portfolio of financial and real assets. SAA not made public.
Korea	Korea Investment Corporation	$20 billion	Other	Launched in 2005 to manage $20 billion of entrusted foreign exchange reserves, of which $17 billion is from Bank of Korea and $3 billion from the government.	Plans to invest in a global asset allocation. SAA not yet available.
Canada	Alberta Heritage Savings Trust Fund	$15 billion (as of March 31, 2007)	Oil	Owned by the government of the Province of Alberta, managed by Alberta Finance.	Invests in a global SAA with 30 percent fixed income, 45 percent equities, 10 percent real estate, and 15 percent alternative assets.
Chile	Economic and Social Stabilization Fund	$9.83 billion (as of July 31, 2007)	Copper	Established in 2006. Owned by the government and managed by the Central Bank of Chile as a fiscal agent.	SAA consists of 72 percent government bonds and 28 percent money market instruments in U.S. dollars, euros, and yen.
	Pension Reserve Fund	$1.37 billion (as of July 31, 2007)	Copper	Established in 2006. Owned by the government and managed by the Central Bank of Chile as a fiscal agent.	SAA consists of 79 percent government bonds and 21 percent money market instruments in U.S. dollars, euros, and yen.
Botswana	Pula Fund[2]	$5+ billion	Diamonds	Owned jointly by the government and the Bank of Botswana. The government's share of the Pula Fund is accounted for on the balance sheet of the Bank of Botswana.	The fund invests in public equity and fixed-income instruments in industrialized economies. The fund does not invest in emerging markets, as they may be highly dependent on commodities.

Sources: Public information from websites; IMF; and Morgan Stanley Research.

Note: Other countries with known sovereign wealth funds include Azerbaijan, Kingdom of Bahrain, Chad, Ecuador, Equatorial Guinea, Gabon, Islamic Republic of Iran, Ireland, Kazakhstan, Kiribati, Libya, Malaysia, Mauritania, Mexico, Oman, Qatar, Sudan, Taiwan Province of China, Timor-Leste, Trinidad and Tobago, Uganda, and Venezuela.

[1]Estimates by Morgan Stanley Research and PIMCO.

[2]In some countries, such as Saudi Arabia and Botswana, there is no formal sovereign wealth fund but the monetary agency manages foreign assets on behalf of various government agencies.

[3]Announced on March 9, 2007, the fund may be established at the end of 2007.

[4]Starting in February 2008, the Oil Stabilization Fund will be divided into two separate funds with distinct policy objectives (Stabilization Fund versus National Welfare Fund).

funds also aim to preserve a minimum amount of capital, in real terms, so that the purchasing power of the funds is guaranteed. Pension reserve funds with explicit liabilities typically design SAA benchmarks that preserve their solvency.

Some Issues for Consideration

The cross-border asset holdings of SWFs raise issues similar to those faced by other international market participants, including their role in global financial markets.

One view is that SWFs enhance market liquidity and financial resource allocation. This view recognizes that SWFs, especially the larger ones, typically use a mix of well-trained in-house expertise and well-regarded international external fund managers, and have longer investment horizons that can accommodate short-term volatility. Consequently, their investment operations may dampen asset price volatility and lower liquidity risk premia, compared with a situation in which these assets were to be managed with shorter duration.

Another view holds, however, that the limited publicly available information on some SWFs, their multiplicity of objectives, and a lack of clarity on their institutional structure and investment management, make it difficult to assess the SWFs' asset management activities and their impact on the capital markets. Without more public accountability, funds may alter their governance structures, perhaps as a result of losses, which, in turn, could lead to sharp changes in investment policies, possibly exacerbating market volatility in some asset classes. The public ownership of SWFs (and other state-owned entities) also raises questions about possible capital account restrictions initiated in recipient countries, especially to avoid certain types of foreign direct investment.

As their size, number, and use grows, and as domestic and international public attention directed toward them increases, SWFs may be faced with several institutional and operational challenges, including:

- *Defining objectives and setting and implementing sovereign asset allocation.* A well-defined SAA within a clearly articulated investment policy is a critical operational component for public investment funds, and as new developments arise, a reassessment of existing objectives and constraints might be needed and reflected in the overall risk tolerance.
- *Institutional arrangements,* including withdrawal and accumulation rules that reflect risk-sharing arrangements between the government and the SWF, or the central bank, and establishing responsibility for investment decisions and their outcomes.[57]
- *Accountability arrangements,* including fiduciary duty to citizens, the legal foundation, and the internal governance structure. In practice, the public disclosure of SWFs varies significantly in terms of the nature of information and its timeliness, providing for more or less public scrutiny of the sovereign assets.

There are a number of voluntary transparency initiatives that are relevant to SWFs.[58] These include the IMF's *Guidelines for Foreign Exchange Reserve Management, Balance of Payments* and *International Investment Position* data, as well as the Coordinated Portfolio Investment Survey, the *Code of Good Practices on Fiscal Transparency,* and the *Guide on Resource Revenue Transparency.* More targeted initiatives include the Joint Oil Data Initiative and the Extractive Industries Transparency Initiative.

References

Baddepudi, Rajeev, 2006, "Key Trends in Asian Hedge Funds," *The Hedge Fund Journal,* Issue 21 (October). Available via the Internet: http://www.thehedgefundjournal.com/commentary/index.php?articleid=26332327.

[57]For instance, in the case of some oil-related SWFs, it is often difficult to determine on which institutions' balance sheet the assets appear.

[58]Further advice on setting up SWFs or alternative uses of reserves is also being provided by the IMF as part of technical cooperation advice or by addressing specific requests from countries.

Bell, Brian, and Peter Dattels, forthcoming, "The Global Financial Stability Map: Concepts and Construction," IMF Working Paper (Washington: International Monetary Fund).

Federal Reserve Board, 2007, "The 2007 Senior Loan Officer Opinion Survey on Bank Lending Practices" (Washington, July). Available via the Internet: http://www.federalreserve.gov/boarddocs/Snloan Survey/200708/default.htm.

Fender, Ingo, and Janet Mitchell, 2005, "Structured Finance: Complexity, Risk and the Use of Ratings," *Bank for International Settlements Quarterly Review* (June), pp. 67–79. Available via the Internet: http://www.bis.org/publ/qtrpdf/r_qt0506f.pdf.

Financial Stability Forum, 2007, "Update of the FSF Report on Highly Leveraged Institutions" (Basel: Bank for International Settlements, May 19). Available via the Internet: http://www.fsforum.org/pub lications/HLI_Update-finalwithoutembargo19May 07.pdf.

Fitch Ratings, 2007a, "Subprime Worries? Financial Guarantors Exposure to Weaker RMBS Originator/ Servicers," Special Report (March 14). Available via the Internet: http://www.afgi.org/pdfs/Subprime Worries_FG_3.14.07.pdf.

———, 2007b, "Hedge Funds: The Credit Market's New Paradigm," Special Report (June 5). Available via the Internet: http://www.fitchrating.com/corpo-rate/reports/report_frame.cfm?rpt_id=299928.

Froot, Kenneth A., Paul G.J. O'Connell, and Mark S. Seasholes, 2001, "The Portfolio Flows of International Investors," *Journal of Financial Economics*, Vol. 59 (February), pp. 151–93.

International Monetary Fund (IMF), 2005, *Global Financial Stability Report*, World Economic and Financial Surveys (Washington, April). Available via the Internet: http://www.imf.org/External/Pubs/FT/GFSR/2005/01/index.htm.

———, 2006, *Global Financial Stability Report*, World Economic and Financial Surveys (Washington, April). Available via the Internet: http://www.imf.org/External/Pubs/FT/GFSR/2006/01/index.htm.

———, 2007a, *Global Financial Stability Report*, World Economic and Financial Surveys (Washington,

April). Available via the Internet: http://www.imf.org/External/Pubs/FT/GFSR/2007/01/index.htm.

———, 2007b, *World Economic Outlook*, World Economic and Financial Surveys (Washington, October).

———, 2007c, "The Role of Fiscal Institutions in Managing the Oil Revenue Boom," IMF Policy Paper (Washington, March 5), SM/07/88. Available via the Internet: http://www.imf.org/external/np/pp/2007/eng/030507.pdf.

Irvine, Steven, 2007, "Why 'Syndicated Investing' Is the New Big Thing," *Finance Asia.com* (May 8).

Kealhofer, Stephen, 2003, "Quantifying Credit Risk I: Default Prediction," *Financial Analysts Journal*, Vol. 59 (January/February), pp. 30–44.

Laurelli, Peter, 2007, "Hedge Fund Industry Asset Flows and Trends," Hedge Fund Asset Flows & Trends Report No. 11 (New York: Channel Capital Group, Inc.). Available via the Internet: http://www.iialternatives.com/AIN/fundflows/sample.pdf.

Moody's, 2007, "U.S. Subprime Market Crisis: Limited Impact on Asian Banks Due to Small Exposures," Special Comment (August). Available via the Internet: http://www.moodys.com/moodys/cust/research/MDCdocs/02/2006800000444201.pdf

Ryback, William, 2007, "Hedge Funds in Emerging Markets," *Banque de France Financial Stability Review*, Special Issue on Hedge Funds, No. 10 (April).

Standard & Poor's, 2007a, "U.S. Bond Insurers Withstand Subprime Stress," *RatingsDirect* (August 2). Available via the Internet: http://www2.standardandpoors.com/portal/site/sp/en/us/page.article/3,1,1,0,1148446441747.html.

———, 2007b, "U.S. Subprime Impact Limited on Rated Asia-Pacific Banks and Insurers," *RatingsDirect* (August 3). Available via the Internet: http://www2.standardandpoors.com/portal/site/sp/en/us/page.article/3,1,1,0,1148446442262.html.

Violi, Roberto, 2004, "Credit Ratings Transition in Structured Finance" (Basel, Switzerland: Bank for International Settlements, Committee on the Global Financial System Working Group on Ratings in Structured Finance, December). Available via the Internet: http://www.bis.org/publ/cgfs23violi.pdf.

DO MARKET RISK MANAGEMENT TECHNIQUES AMPLIFY SYSTEMIC RISKS?

This chapter assesses how market risk management techniques may have contributed to the benign financial environment of recent years, and whether seemingly prudent behavior by individual firms, reacting to similar market risk systems, could serve to amplify market volatility in periods of stress beyond what would otherwise have occurred. Based on simulations and observed risk management practice, there are grounds for believing that this could be the case. Results of the simulations suggest that, in a period of stress, having a variety of risk models is more stabilizing than uniformity. Perhaps more important, however, is the presence of a variety of types of financial institutions with differing investment horizons and risk appetites, as well as the scope to take offsetting positions when prices overshoot and "fire sales" occur.

From 2002 to early 2007, the decline in volatility in the global economy and financial markets was reflected in lower measures of market risk, which encouraged firms to increase their risk-taking, thereby enhancing market liquidity and resulting in even lower levels of volatility (Figure 2.1). Conversely, shocks in an environment of heightened risk-taking could result in a rapid deterioration of such a benign environment, as reductions in risky positions lead to rising volatility and asset correlations, a reduction in market liquidity, and a further retrenchment in risk-taking.[1] As similar market risk measurement techniques spread across more institutions, the question arises as to whether the potential for reinforcing behavior has increased, given that past and current episodes of stress indicate that many financial institutions react by following the basic tenets of their risk management systems by selling risky assets, calling in higher-quality collateral, and increasing margin requirements.[2]

Certainly, over the last decade, the risk management techniques of financial institutions have greatly improved, been used more broadly, and may, along with specialized instruments, have contributed to the lower volatility and less pronounced disruptions of markets. Over time, financial institutions have taken a more holistic view of their risks and have instituted better risk management practices. These have included improved internal and external reporting of various types and measures of risk, better decision-making structures, and greater involvement of boards of directors in setting the risk appetite of the firm and overseeing risk management policies. Moreover, the use of more rigorous risk modeling has made firms more sensitive to, and aware of, their risks—the first defense against systemic problems.

Value-at-risk (VaR) methods are now used almost universally by banks, as well as by many hedge funds, to measure market risk. Put simply,

Note: This chapter was written by John Kiff, Laura Kodres, Ulrich Klueh, and Paul Mills, with the aid of Jon Danielsson on risk modeling. Yoon Sook Kim provided research support.

[1]See Persaud (2000 and 2003) for early expressions of this possibility.

[2]This chapter focuses primarily on market risk in the trading books of large investment and commercial banks.

Trading book positions are held with the intention of profiting from transaction fees or short-term changes in valuations. Banks hold credit and interest rate risk (a component of market risk) in their banking books, where the intention is to hold the position for more than one year. For many commercial banks this can be where their greatest risks lie. Aggregation problems across risk categories are discussed later in this chapter.

VaR is an estimate of the expected loss that an institution is unlikely to exceed in a given period with a particular degree of confidence. VaR is usually supplemented with other tools, and risk managers say that they do not (and will not) react to the signals from any one of their risk models mechanistically. Nonetheless, most market participants maintain position limits, some of which are connected to the measures discussed in this chapter, and these and similar risk mitigation techniques may reinforce the natural inclination for firms to close positions during periods of price pressures and liquidity strains.

This chapter focuses particularly on VaR not only because it has become the most widely used measure for market risk management among banks, but also because it is an archetype of other risk management techniques—the factors that influence VaR also drive other risk measures. In addition, VaR forms the basis for a number of risk controls (e.g., position limits and margin requirements) as well as for regulatory market risk capital, and shares many of the same traits as banks' economic risk capital (ERC) models.[3] Showing what happens to VaR measures in benign and stressful periods should illustrate the signals other risk management measures are giving to banks and hedge funds. For instance, the characteristics of standardized VaR techniques—their backward-looking nature and treatment of tail events—are shared by other approaches that, if used instead, could also lead to the amplification of volatility.

The first part of this chapter reports the results of VaR simulations to demonstrate that, even when calculated with differing sets of parameters, VaR measures react similarly in periods of both low volatility and stress. This sug-

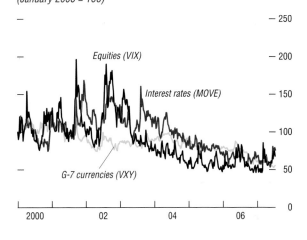

Figure 2.1. Implied Volatility Indices
(January 2000 = 100)

Source: Bloomberg L.P.
Note: VIX is the Chicago Board Options Exchanges S&P Volatility Index. MOVE is the Merrill Lynch Option Volatility Estimate Index. The JPMorgan VXY index measures volatility in a basket of G-7 currencies.

[3]ERC models measure the amount of capital required to absorb losses from extremely unlikely events over long time horizons. For example, typical ERC models use confidence intervals of up to 99.97 percent (versus 95 to 99 percent for VaR models) and horizons of up to one year (versus one to 10 days for VaR models). ERC calculations account not just for market risk, but also for credit and operational risks, and may make provision for liquidity, legal, and reputational risks.

gests that risk management systems *could* lead to similar reactions by market participants. A new type of exercise is then described in which a set of firms adjust their asset holdings in response to risk perceptions based on VaR estimates. The *collective* impact of their reactions demonstrates that market price dynamics can be amplified by the models during stressful times.

The second part of the chapter investigates the extent to which market risk measures may be adhered to during stressful periods and how they could amplify market stresses. Given that the simulation results are only suggestive, the connections between market risk models and firms' behavior are critical to understanding the potential for amplification of volatility and herding behavior.[4] It is comforting that most risk managers say they understand the shortcomings of their models and believe that they have the latitude to make an independent assessment of their risk-taking during a period of stress. However, some firms have less well-developed risk management systems and may be prone to interpret their models more rigidly.

To circumvent the potential for a mechanistic reaction to risk model signals to amplify shocks, rather than just a diversity of risk models, it seems more important to have a range of underlying positions being taken by financial institutions, or other market participants who are able to step in, with sufficient capital, to take risky positions during such periods. Hedge funds are one such set of institutions where market risk models are used more flexibly and position limits tend to be less binding. While not the focus of this chapter, other institutions—such as pension funds and insurance companies—also have different investment horizons and strategies, which may allow them to ride out a stressful period without adding to dislocations (IMF, 2004).

Three important policy implications flow from this chapter's examination of market risk management techniques and models:

---

[4]"Herding" arises in financial markets when market participants' investment decisions are made on the basis of the short-term actions of others, rather than on fundamental characteristics.

- While continuing to raise the overall quality of market risk management, supervisors and other policymakers need to acknowledge and encourage risk management approaches that reflect firms' particular business and risk profiles and that can be tested with relevant stress scenarios.
- Financial institutions could be more transparent and disclose to investors and counterparties how their market risk management systems would react and could be managed in a stressed environment, rather than simply reporting aspects of a single risk metric, such as VaR.
- Policymakers should recognize that a diversity of market participants with differing investment strategies and horizons, and with different risk management systems, is more likely to be conducive to market stability.

To help mitigate the collective action problems potentially caused by the similarity of responses to market risk models (or risk limits) in periods of systemic stress, more financial institutions need to become aware beforehand that such events can take place and make provision for such circumstances, allowing them to react more flexibly at such moments.

VaR and Other Risk Management Techniques

While typical market risk management frameworks use a complex set of different techniques, the VaR measure is at the heart of current practice in most financial institutions. VaR was first used by major financial institutions in the late 1980s. JPMorgan's release of its VaR methodology as RiskMetrics™ in 1994 brought it into mainstream practice. Since then it has become the primary quantitative measure of market risk within most financial institutions—especially for fixed-income, equity, and foreign exchange positions—and is the cornerstone of the 1996 market risk amendment to the Basel Accord (BIS, 1996). VaR is a useful standardized yardstick across portfolios within a firm over time, and its basic concepts have been extended to more recent ERC measures (Box 2.1).

Box 2.1. Criticism of VaR-Based Risk Management Models and Alternatives

While VaR constitutes the cornerstone of most market risk management systems, it has been criticized for saying nothing about the size of potential large gains or losses in the tail of the profit and loss (P&L) distribution. This has prompted a number of efforts to examine the more extreme possible outcomes.

Expected shortfall (ES), which measures the expected loss if losses exceed the VaR, has been suggested as an alternative that overcomes this criticism (Artzner and others, 1999). Whereas VaR at a given confidence level, α, is defined as the maximum loss expected to occur with probability, $p = (1-\alpha)$, ES is the conditional expectation of loss given that the loss is beyond the VaR level. Liang and Park (2007) find that hedge fund returns are better explained by ES because they are more likely to be exposed to the tails of P&L distributions.[1]

VaR may also not be appropriate for P&L distributions with "fat" and "super fat" tails—portfolios containing assets that change very little in price most of the time but occasionally jump, such as loans that rarely default and some option positions (Danielsson and others, 2006). Much of the academic literature has therefore focused on improving VaR through the use of more appropriate distributional assumptions and extreme value theory. Bams, Lehnert, and Wolff (2005) evaluate a number of these approaches against more standard techniques.

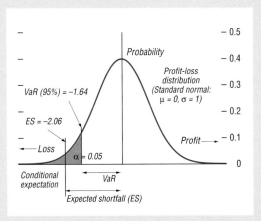

However, their findings suggest that more sophisticated tail modeling often leads to VaR being estimated with a higher degree of uncertainty because there are too few underlying tail observations for precise estimates.[2]

Generally, these other measurement techniques have not been widely applied in financial institutions. Many firms recognize that VaR does not adequately capture episodes of extreme volatility and market illiquidity, but the alternatives are typically data intensive, difficult to verify through backtesting, and hard to explain to senior management. Thus, financial institutions tend to complement VaR measures with more straightforward stress tests to assess the impact of tail events.

[1]See Lo (2001) for a list of other reasons why VaR may not be an appropriate hedge fund risk measure.

[2]See ECB (2007) for a more detailed review of alternatives to VaR, and Bervas (2006) for a summary of recent work on VaR measures that incorporate liquidity risk ("L-VaRs").

Technically, VaR is an estimated portfolio loss that a firm or portfolio is unlikely to exceed, over a given time horizon, at a given probability level. It is expressed in the monetary units of the firm's accounts or the portfolio's value. For instance, if a firm's one-day estimated VaR is $10 million, at a confidence level of 95 percent, this implies that a loss of $10 million or greater is expected on five trading days out of 100. The

time horizon chosen usually ranges from one to 10 days, depending on how long it is estimated it would take to liquidate or hedge a position or portfolio. The level of statistical confidence is usually set at between 95 and 99 percent—the higher the confidence level, the more cautious the measure. The Basel II Accord stipulates that, for the purpose of establishing bank regulatory market risk capital, a 99 percent (one-tailed) confidence interval be used over a 10-day horizon.[5]

To calculate a VaR, one needs two elements—a set of positions in financial instruments (the portfolio) and their prospective returns (or price changes). Typically, the positions are taken as fixed for the time horizon under consideration (e.g., for one or 10 days), and so the critical assumption concerns the distribution of expected price changes. Different assumptions

give rise to alternative measurements of VaR (see Box 2.2 for the two measures used below).

VaR is best suited to quantify portfolio risks under typical market conditions. And, as is true of most statistical models, VaR assumptions about future price changes are derived from actual changes in the recent past, suffering similar weaknesses as other models (Box 2.1). Stress tests are a way to assess potential portfolio impacts of atypical events (BIS, 2005) and entail either scenario or sensitivity analysis.[6]

---

[5]The accord also stipulates that the probability calculation's statistical inputs (market value volatilities and correlations) be based on at least one year of profit and loss data—if calculated over shorter horizons, banks must scale them up to a 10-day horizon by the "square root of time rule." For example, a $100 million one-day VaR is scaled up to a $316 million 10-day VaR by multiplying by the square root of 10 (3.16). See Danielsson and Zigrand (2006) for a critique of this scaling rule.

[6]When the IMF conducts a Financial Sector Assessment Program (FSAP) of a member country's financial system, country authorities and IMF staff jointly conduct "stress tests." These, however, differ from banks' usual scenario or sensitivity analyses in that they test a *(cont.)* country's vulnerability over the medium term to a macroeconomic or system-wide shock, rather than a short-term extreme movement in market prices.

Box 2.2. The Basics for Constructing VaR Measures

In the simulation exercises reported, two alternative ways of constructing VaR are considered: exponentially weighted moving average and historical simulation. In each method, the proportions of the assets in the portfolio are considered fixed and the price changes (return) variances and their covariances across the assets take on different assumptions.

Exponentially weighted moving average: This method assumes that each asset's price change (or return) can be characterized by a variance that changes over time. The variance is updated each day using a weighted average of yesterday's estimated variance and yesterday's squared return of the asset:

$$h_t = \lambda \, h_{t-1} + (1 - \lambda) \, r_{t-1}^2,$$

where h_t is the variance of the asset at time t and r_{t-1} is the return at time $t{-}1$. An initial variance, h_0, is constructed using an early part of the sample, say, the first 30 days. The weight (λ), usually between 0.86 and 0.98, is chosen to put more weight on the most recently estimated variances. A similar method weights the covariance between every two assets in the portfolio. These variances and covariances, along with the

portfolio proportions, are used to construct a portfolio value and variance. This conditional variance, along with an assumption of normality, is used to construct the VaR estimate for the next day. Typically a 95th or a 99th percentile of a normal distribution is used.

Historical simulation: The second approach assumes that the history of price changes for the assets in the portfolio over some past period (say the last 300 days) is a good guide to what the price changes will be tomorrow. These price changes are then applied to the portfolio's positions to produce a range (or distribution) of possible portfolio outcomes. From that distribution, the 95th or the 99th percentile defines the VaR obtained by taking the 15th smallest observations from the historical sample (in the case of the 95th percentile VaR with a sample size of 300 days). The historical data "window" moves through time so the most recent days are used. A long enough window is needed so that the 95th (or other percentile) corresponds to an integer data observation with at least a few other tail observations to reduce statistical uncertainty.

Scenario analysis usually draws from historically stressful events such as the October 1987 stock market crash, the 1997 Asian crisis, or the bursting of the technology stock bubble and estimates the current portfolio's maximum loss and/or VaR if similar circumstances were to be repeated. Sensitivity analysis quantifies the impact of standardized large movements in the relevant financial instruments, so that vulnerabilities to hypothetical extreme events can be identified.

Assessing Amplification Effects in a Stylized Market Risk Management Framework[7]

Analytical Framework

The objectives of this section are twofold: first, to analyze the behavior and performance of VaR measures for different portfolios in two types of environments—the recent period of falling volatility and a hypothetical stressful period; and second, to examine whether VaR-based risk management procedures have the potential to destabilize price dynamics. To set such cycles in motion, linkages between VaR-type measures and trading behavior would need to function, at least partly, in a mechanistic way, through trading limits based on VaR, margin requirements and capital regulation, or behavioral channels. In addition, risk measures across institutions would need to become sufficiently similar, resulting in more correlated behavior than otherwise. Finally, the VaR measures would then need to react to the market dynamics resulting from the correlated behavior to produce a feedback mechanism.

The first exercise gauges the sensitivity of VaR measures to changes in the volatility of the market environment by examining two distinct scenarios:[8]

- *The decline in volatility of many financial assets over the past several years.* To what extent has falling volatility resulted in declining VaR measures on unchanged portfolios? Are different portfolios characterized by similar adjustment paths, and how does the choice of alternative VaR techniques affect the results?
- *An episode of financial market distress, when volatilities and correlations strongly increase in an abrupt fashion.* What are the adjustment paths and liquidation pressures that unfold during extended periods of distress, and how are these dynamics influenced by the choice of sample period and other assumptions?

The exercise is conducted with three portfolios that resemble stylized positions that may be taken by an investment bank's proprietary trading desk:[9]

- A broad portfolio with wide-ranging asset classes, including long positions in mature market stocks from several countries, emerging market stocks, 10-year fixed-income securities, exposures to commodity price fluctuations, and long foreign currency and two-year interest rate swap positions;
- A portfolio with greater exposure to emerging market risks, with a geographic focus on Asia and Latin America;[10] and
- A portfolio with greater exposure to riskier mature market instruments, particularly equities and high-yield debt instruments.

The VaR of a portfolio reflects daily profit and loss (P&L) (reported here in U.S. dollars), meaning that currencies have to be added as an additional asset for each nondollar asset. The value of each portfolio is fixed at $1,000. The two choices of VaR methodology were guided by actual industry practice and the need for sufficiently distinct approaches to generate meaningful comparisons (Box 2.2):

---

[7]This discussion summarizes the methodology and results of a VaR simulation exercise. A fuller description and analysis is provided in Danielsson, Klueh, and Zigrand (forthcoming).

[8]This first exercise builds on the approach taken in Bank of England (2007).

[9]None of the portfolios involve options or other positions with nonlinear payoffs.

[10]These regions were chosen to represent emerging markets where investment banks and hedge funds had greatest exposures over the data period, which includes the Asian and Long-Term Capital Management crises.

Figure 2.2. Backtesting Results: Broad Portfolio, October 1997 to October 1998

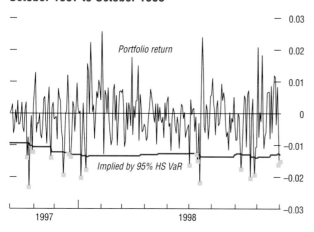

Sources: Bloomberg L.P.; and IMF staff estimates.
Note: HS VaR = historical simulation of value-at-risk. Yellow squares indicate VaR violations.

Figure 2.3. Backtesting Results: Broad Portfolio, June 2006 to June 2007

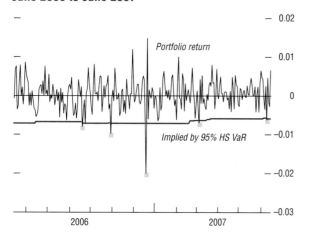

Sources: Bloomberg L.P.; and IMF staff estimates.
Note: HS VaR = historical simulation of value-at-risk. Yellow squares indicate VaR violations.

- The historical simulation (HS) methodology assumes that recent price changes will be representative of changes in the future. It uses actual P&L observations over the previous 400 days to estimate the theoretical quantiles of the P&L distribution one day into the future.

- The exponentially weighted moving average (EWMA) methodology applies exponentially declining weights to the underlying variances and covariances of the asset returns. A higher value for the weighting parameter, λ, implies a more persistent reaction to a given shock. Here, λ is set to 0.94—a standard market practice inspired by RiskMetrics™ (JPMorgan, 1993). The covariance matrix, combined with an assumption of conditional normality, is then used to calculate a VaR forecast one day into the future.

A number of validation exercises (referred to as "backtesting") confirm that the number of loss exceptions to the estimated VaR is generally in line with the model's intended construction. For example, at a confidence level of 95 percent, losses exceeding the one-day VaR should occur on around five days out of 100.

VaR at the Firm Level in a Period of Declining Volatility

While the decline in volatility over recent years is well established for many asset classes, it is interesting to see how it translates into lower VaR estimates, and how the observed adjustment paths of VaR depend on the actual estimation approach. The backtesting exercises show how the decline in historical asset volatilities affects the number of VaR exceptions. Using the HS method and constant proportions of assets in the broad portfolio, there is a clustering of exceptions during the turbulent 1997–98 episode (Figure 2.2) and a paucity of violations during the recent calmer period (Figure 2.3).

For all portfolios, both HS (upper panel of Figure 2.4) and EWMA (lower panel of Figure 2.4) methods yield a decrease in the VaR. It is also noteworthy that the VaR of the emerging market portfolio is now similar to the level of the mature market portfolio in the late 1990s. The fact that major trends in VaR are replicated in similar ways and that recent years have seen a pronounced convergence of estimates, despite the fact that the portfolios and methods differ markedly, reflects the convergence of volatility across a number of asset classes, due in part to lower economic, or fundamental, volatility.[11]

Nonetheless, it is interesting to see how the backward-looking nature of VaR can lead to markedly different results with respect to turning points. Figure 2.5 illustrates that HS's equally weighted historical daily prices can lead to higher VaRs over a prolonged period of volatility declines. At the same time, HS occasionally produces stepwise or very abrupt changes.

VaR Measures at the Firm Level During Stressful Periods

The aim of the exercise reported here is to demonstrate the behavior of VaR measures during episodes of financial turmoil. To stress the VaR estimates, two alternative approaches are employed. The first is based on estimates of the return distribution during a particular stress event, and assumes the returns follow either a normal or a fatter-tailed *t*-distribution. The other analyzes the impact of the stressful episode on VaR by separating out the effects of volatility and asset correlations.

Figure 2.6 presents the results of stressing the VaR estimates for the emerging market portfolio, using data from the 1997 Asian crisis. It compares the VaR during the baseline period (January 1999 to June 2007) with the VaR derived from the stressful period (October to December 1997), using alternative assumptions about the underlying distribution of P&Ls. The results indicate a high degree of sensitivity to

[11]In this context, the analysis assumes constant position sizes. Declining VaR measures for an actual portfolio or institution could reflect decreasing volatility, lower exposures, and/or greater diversification.

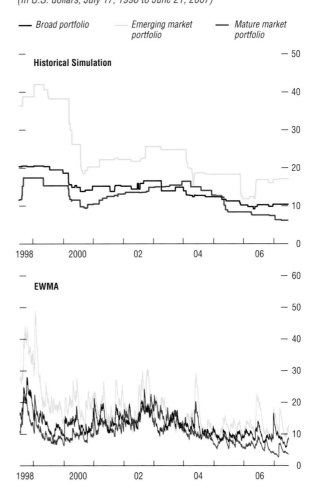

Figure 2.4. VaR in an Era of Declining Volatilities
(In U.S. dollars; July 17, 1998 to June 21, 2007)

—— Broad portfolio   —— Emerging market portfolio   —— Mature market portfolio

Sources: Bloomberg L.P.; and IMF staff estimates.
Note: VaR = value-at-risk; EWMA = exponentially weighted moving average. The window size for historical simulation is 400 days and the smoothing constant for EWMA is 0.94. The figure shows the VaR for a portfolio value of $1,000.

Figure 2.5. VaR Measures: Historical Simulation versus EWMA

(In U.S. dollars; July 17, 1998 to June 21, 2007)

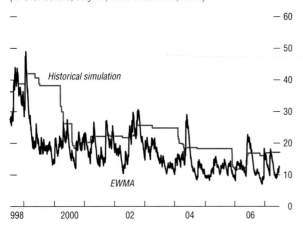

Sources: Bloomberg L.P.; and IMF staff estimates.
Note: VaR = value-at-risk; EWMA = exponentially weighted moving average. The window size for historical simulation is 400 days and the smoothing constant for EWMA is 0.94. The figure shows the VaR for a portfolio value of $1,000.

Figure 2.6. Asian Crisis: Stressed VaR Estimates at the 99 Percent Confidence Level

(In U.S. dollars)

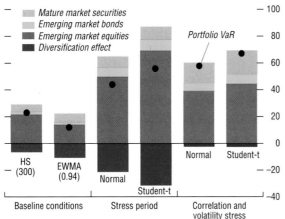

Sources: Bloomberg L.P.; and IMF staff estimates.
Note: VaR = value-at-risk; HS = historical simulation; EWMA = exponentially weighted moving average. Baseline conditions refer to the period from January 1, 1999 to June 21, 2007 and the stress period ranges from October 1, 1997 to January 1, 1998. The figure shows the VaR for a portfolio value of $1,000. The right-hand bars show the VaRs when the correlations between asset classes are increased by 78 percent and the volatilities by 76 percent compared with the baseline scenario.

the stress event, with the portfolio's VaR at least doubling. To gauge the sensitivity of VaR to more extreme changes in correlations, we calculated the portfolio's VaR during a hypothetical scenario in which a pronounced increase in volatility (75 percent) is combined with an extreme rise in asset correlations (78 percent).[12] Again, the portfolio's VaR more than doubles, as the diversification effect falls away with the rise in correlations.

Figure 2.7 shows estimates of the VaR for the Russian crisis of 1998 with correlations increasing to extreme levels. The experiment is applied to a broad range of asset classes and over a more sustained period of time. In this case, the amplification effect of such a scenario is severe, leading to nearly a fourfold increase of the VaR relative to the baseline scenario for the *t*-distribution.

A disadvantage of this exercise is that the VaRs for stress and nonstress periods are based on different estimation strategies. Specifically, the baseline periods use HS and EWMA, while the other two exercises estimate normal and *t*-distributions from the P&L data during the stressful episode and calculate VaRs at the 99th percentile of the lower tail. In a final step, we add data from the stress period to the end of the nonstress data set. For example, one might be interested in how today's VaR would behave if the Russian crisis were to recur now. This allows an examination of the dynamic response of different risk measures when moving into an extreme shock.

Figure 2.8 shows the effect of a sustained increase in volatility and correlations at a more recent point in time, thus taking into account that the volatilities embodied in current VaRs have been exceedingly low. The figure shows

[12]One advantage of VaR is its ability to take account of correlations across the portfolio's assets that lower risk (a "diversification effect"). Formally, this effect is measured as the sum of the individual component VaRs less the VaR for the portfolio. Note that in Figures 2.6 and 2.7, the observed diversification effect remains substantial in the stressed VaR due to the portfolios' very diverse sets of asset classes.

that the EWMA picks up the increasingly unstable environment at the outset, while the HS remains constant over most of the episode. However, when more extreme movements occur toward the end of the observation period, the HS-VaR increases abruptly, and by a similar magnitude to the EWMA-VaR. The fact that both measures, though based on different estimation strategies, produce a jump that occurs simultaneously, suggests that the use of different VaR estimation techniques would not necessarily prevent a common result arising from market stress.

When a Number of Firms Use VaR Measures

Having analyzed VaR measurement at an individual firm level, a new stylized model of the interaction between different institutions employing VaR-based techniques is now developed. The purpose is twofold.

First, the model demonstrates how the mechanistic application of risk management systems *could* give rise to unduly large price movements and feedback effects. The analysis employs a model that derives institutions' demands for specific assets using a standard portfolio choice model (mean-variance optimization) and by specifying a given risk appetite. Institutions also attempt to maintain a certain level of capital in accordance with perceived risks. A shock to prices changes their VaR measure, which then alters their preferred portfolio (including for a risk-free security linked to their desired capital level). The changes in demand for risky and risk-free assets result in changes in market prices and a feedback to VaR measures.

Second, the model is able to consider the effects of VaR model heterogeneity. To this end, two cases are considered, one in which all actively trading institutions use the same approach, and one in which different segments of the market use alternative models.

The model setup is such that, each day, a financial institution compares its actual level of capital with its desired level. The latter is a combination of its required capital—expressed as a multiple of the financial institution's VaR—plus

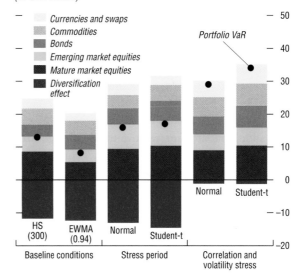

Figure 2.7. August 1998: VaR Estimates at the 99 Percent Confidence Level
(In U.S. dollars)

Sources: Bloomberg L.P.; and IMF staff estimates.
Note: VaR = value-at-risk; HS = historical simulation; EWMA = exponentially weighted moving average. Baseline conditions refer to the period January 1, 1999 to June 21, 2007 and the stress period ranges from July 10, 1998 to August 10, 1998. The figure shows the VaR for a portfolio value of $1,000. The right-hand bars show the VaRs when the correlations between asset classes are increased by 80 percent and the volatilities by 95 percent compared with the baseline scenario.

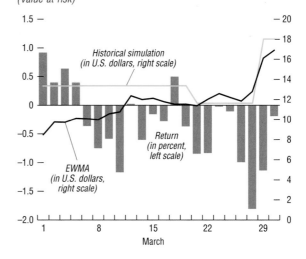

Figure 2.8. Long-Term Capital Management Scenario: EWMA versus Historical Simulation, March 2007
(Value-at-risk)

Sources: Bloomberg L.P.; and IMF staff estimates.
Note: EWMA = exponentially weighted moving average. The window size for historical simulation is 400 days and the smoothing constant for EWMA is 0.94. The figure shows the value-at-risk for a portfolio value of $1,000. For historical simulation and EWMA, the LTCM scenario for March 2007 is calculated for a 99th percentile VaR.

a buffer. This then directly links an institution's VaR to its demand for risky assets and capital.[13] A reduction in VaR due to lower volatilities frees capital and enables the institution to increase its holdings of risky assets. Conversely, an increase in VaR implies undercapitalization relative to the target level, inducing the institution to exchange risky for safe assets. Since the institution is assumed to be a significant market participant, its trading decisions will alter prices by an additional amount, relative to the average-sized participant, under normal market conditions.

The basic idea is that an adverse shock to the covariance matrix of returns (i.e., higher absolute correlations of returns) results in higher VaR estimates and thus higher target capital levels, inducing sales of risky assets by one institution. This then results in an excess supply of risky assets, assuming other institutions do not increase their holdings by at least the same amount, implying prices of risky assets will fall to clear the market. The institution's action to rebalance its portfolio thus results in additional price pressures. In the model, such price changes also lead to an increase in correlations, as the institution simultaneously sells different types of risky assets. These effects, in turn, feed back into revised VaR measures and renewed portfolio rebalancing.

Results

The impact of the activity described above using a broad portfolio is distinguished for three different situations: one in which all institutions employ HS, one in which all rely on an EWMA measure, and one in which both methods are used in equal proportions. The main focus is on the price dynamics during periods of stress and so, to this end, the data for August 1998 are extracted from the entire sample period and provide the baseline for the exercise.

---

[13]The multiple used in the model (three) is the same as the Basel market risk framework, in which regulatory capital is three times the VaR measure.

In addition to the parameterization of VaR techniques (the choice of HS window size and EWMA smoothing constant), it is necessary to specify both the institution's risk tolerance and the degree of price impact the institution has in the market. All else being equal, if risk tolerance is very low, the institution will exit the market at the first sign of uncertainty; if risk tolerance is very high, the institution will always seek to increase its risk. Similarly, if its price impact is low, the institution does not affect prices, whereas if its price impact is very high, its trades will dominate price movements. Alternative parameter values can produce both cases in which multiple institutions have no interactive effects and cases in which destabilizing behavior is observed. Parameter values were chosen to reflect information obtained from actual users and industry practice.

The model findings can be summarized as follows:

- Having institutions that employ the same risk model is destabilizing both in terms of covariance structure and volatility of returns, relative to the historical baseline. Conversely, there is a greater tendency toward stability if institutions use different models. As can be seen from Figure 2.9 for the case of one particular asset price, deviations from the historical series are negligible in the case where some institutions use EWMA and others use HS measurement techniques. In contrast, the model with universal use of HS yields markedly different selling and buying patterns when volatility surpasses a certain level.

- Relative to the historical baseline, the model shows how institutions' actions, in accordance with their use of different VaR models, affect the correlation structure of returns (Table 2.1). The positive correlation across the risky assets (the S&P 500 and FTSE 100 indices) increases markedly, while the correlations between this group and the safe asset (10-year U.S. treasuries) generally decline, as the "flight to quality" effect is intensified.

- Volatilities tend to increase relative to the baseline, but only marginally if both VaR methods are used in equal proportion (Figure 2.10). If only one type of VaR method is employed, volatilities increase dramatically for the risky assets.

- Lower levels of risk tolerance imply a more pronounced tendency toward destabilization. This effect is particularly strong when both institutions employ the same risk model.

Overall, the results of both simulation models show that VaR-based systems provide the scope for self-reinforcing mechanisms to arise. The model in which firms interact shows that diversity across VaR measures is helpful in dampening asset volatility.

Developments in Market Risk Management Practices by Banks and Hedge Funds

This section reviews market risk measurement and management practices, as disclosed in publicly available documents and through staff discussions with individuals from commercial and investment banks, hedge funds, and rating agencies.

Risk Appetite and Governance

Investment banks and commercial banks active in financial markets explicitly recognize that their business is to take informed risks. To establish its "risk appetite," a board of directors typically reviews the firm's risk-taking periodically in terms of a VaR or ERC framework, while entertaining bids for risk capital (or the risk "budget") from business unit managers reflecting the opportunities they see.

Risk managers today are increasingly involved in assessing risk-taking proposals by business units. Ten years ago, risk management was viewed as a compliance function to police risk limits on traders. Risk managers now increasingly and appropriately regard themselves as being on an equal footing with traders, working to promote and control profitable risk-taking. They often articulate their main objectives as ensuring that there are no P&L "surprises"

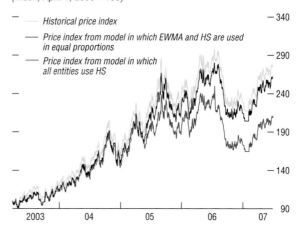

Figure 2.9. Asset Price Dynamics Under Alternative Model Specifications
(Index; April 1, 2003 = 100)

Historical price index

Price index from model in which EWMA and HS are used in equal proportions

Price index from model in which all entities use HS

Sources: Bloomberg L.P.; and IMF staff estimates.
Note: EWMA = exponentially weighted moving average; HS = historical simulation. The price indices refer to the Commodity Research Bureau energy futures index, one of the assets included in the VaRs of the simulated financial institutions.

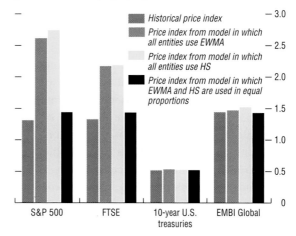

Figure 2.10. Selected Asset Volatilities Under the Interactive Model
(Standard deviations; in percent)

Historical price index

Price index from model in which all entities use EWMA

Price index from model in which all entities use HS

Price index from model in which EWMA and HS are used in equal proportions

Sources: Bloomberg L.P.; and IMF staff estimates.
Note: EWMA = exponentially weighted moving average; HS = historical simulation. The standard deviation is calculated over the stress period August 1998.

Table 2.1. Selected Correlation Coefficients Between Asset Classes in the Interactive Model

	S&P 500	FTSE 100	10-Year U.S. Treasuries	EMBI Global
Baseline Results				
S&P 500	1.00	0.34	0.35	−0.25
FTSE 100		1.00	−0.14	−0.06
10-year U.S. treasuries			1.00	0.22
EMBI Global				1.00
All Entities Use EWMA				
S&P 500	1.00	0.79	−0.02	0.05
FTSE 100		1.00	−0.26	0.12
10-year U.S. treasuries			1.00	0.16
EMBI Global				1.00
All Entities Use HS				
S&P 500	1.00	0.79	0.19	0.14
FTSE 100		1.00	−0.07	0.20
10-year U.S. treasuries			1.00	0.22
EMBI Global				1.00
EWMA and HS Used in Equal Proportions				
S&P 500	1.00	0.45	0.20	−0.26
FTSE 100		1.00	−0.22	−0.07
10-year U.S. treasuries			1.00	0.21
EMBI Global				1.00

Sources: Bloomberg L.P.; and IMF staff estimates.
Note: EWMA = exponentially weighted moving average; HS = historical simulation.

outside the board's risk tolerance and that their traders have risk-taking capacity when opportunities arise.

A hedge fund's risk appetite and management culture derives primarily from how it markets itself to investors—its desired risk-return trade-off and resultant strategies—as articulated in the initial offer document and periodic reports. As a whole, hedge funds tend to view their risk appetite more flexibly, with some deliberately positioning themselves to take advantage of volatile or unstable conditions. The absence of direct regulation of the funds facilitates the relative freedom of their approach.

Hedge fund risk managers appear to work more closely with traders than do regulated entities. They modify risk-taking in light of market opportunities, while reinforcing the discipline to stay out of markets if profitable opportunities do not exist (Bookstaber, 2007). Where funds employ purely quantitative strategies, risk control is often built into the process of strategy selection and implementation.

Risk Measurement and Analysis

All of the major investment banks now use VaR as one of their market risk measures, primarily using an HS methodology (Box 2.2) with significance levels ranging from 95 to 99 percent, and holding periods of one to 10 days. Banks use from one to five years of market data to calculate risk factors, with some giving more weight to the most recent observations. Others deliberately use longer time horizons in order to capture more volatile periods.

Published VaRs cannot be meaningfully compared between firms due to the different assumptions that go into their calculations. However, they can provide a useful consolidated guide to a firm's risk profile over time if calculated on a consistent basis (Box 2.3). Also, investment banks have become increasingly transparent and sophisticated in publishing their VaR out-turns and P&L exceptions, although further details—particularly of stress test results—would help investors and credi-

Box 2.3. Risk Measurement and Disclosure Practices of Financial Institutions

All of the major regulated financial institutions publish value-at-risk information with various degrees of detail. The figure shows the recent development of average VaRs for the main U.S. investment banks.[1] Average VaRs have generally been rising as, for instance, these banks have diversified into additional business lines (e.g., commodity dealing and leveraged loans). However, when scaled to tangible equity, VaR measures have been more stable.[2] Nevertheless, given that VaR volatility inputs have been declining, the slightly increasing VaR/tangible-equity trend suggests that outright risk-taking has been rising.

Investment banks typically publish their high, low, and average VaRs for the reporting period broken down into various risk classes (usually interest rate, currency, equity, and commodity risks), plus an implicit diversification benefit. Some also include sensitivity tests (VaR at different horizons, confidence intervals, and using different underlying factor data), and backtesting details (for instance, UBS AG presents its VaR assumption sensitivities and backtesting

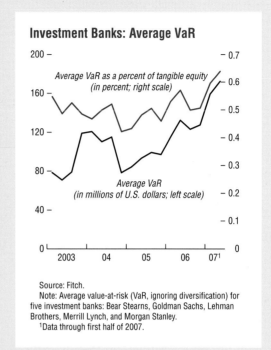

Investment Banks: Average VaR

Average VaR as a percent of tangible equity (in percent; right scale)

Average VaR (in millions of U.S. dollars; left scale)

Source: Fitch.
Note: Average value-at-risk (VaR, ignoring diversification) for five investment banks: Bear Stearns, Goldman Sachs, Lehman Brothers, Merrill Lynch, and Morgan Stanley.
[1]Data through first half of 2007.

results). However, only a few institutions currently publish the details of their stress tests and scenario analysis in their annual reports—Société Générale and BNP Paribas being two notable examples.

In addition, most firms assess vulnerabilities to ad hoc shocks (e.g., a 10 to 20 percent stock market crash, or a volatility and/or correlation spike), and across product lines—some institutions even use shock correlations (e.g., assuming a correlation structure of +/−1.0 across all assets). Some firms include these in their published reports, but most do not. Additional disclosure along these lines should be encouraged.

---

[1]The main U.S. broker-dealers are now regulated by the Securities and Exchange Commission under the "Consolidated Supervised Entity" regime. This requires them to maintain regulatory capital based on VaR-type measures, emulating a number of the capital and risk management features of the Basel II Accord for banks.

[2]Tangible equity is defined as the book value of a firm's common equity (share capital, additional paid-in capital, and retained earnings) minus intangible assets. Similar trends are apparent in the VaRs of the 20 largest U.S. and European commercial banks (Jeffrey, 2006).

---

tors more thoroughly assess bank exposure to extreme events.[14]

---

[14]Pérignon and Smith (2006) find that VaR disclosure by the largest global commercial banks systematically improved over the decade to 2005, with those in Spain, Canada, and the Netherlands being the most transparent. However, there is a wide divergence of practices, with some of the largest banks publishing very little. Pérignon,

All major investment banks are working to supplement their VaR calculations with ERC measures designed to ensure that the firm has

---

Deng, and Wang (2007) find that VaRs published by Canadian banks are persistently too conservative—a conclusion reached by others—as a result of the relative scarcity of exceptions to VaR limits (Jeffrey, 2006).

sufficient capital to survive extreme and pro-longed market stress events and meet regulatory requirements, although far less is published about such calculations. The ERC measures are based on VaR principles, but include a wider set of risks (e.g., credit, liquidity, operational, legal, and reputational risks) assessed at higher confidence intervals. These ERC measures are then used to allocate capital to various business units of the institution, linking the expected rate of return and its risk. A few firms are starting to relate traders' remuneration to their ERC measures, rather than outright P&L, given that traders should be rewarded according to their risk-adjusted returns rather than absolute profit if risk measures accurately measure the riskiness of returns and cannot easily be manipulated.

Simulations and stress tests are now nearly universally used by banks to investigate the extreme tails of possible P&L distributions and to condition their risk appetite or add capital. Investment banks tend to run very similar suites of historical stress tests and hypothetical simulations, in part because senior management may dismiss very extreme scenarios as unrealistic. Typical episodes usually include recent equity market crashes or downturns (e.g., 1987, 2001–02), fixed-income and credit stresses (e.g., 1994, 2005), emerging market crises (especially 1997), liquidity stresses (e.g., the collapse of Long-Term Capital Management, the 9/11 terrorist attacks), an oil price shock, and sometimes a pandemic flu scenario.

Sophisticated firms select scenarios that are most suitable for exploring the risks specific to their portfolios and positions. They also adapt historical data from stress periods to take account of market innovations and developments, and make allowance for liquidity risk by assuming that they are unable to trade their position for a period, often at least 10 days, in stressed circumstances. However, there is a tendency to assume that monetary authorities will act to mitigate the severity of a crisis through the provision of emergency liquidity.

The connection between the use of VaR, ERC, and stress tests and limitations on market risk-taking is complex. Position limits are the most common. Investment banks tend to set relatively conservative position limits for untested traders, making sure either the VaR limit or a "stress limit" (or other limit) is close enough to actual positions that it induces periodic and prompt discussions between risk officers and traders about whether further risk-taking is warranted, with somewhat more lenient limits for experienced, successful traders. While flexibility to raise limits at short notice is often delegated to managers, a sharp or sustained rise in volatility is likely to trigger multiple limit breaches across the firm and require a firm-wide reassessment of appropriate exposures.

Most hedge funds calculate a VaR measure, but they tend to put less emphasis on it as a risk measure than do the banks and securities firms, adding other measures to reports to investors. This is because VaR fails to adequately capture the liquidity or credit risks associated with some funds' strategies and positions. According to recent survey evidence, 46 percent of the larger hedge funds use VaR as their primary market risk measure, 40 percent use some sort of volatility metric, and 9 percent use potential future exposure—that is, the potential amount of credit exposure that could be subject to loss following a future default, and so most appropriate for credit funds (Mercer Oliver Wyman, 2006). Other measures can include net asset value (NAV) volatility, leverage (measured by gross assets to NAV), and exposure to changes in market rates (e.g., yield curve shifts).

Since the collapse of Long-Term Capital Management, hedge funds have placed more emphasis than investment banks on stress tests and scenario analyses relative to VaR. Funds frequently supplement the historically stressful scenarios by a suite of hypothetical scenarios that are tailored to the specific risks faced by the fund. Hedge funds are often able to subject their positions to more complex and numerous stress tests with greater frequency than banks, as a result of having far fewer trading positions, more integrated risk management information technology systems, and shorter reporting lines than the trading desks of regulated banks. Compared with most investment banks, hedge funds tend to control risk more flexibly, setting more generous position limits for trusted, active traders to take advantage of opportunities that may arise.

Market Risk Management Challenges

Market Liquidity Risk Management

While both investment banks and hedge funds are fully cognizant of the risks of being caught in "crowded trades," it is difficult to manage liquidity risk in a quantitative manner.[15] Some banks and funds try to assess competitor dynamics when setting limits on their own positions and use various metrics (bid-offer spreads, turnover, surveys of investor risk appetite, and observed order flow) to do so. However, these factors tend not to be formally incorporated into their market risk measures, with most institutions focusing on limiting their own exposure relative to the total market and not taking into account potentially interactive effects. (See Box 2.4 for a review of the Amaranth hedge fund case.) Many use similar, often simple, rules of thumb to constrain position-taking (e.g., a maximum position of 10 percent of average daily turnover in an emerging market security). Comfort from such limitations could prove illusory if a large number of institutions follow the same rule.[16] Indeed, if average turnover is assessed using only the most recent data, position limits could be relaxed as market turnover rises in a crowded trade, only to tighten rapidly when turnover drops in a stressed environment. Risk managers need to factor in the consequences if others follow similar rules for position limits—not all can be the first to exit the burning building.

To protect themselves against forced liquidations in illiquid markets, prudent institutions try to carefully manage their maximum liquidity requirements. For most, this is achieved by keeping a proportion of assets invested, unleveraged, and in liquid assets, and by factoring in extra time that may be required to liquidate assets. For hedge funds, requiring investors to submit to initial lock-ups and three-to-six-month notice periods for withdrawals, and retaining the ability to impose "gates" that limit total withdrawals per month as a proportion of NAV, are also used. However, some hedge funds are concerned that their counterparts operate with too great a liquidity mismatch—providing their investors with the ability to withdraw funds too quickly relative to the illiquidity of their assets (e.g., structured credit products), which can potentially lead to panic selling if redemptions are abnormally high.[17] Some hedge funds—especially funds of funds and those trading in liquid markets—offer monthly redemptions to investors and could quickly find themselves forced to liquidate positions in falling markets if investors were to seek withdrawals en masse.

Trading and Banking Book Risks

One of the greatest challenges currently facing investment bank risk officers is how to consistently evaluate and aggregate risks across both their trading and banking books. This can be an issue of methodology—it is not appropriate, for instance, simply to add market and credit VaRs together, but calculating an aggregated VaR is technically challenging. More importantly, with the growing use of securitization and credit derivatives, credit risk is less exclusively a bank-

---

[15]In a recent survey of large financial institutions, a majority of firms had yet to include liquidity risk in their ERC calculations (Deloitte, 2007a).

[16]See IMF (2007a, p. 92) for a description of the crowded trade that developed in the Brazilian inflation-linked government bond market in May–June 2006.

[17]The problems of the Bear Stearns–sponsored high-yield hedge funds in the summer of 2007 were prompted by requested investor withdrawals and margin calls requiring the potential sale of illiquid asset-backed securities collateralized debt obligations (ABS CDOs) (see Chapter 1). A recent study of 60 hedge funds found that a third did not monitor their liquidity requirements at all (Deloitte, 2007b). About 54 percent of hedge funds use gates or locks to manage investor withdrawals (Mercer Oliver Wyman, 2006).

Box 2.4. The Amaranth Hedge Fund Failure and Liquidity Risk

"We viewed the probability of market movements such as those that took place in September [2006] as highly remote, and our energy-risk models correspondingly discount the [Amaranth] Funds' exposures to the losses associated with such scenarios...But sometimes, even the highly improbable happens...It was not, however, for lack of applying resources or personnel to energy risk analysis that our funds experienced this severe drawdown. For as long as we have had a significant energy business, we have assigned full-time, well-credentialed and experienced risk professionals to model and monitor our energy portfolio's risks."

– From the transcript of a conference call between Nick Maounis, Amaranth CEO, and fund investors, on September 22, 2006

In September 2006, the multistrategy hedge fund Amaranth Advisors lost approximately $6 billion of its $9 billion net asset value (NAV) through trading losses incurred in the natural gas futures markets. This resulted in the fund liquidating its remaining positions to crystallize the largest NAV loss incurred by a hedge fund. What went wrong with Amaranth's risk management?

The fund appears to have significantly underestimated the magnitude of potential losses during an extreme liquidation event. Amaranth's primary trading strategy at the time involved natural gas calendar spread trades (e.g., long March and short April contracts). Forensic risk analysis indicates that its positions had become massive compared with the prevailing open interest in the exchange-traded gas futures markets. For example, Chincarini (2007) estimated that Amaranth's positions may have represented up to 80 percent of the natural gas derivatives open interest on the NYMEX, although potentially spread between positions on two exchanges and over-the-counter transactions. Also, some of Amaranth's positions are estimated to have been hundreds of times greater than average daily trading volumes in some contracts. Liquidity risk may have been particularly acute in some of the fund's 2008–10 positions (Finger, 2006). Once Amaranth's initial losses became known, the terms being offered to unwind its positions deteriorated significantly.

However, Amaranth's positions were nevertheless consistent with running a substantial VaR. Chincarini (2007) estimated that Amaranth's losses were consistent with a 99 percent one-day VaR of between $3 billion and $4 billion on its $9.2 billion of assets, depending on the assumptions used regarding its daily P&L probability distribution. The fund was estimated to be leveraged seven times over. This was incurred in pursuit of a $1 billion expected monthly profit. In other words, "they were chasing an 11% return... for a 'worst-case' [1 percent probability] scenario of a loss of 36%" (Chincarini, 2007, p. 22). In a similar analysis, Finger (2006, p. 5) concluded that the actual $6 billion loss was "well within the realm of the large moves that policies built on [VaR] models are meant to address." Perusal of the fund's monthly P&L data would have indicated that a $6 billion monthly loss was not a remote possibility (Till, 2006).

The absence of wider market disruption from Amaranth's September 2006 closure resulted from the willingness of other market participants with sufficient capital to assume the fund's positions with relative ease. The episode highlights the importance of making allowance for liquidity risk. Nevertheless, if a firm's principals are determined to take substantial risks to achieve high returns, the potential for failure exists, however sophisticated the risk management procedures.

ing book risk and could legitimately be allocated to the trading book.

A particular issue at present is the appropriate treatment of leveraged loans and commitments.

Investment banks' credit exposure in such transactions is intended to be short-term and so would naturally be included in the trading book, but since the commitments cannot be traded or easily hedged it is difficult to include them in the market VaR calculation. It appears that most banks assess these transactions on an ad hoc basis, taking into account the existing credit exposure to the borrower and concentration of potential commitments. Nevertheless, the danger is that reported VaR numbers significantly understate the risk that banks are incurring through leveraged loan activities.

Recent events in credit markets have underscored the difficulties risk managers face in adapting their systems to the increased ability to trade credit risk, while taking account of the potential fragility of market liquidity under stressful circumstances.

Observations

While difficult to generalize across banks and hedge funds, there seem to be a number of trends observable in risk management approaches from which one can draw policy implications.

Overall, risk management systems at the largest institutions are varied, and risk managers appear cognizant of the implications of the risk measurement models they employ. This increases risk awareness and prevents problems from building up. That said, there are a number of factors that tend toward narrowing the range of risk management practices and approaches, particularly at commercial and investment banks:

- The Basel I and II Accords, as well as other regulatory influences, tend to focus on minimum standards that banks must meet to satisfy risk management requirements—these raise the standard at smaller institutions but could then result in less well-resourced institutions just settling for the minimum risk management systems;
- Rating agencies scrutinize banks' risk management processes using a prescribed methodology as an important element in the rating process;[18]

- Banks employ similarly-trained risk modelers from a limited number of academic institutions;
- Best practices are transferred between institutions through the job mobility of risk professionals; and
- Medium-sized and small banks employ a limited range of risk consultancies to design and build their risk management systems, with a tendency to use "off-the-shelf" risk management packages.

Undoubtedly, these factors raise the quality of risk management at many individual firms and increase their resilience to firm-specific shocks for a given level of capital. But while the risk management "bar" is being raised, the variance around that bar may have narrowed somewhat, especially as new entrants to some markets strive to compete with existing players. This suggests that, if a significant market-wide stress event occurs, the likelihood of a number of the banks acting in similar ways may have increased.

The diversity of strategies and flexibility with regard to risk management approaches used by hedge funds has helped to stabilize markets when stressed in the recent past. For instance, hedge funds bid for distressed assets in the resolution of the Refco brokerage insolvency in 2005 and the Amaranth liquidation in 2006. However, even here, the growing institutionalization of investors (through the participation of pension funds and funds of funds), and the small but growing number of funds issuing publicly traded securities and seeking ratings, could lead to greater similarities in risk management approaches. Regarding systemic stability, this highlights the importance of hedge funds retaining flexibility over strategy or risk-taking in periods of market stress.

The fundamental question is whether this possible convergence of some types of risk management technique actually matters in practice when it comes to amplifying systemic risk. The key issue

[18]An example is Standard & Poor's (2005). The difficulty for supervisors in retaining experienced risk management expertise may also encourage a "check-box" approach rather one that can fully analyze a range of idiosyncratic models.

is how each firm's senior management and risk officers interpret their risk measures to condition their risk appetite in volatile or crisis conditions. Indeed, when asked directly, both banks and hedge funds maintain that they will *not* mechanistically follow VaR-based risk limits when deciding how to react to volatile conditions.

Even if these intentions are carried out, there are a number of other routes whereby risk management techniques could reduce firms' collective ability to take risk in stressful circumstances.

Margin calls. When setting margin requirements for hedge funds and other counterparties, prime brokers often use VaR-based approaches and therefore require a lower percentage of up front collateral if the volatility of the underlying asset is low. This permits counterparties to incur positions with greater leverage. If asset values then fall and volatility spikes up, "variation" margin calls are made first, as the borrower's exposure increases, and margin requirements are raised in the future, as the asset has become riskier. The result is that borrowers are forced to find cash or liquidate other assets to meet the increased margin calls, and lending conditions are tightened, just as asset market conditions become more volatile.[19] If margin requirements were initially set more conservatively, but were less risk sensitive, market dynamics would be more stable.

Large hedge funds address this potential danger by negotiating margin "locks" with their prime brokers. In return for relatively higher margin ratios, prime brokers concede the right to increase margin requirements at short notice, which also cements longer-term relationships with the counterparty.[20]

However, such long-term behavior is likely to be followed only by the well-established prime brokers and their most creditworthy counterparts. Recent competition to provide brokerage services to hedge funds has allegedly resulted in more generous up front margin requirements from new entrants, although the banks concerned fully expect to tighten these requirements as volatility rises, and in some recent cases have allegedly done so.[21]

The commonality of stress tests. As noted earlier, major banks tend to run a similar suite of stress scenarios. However, to prepare adequately for an unprecedented stressful event, an individual firm would need much higher levels of capital to protect itself fully. In the process, the firm could become uncompetitive.

Regulatory capital requirements. With the growing adoption of risk-based bank capital requirements, there is the potential that adverse movements in market risk factors could result in a coincident erosion of regulatory capital—at least among those firms primarily exposed to market risk. Hypothetically at least, sufficiently adverse market moves could begin to erode the cushion of ERC that firms hold above regulatory minima. In turn, this may prompt firms to raise additional capital or reduce the riskiness of their operations (e.g., by closing their most risk capital-intensive positions or assets).[22] Market-makers will find inventory more capital-intensive to hold in volatile conditions and so widen

---

[19]The process could be exacerbated further by the practice of some brokers that use VaR-based margining across the portfolio of a counterparty's exposures. This saves margin at the outset as the counterparty receives the benefits of netting and diversification in its exposure to a broker, but means that margin requirements could rise swiftly in stressed circumstances if the volatility or correlation of those positions rises.

[20]A similar outcome results if prime brokers calculate average market volatility over prolonged data periods and set the initial margin on the basis of "stressed" liquidity

(so reducing the likelihood of having to increase the margin in volatile conditions).

[21]In June 2007, the volatility of the ABX (an index of ABS credit default swaps with significant U.S. subprime exposure) settled at 10 times higher than its pre-February 2007 level (Rosenberg, 2007). As a result, King (2007) estimates that initial margin requirements on the various ABS tranches rose between two and five times.

[22]A comparable scenario transpired in the United Kingdom in 2002–03 when life insurance regulatory requirements interacted with equity declines to encourage insurers to sell equities into falling markets due to their relatively high capital charge. The decision by the Financial Services Authority to offer waivers from the regime prior to reform (Tiner, 2003) contributed to stabilizing the U.K. equity market.

spreads or quote smaller size available to trade as a result, thus reducing market liquidity.

Automatic position and stop-loss risk limits. The prevalence of automated portfolio insurance trading strategies, whereby equities were automatically sold if prices fell a specified amount, exacerbated the equity market sell-off in October 1987.[23] A similar self-reinforcing dynamic could be recreated if sufficient numbers of firms and funds were to manage liquidity risk through automated position limits relative to market turnover or through automated stop-loss orders.[24]

Risk managers' reaction to significant market losses. Ultimately, whatever the degree of sophistication of risk measurement, the behavior of firms will depend on how bank risk committees react to recent significant losses resulting from market volatility. Much depends, of course, on the firm's peer group, regulators' expectations, equity analyst reactions, and the margin of risk capital above regulatory minima. For example, if a regulated entity experiences a cluster of VaR exceptions, an initial reaction may be to reduce risky positions to avoid having to explain the violations to the regulator.

Hedge funds' ability to react flexibly. Hedge fund reactions will depend on how they have expressed their risk appetite and limits to investors. If these are relatively tightly defined around specified risk measures or leverage usage, then the franchise value of the fund will depend on adhering to these prior commitments to investors and potentially closing out their long or short positions in stressful conditions. Conversely, hedge funds with greater risk tolerance, low exposures, or access to resilient sources of capital or funding could well take the opportunity to increase their risk-taking positions.

Policy Implications

Systemic risk is addressed both by improving risk management at individual financial institutions (to reduce counterparty risk for others) and by facilitating diversity in terms of both the risk management approach and market participants, with a view to broadening the scope for contrarian behavior during periods of stress.[25] In addition, while some institutions have specific plans in place, others would benefit from considering beforehand how they would react to stressful scenarios and making provision in benign periods for such events.

A number of implications for policymakers and risk managers arise from the preceding analysis.

Stress tests to augment market risk models more systematically. Banks' market risk-based models can be augmented with stress tests to establish the appropriate level of capital. As has been shown in this chapter, VaR and related ERC models generally cope well when outcomes remain within the normal range of experience, but they have well-known limitations when stressed. Hence, as is becoming standard practice, regulators need to use their discretion under the second pillar of the Basel II Accord to ensure that their systemically important institutions assess their exposure to extreme events. As product innovation enables more of a bank's banking book to be hedged or traded, stressing risk exposures (both on- and off-balance-sheet) for credit spread widening and liquidity shocks will become especially important, including attempting to anticipate the actions of other firms when modeling liquidity shocks.[26]

[23]Presidential Task Force on Market Mechanisms (1988); New York Stock Exchange (1990).
[24]Garleanu and Pedersen (2007) describe a model whereby markets in which traders are constrained by VaR-based risk limits display lower prices when volatility increases.

[25]Stabilizing speculators need both available risk capital and appetite to enter into volatile markets to take positions when they believe prices are significantly different from their fundamental value. If risk capital is unavailable, prices may diverge from fundamentals for prolonged periods (Shleifer and Vishny, 1997).
[26]"Liquidity-adjusted" VaRs were conceptualized in the late 1990s and are now being implemented. At their simplest, L-VaRs impose limits on trading positions linked to the markets' underlying turnover. At their most complex, L-VaRs incorporate liquidity-inspired adjustments into the VaR's volatility and correlation structures.

Stress tests to be adapted to the most relevant scenarios. Some regulators are already aware of the tendency of firms to take suggestions from regulators as to what the scenarios are that they are "expected" to run rather than the threats most relevant to their institution, and thus avoid providing such suggestions. For their part, authorities need to maintain a "constructive ambiguity" about their reaction in a crisis to ensure that firms do not automatically assume in their stress tests that intervention or regulatory relief will automatically be forthcoming.

Reactions to stressful events better anticipated. Supervisors and central banks can consider how they would expect financial institutions to react in stress scenarios and what their own response would be. Given the potential for firms' collectively to be vulnerable to systemic stress, it would be prudent for monetary authorities and bank regulators to include within their own private risk management plans scenarios where system-wide liquidity injections and regulatory relief may be necessary, and to have thought through the circumstances in which such action may be appropriate (e.g., in internal "crisis simulations").

Supervisors remain flexible when assessing risk management systems and models. When assessing banks' capital models and risk management systems, regulators can recognize the tendencies that push firms toward standardization on what is currently believed to be best practice. While maintaining sound minimum requirements, bank supervisors can avoid being too rules-based with regard to model details and use the discretion they retain under international agreements to allow firms to tailor models to their own requirements and parameters in order to foster innovation and a diversity of approaches.

Banks improve their risk management reporting. Consistent with the spirit of the second pillar of the Basel II Accord, banks themselves can further improve the comprehensiveness of their risk management reporting in order to provide assurance to counterparties, creditors, and shareholders as regards their exposure

to tail events and the contingency plans and preparations they have made. In particular, external assessment of the robustness of VaR models would be aided by publishing more results of backtesting exercises and exception reporting.[27] Also, the understanding of a firm's vulnerability to tail events would be facilitated by publishing the details and results of a selection of stress tests (Box 2.3) as well as a firm's VaR under a hypothetical extreme market stress event.[28]

Stabilizing benefits of hedge funds be taken into account. Regulatory authorities can consider the stabilizing benefits that hedge funds can bring in times of stress when assessing risk management requirements. Unregulated liquidity providers (i.e., hedge funds) often provide bids or offers in stressed circumstances when assets are deemed to be fundamentally misvalued and they have access to sufficient capital. Because they are not required to calculate and hold a minimum of economic capital, such pools of private capital can have the freedom to take advantage of the possible herd behavior of others that could result from those that apply more rigid risk management procedures required of regulated institutions. Naturally, some hedge funds have managed risk injudiciously, and no doubt others will occasionally do so, and it is not yet clear whether, overall, hedge funds have a stabilizing or destabilizing influence in markets. But it is the primary responsibility of their investors and counterparties to ensure that hedge funds' risk man-

---

[27]As an example of how detailed stress test disclosure can be, Société Générale's annual report lists 11 of its 18 historical stress tests and displays the year-end potential losses associated with these and seven other extreme, but plausible, hypothetical scenarios.

[28]In order roughly to approximate "stressed VaRs" to compare across firms, rating agencies are forced simply to add VaRs across business units, assuming correlation structures go to unity in a crisis (Fitch Ratings, 2007). When considering U.S. bank holding companies with large trading operations, Hirtle (2007) finds that greater transparency, particularly over stress test results and VaR components, is associated with significantly higher risk-adjusted returns by the bank—although the direction of causation was not determined.

agement systems are sufficiently robust, and they should require that such information be available for this purpose. Consequently, care needs to be taken when devising industry or supervisory "codes of hedge fund best practice" to ensure that those codes do not inadvertently restrict how funds model and manage their risk-taking, while appropriately providing guidance in other areas, such as disclosure and customer protection.

Conclusions

Do market risk management techniques amplify systemic risks?

Not surprisingly, there is no straightforward answer to this question. First, it is important to emphasize that, particularly in less volatile environments, financial systems are more stable if firms are risk-sensitive and react to the signals their models are sending. If firms were not generally risk-sensitive, the likelihood of asset bubbles and crises would be even greater. VaR-type techniques reveal aspects of a firm's risk-taking, particularly regarding correlated exposures, that would not necessarily be apparent if risks were managed in silos within a firm.

Having said this, risk management techniques are not a panacea for all ills. The modeling work presented in this chapter suggests that a VaR-type risk management framework certainly has the potential to encourage firms to increase their risk appetite in a benign environment, as well as to reverse it when volatility returns. This result holds with a surprising degree of uniformity even when varying the timeframe over which the data are selected or the weights given to recent data. The model of price dynamics involving multiple firms using VaR measures also demonstrates that there is potential for a destabilizing feedback mechanism to develop whereby the movement of market prices is amplified. Results from the model indicate that a diversity of risk management models can be a stabilizing influence.

The question is: Do the principal institutions actually operate in ways whereby these theo-

retical results could hold? To put it another way: Will enough firms be constrained to follow their risk management measures sufficiently closely to amplify market volatility by their actions? When risk managers at major institutions are asked the question directly, the answer is most definitely that they do not follow their risk management systems inflexibly. They claim to understand the limitations of their VaR and ERC models and to apply judgment to these outputs when deciding whether the firm's risk appetite should be curtailed in stressed circumstances.

Other evidence, however, suggests that price pressures and risk management systems could interact in a destabilizing manner. First, VaR-type measures are now nearly universal in banks, and nearly all use short time-period HS.

Second, published investment bank VaRs have been generally rising over the past three to four years despite falling volatility, indicating they have added to their risky positions. The surprising lack of exceptions to their daily VaR limits that firms publish indicates that either (1) their models are too conservative and are not calibrated finely enough to show exceptions in practice; (2) banks prefer to show a high VaR with few exceptions; or (3) their models have been overly influenced by benign conditions to report low VaR usage in practice. The danger is that, with the recent move to higher volatility, some firms will recognize that their underlying positions were much riskier than they perhaps realized and cut them.

Third, as described above, there are a number of indirect ways in which greater volatility can encourage selling into falling markets—from automatic stop-loss triggers and rules of thumb to ERC minimum requirements. It is worth highlighting the potential interaction of the exposure of some leveraged hedge funds to increasing volatility, triggering both margin calls from prime brokers and redemption requests from investors at a time of reduced trading liquidity. Long-Term Capital Management and Amaranth highlighted how quickly supposedly well-resourced risk management architectures can be overwhelmed in unfavorable market conditions. Given the difficulty of incorporating liquidity risk into the market risk management systems of large trading institutions, more risk managers also need to consider what the market dynamics will be if the majority of their counterparts are also following similar rules.

One should not lose sight of the improvements in risk measurement and control over the last decade and the positive role of these improvements in reducing the likelihood of idiosyncratic failure from uninformed risk-taking. These advances should induce greater risk sensitivity on the part of financial institutions, leading to early unwinding of unanticipated exposures and better risk control. At the same time, it is important not to place undue confidence in all aspects of firms' risk management systems—for instance, the ability to measure and assess vulnerability to extreme events is still not well developed. Also, the co-vulnerability of firms seems to have increased so that, when systemic firms come under pressure, they are more likely to be under stress together rather than alone (Chan-Lau, Mitra, and Ong, 2007; and IMF, 2007b). Raising the general quality of market risk management, while reducing its variance, has probably reduced the likelihood of failure of individual systemically important institutions, while possibly increasing the tendency of institutions to act similarly in stressful periods. In such circumstances, from a systemic perspective, it is important to ensure that there are market participants that are either sufficiently disparate in their holdings and strategies, or are able to take large contrarian positions during periods of stress. Over the medium term, the general trend toward greater involvement of an increasing variety of players in global financial markets should help to improve market resilience.

References

Artzner, Philippe, Freddy Delbaen, Jean-Marc Eber, and David Heath, 1999, "Coherent Measures of Risk," *Mathematical Finance*, Vol. 9, No. 3, pp. 203–28.

Bams, Dennis, Thorsten Lehnert, and Christian C.P. Wolff, 2005, "An Evaluation Framework for Alternative VaR-Models," *Journal of International Money and Finance*, Vol. 24 (October), pp. 944–58.

Bank for International Settlements (BIS), 1996, "Amendment to the Capital Accord to Incorporate Market Risks" (Basel: Basel Committee on Banking Supervision, January).

———, Committee on Global Financial System (CGFS), 2005, "Stress Testing at Major Financial Institutions: Survey Results and Practice," CGFS Publication No. 24 (Basel, January).

Bank of England, 2007, "Assessing the Sensitivity of Value-at-Risk to Measures of Stress," *Financial Stability Report*, Vol. 21 (April), p. 33.

Bervas, Arnaud, 2006, "Market Liquidity and Its Incorporation into Risk Management," *Financial Stability Review*, No. 8 (May), pp. 63–79.

Bookstaber, Richard, 2007, *A Demon of Our Own Design: Markets, Hedge Funds, and the Perils of Financial Innovation* (Hoboken, New Jersey: John Wiley and Sons).

Chan-Lau, Jorge A., Srobana Mitra, and Li Lian Ong, 2007, "Contagion Risk in the International Banking System and Implications for London as a Global Financial Center," IMF Working Paper 07/74 (Washington: International Monetary Fund).

Chincarini, Ludwig B., 2007, "The Amaranth Debacle: A Failure of Risk Measures or Failure of Risk Management?" Social Science Research Network Working Paper (April). Available via the Internet: http://ssrn.com/abstract=952607.

Danielsson, Jon, and Jean-Pierre Zigrand, 2006, "On Time-Scaling of Risk and the Square-Root-of-Time Rule," *Journal of Banking & Finance*, Vol. 30 (October), pp. 2701–13.

Danielsson, Jon, Ulrich Klueh, and Jean-Pierre Zigrand, forthcoming, "Asset Price Volatility, Correlation, and Value-at-Risk-Based Capital Constraints," IMF Working Paper (Washington: International Monetary Fund).

Danielsson, Jon, Bjorn N. Jorgensen, Mandira Sarma, and Casper G. de Vries, 2006, "Comparing Downside Risk Measures for Heavy Tailed Distributions," *Economics Letters*, Vol. 92 (August), pp. 202–08.

Deloitte, 2007a, "Global Risk Management Survey: Accelerating Risk Management Practice" (Deloitte Research, 5th ed.). Available via the Internet: http://www.deloitte.com/dtt/article/0,1002,cid%253D151057,00.html.

———, 2007b, "Risk Management and Valuation Practices in the Global Hedge Fund Industry: Precautions That Pay Off" (Deloitte Research, January). Available via the Internet: http://www.deloitte.com/dtt/research/0,1015,cid%253D141897,00.html.

European Central Bank (ECB), 2007, "Market Risk Measurement: Beyond Value at Risk," *Financial Stability Review* (June), pp. 108–10.

Finger, Christopher C., 2006, "The Lights Are On," RiskMetrics Group *Research Monthly* (October). Available via the Internet: http://www.riskmetrics.com/research_monthly.html?article_id=84.

Fitch Ratings, 2007, "Securities Firms: YE06 Peer Data," Fitch Ratings Special Report (March).

Garleanu, Nicolae B., and Lasse H. Pedersen, 2007, "Liquidity and Risk Management," NBER Working Paper No. 12887 (Cambridge, Massachusetts: National Bureau of Economic Research).

Hirtle, Beverly, 2007, "Public Disclosure, Risk, and Performance at Bank Holding Companies," Staff Report No. 293 (New York: Federal Reserve Bank of New York, July).

International Monetary Fund (IMF), 2004, "Risk Management and the Pension Fund Industry," Chapter III, *Global Financial Stability Report*, World Economic and Financial Surveys (Washington, September). Available via the Internet: http://www.imf.org/External/Pubs/FT/GFSR/2004/02/index.htm

———, 2007a, "Changes in the International Investor Base and Implications for Financial Stability," Chapter II, *Global Financial Stability Report*, World Economic and Financial Surveys (Washington, April). Available via the Internet: http://www.imf.org/External/Pubs/FT/GFSR/2007/01/index.htm.

———, 2007b, "The Globalization of Financial Institutions and Its Implications for Financial Stability," Chapter III, *Global Financial Stability Report*, World Economic and Financial Surveys (Washington, April). Available via the Internet: http://www.imf.org/External/Pubs/FT/GFSR/2007/01/index.htm.

Jeffrey, Christopher, 2006, "VAR Breakdown," *Risk Management* (July), pp. 43–48. Available via the Internet: http://www.risk.net/public/showPage.html?validate=0&page=risknet_login2&url=%2Fpublic%2FshowPage.html%3Fpage%3D335597.

King, Matt, 2007, "Short Back and Sides: Subprime Haircuts—Too Much off the Top?" (Citigroup Research, July 3).

Liang, Bing, and Hyuna Park, 2007, "Risk Measures for Hedge Funds: A Cross-Sectional Approach," *European Financial Management*, Vol. 13 (March), pp. 333–70.

Lo, Andrew W., 2001, "Risk Management for Hedge Funds: Introduction and Overview," *Financial Analysts Journal*, Vol. 57 (November/December), pp. 16–33.

Mercer Oliver Wyman, 2006, "Risk-Taking and Risk Management in the Hedge Fund Industry: Review of Market Practices" (unpublished; New York, July).

New York Stock Exchange, 1990, "Market Volatility and Investor Confidence Panel," Report to the Board of Directors of the New York Stock Exchange, Inc. (New York, June).

Pérignon, Christophe, and Daniel R. Smith, 2006, "The Level and Quality of Value-at-Risk Disclosure by Commercial Banks," Social Science Research Network Working Paper (December). Available via the Internet: http://ssrn.com/abstract=952595.

Pérignon, Christophe, Zi Yin Deng, and Zhi Jun Wang, 2007, "Do Banks Overstate Their Value-at-Risk?" Social Science Research Network Working Paper (May). Available via the Internet: http://ssrn.com/abstract=929750.

Persaud, Avinash D., 2000, "Sending the Herd off the Cliff Edge: The Disturbing Interaction Between Herding and Market-Sensitive Risk Management Practices" (Washington: Institute of International Finance, December). Available via the Internet: www.erisk.com/ResourceCenter/ERM/persaud.pdf.

———, 2003, "Market Liquidity and Risk Management," in *Liquidity Black Holes: Understanding, Quantifying and Managing Financial Liquidity Risk*, ed. by A. Persaud (London: Risk Books).

Presidential Task Force on Market Mechanisms, 1988, *Report of the Presidential Task Force on Market Mechanisms: Submitted to the President of the United States, the Secretary of the Treasury, and the Chairman of the Federal Reserve Board* (Washington: U.S. Government Printing Office).

Rosenberg, Jeffrey, 2007, "The Repo Man," Cross Product Debt Research, Bank of America, June 22, pp. 3–7 (unpublished).

Shleifer, Andrei, and Robert Vishny, 1997, "The Limits of Arbitrage," *Journal of Finance*, Vol. 52 (March), pp. 35–55.

Standard & Poor's, 2005, *Enterprise Risk Management for Financial Institutions: Rating Criteria and Best Practices* (New York: McGraw-Hill).

Till, Hilary, 2006, "EDHEC Comments on the Amaranth Case: Early Lessons from the Debacle" (Nice, France: École de Hautes Études Commerciales du Nord, Risk and Asset Management Research Centre, October). Available via the Internet: http://www.edhec-risk.com/features/RISKArticle.2006-10-02.0711/view.

Tiner, J., 2003, "Required Minimum Margin: Letter to CEOs of Life Insurance Companies," FSAP Press Release (London: Financial Services Authority, January 31). Available via the Internet: http://www.fsa.gov.uk/Pages/Library/Communication/PR/2003/017.shtml.

THE QUALITY OF DOMESTIC FINANCIAL MARKETS AND CAPITAL INFLOWS

This chapter finds that—over the medium term—a more developed domestic financial market increases the volume and helps reduce the volatility of capital flows to emerging markets. Specifically, the estimation results find that, although growth is the primary determinant of the level of capital inflows, equity market liquidity and financial openness also help attract capital inflows. Moreover, financial openness is associated with lower capital inflow volatility. These results, which are consistent with the views expressed by institutional investors, point to the advantages of focusing on the medium-term goal of improving the quality of domestic financial markets. By adopting such a focus, emerging market countries will be in a better position to maximize the benefits of capital inflows while dealing with their potential volatility.

The recent surge in capital flows to emerging market economies has stirred an intense debate about the appropriate policy response to this development. On the one hand, capital inflows are welcome because they encourage investment, help deepen financial intermediation, and, therefore, enhance economic development. However, in large sums over short time spans they can also impose policy challenges relating to upward pressure on the exchange rate, overheating of the economy, and asset price bubbles. They also pose the risk of an abrupt reversal, potentially having negative real economic effects.

This chapter analyzes the domestic determinants of capital inflows, with a view to assessing what actions emerging market countries can take to maximize the benefits of those inflows while minimizing the threat to financial stability. In particular, the chapter examines the influence of domestic financial markets on capital inflows, putting the large capital inflow increases to emerging markets that have occurred since 2002 within a medium-term perspective.

Beginning in 2002, capital flows have been on a strong upward trend worldwide in both gross and net terms, with flows to emerging markets growing almost sixfold in five years (Figure 3.1).[1] Contrary to the early 1990s, the recent surge of capital flows to emerging markets has coincided with generally stronger economic policies and performance in those markets, including current account surpluses and improved debt management. In terms of composition, bonds and bank loans account for the bulk of the growth in capital flows; for emerging markets, although foreign direct investment (FDI) flows continue to be the single largest and relatively stable part of inflows, the FDI contribution to total inflows has declined as the other components have been rising more rapidly in recent years (Figure 3.2).[2] As noted in *Global Development Finance*, capital flows to all developing countries have continued to shift in composition from official to private sources, and from debt to equity financing (World Bank, 2007). FDI

Note: This chapter was written by Shinobu Nakagawa and L. Effie Psalida with research assistance provided by Oksana Khadarina. Badi Baltagi provided consultancy support.

[1]For a sample of 56 developed and emerging market economies (comprising 81 percent of world capital inflows in 2005), and 41 emerging market economies, respectively.

[2]The lines between FDI and portfolio investment are becoming increasingly blurred because some portfolio-type inflows show up as FDI. This may partly explain why FDI flows have not always been stable.

Figure 3.1. Total Capital Inflows
(In billions of U.S. dollars)

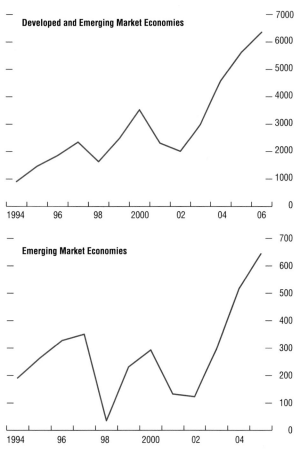

Source: IMF, *International Financial Statistics* database.

inflows continue to expand, keeping pace with strong GDP growth, while in 2006 portfolio equity flows reached record levels. As financial markets become increasingly integrated, capital inflows are often matched by emerging market outward investment, particularly in Asia but also in Latin America (Box 3.1).

Despite the growth of outward emerging market investment, large capital inflows pose policy challenges to many emerging markets. These flows can be explained both by stronger domestic performance (pull factors) and by global financial factors such as the high liquidity, low volatility, and compressed yields of recent years (push factors).[3] However, although there may be cyclical downturns, over the longer term countries will need to cope with rising capital flows, as globalization is likely to proceed apace. The question posed here, therefore, is: What financial policy actions can emerging market countries themselves take to best deal with capital flows over the longer term?

Specifically, this chapter asks whether—in addition to strong macroeconomic fundamentals—a well-functioning domestic financial market increases the level of capital inflows and reduces their volatility. This issue is analyzed in two ways.

First, the chapter identifies and estimates domestic "micro" financial factors that help determine the volume and volatility of capital inflows for a sample of 56 economies over 30 years. Panel regression estimations are used, the results of which are discussed later in the chapter.

This long-term empirical analysis is then augmented by examining the ongoing challenges and risks associated with the recent bout of capital inflows for countries that are at different stages of domestic financial market development. Their financial policy options are discussed by concentrating on five country examples.

The chapter finishes with a discussion of the key results, and draws some policy conclusions.

---

[3]See Chapter II of the April 2007 GFSR for a discussion of the supply factors determining capital flows and the broadening and diversification of the international investor base into emerging markets (IMF, 2007a).

Does Domestic Financial Development Help Determine Capital Inflows?

There is an extensive body of applied literature on the growth and investment impact of capital account openness and stock market liberalization, but, contrary to economic theory, the empirical results—derived primarily from cross-country macroeconomic analysis—are ambiguous and inconclusive.[4] In search of more robust results, recent literature has turned to the use of microeconomic data, although this approach is still at an early stage largely due to data limitations.[5] Another branch of the applied literature investigates the implications for financial stability of the links between capital flows and "micro" domestic factors such as institutional quality.[6] This chapter extends the work along this branch of the literature in order to understand the financial and institutional factors that attract capital flows to emerging markets. Further, it assesses the implications for financial stability by examining the links between these factors and the volatility of inflows. The accepted wisdom is that a well-functioning and deep financial system should help attract inflows and provide less incentive for rapid outflows, thereby lowering volatility and mitigating any negative effects on the real economy. Although the common wisdom prevails, few empirical studies verifying these conjectures have been conducted to date.

This chapter develops an empirical framework for assessing the determinants of the

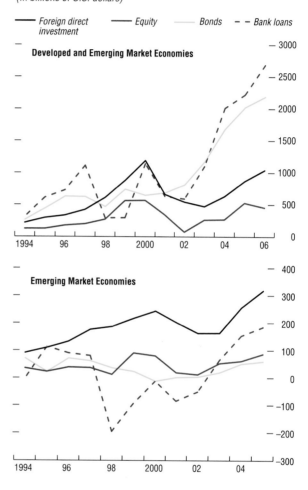

Figure 3.2. Composition of Capital Inflows
(In billions of U.S. dollars)

—— Foreign direct investment   —— Equity   —— Bonds   – – Bank loans

Source: IMF, *International Financial Statistics* database.

---

[4]See the surveys by Eichengreen (2001) and Prasad and others (2003). The latter note that: "…the literature suggests that there is no strong, robust, and uniform support…that financial globalization per se delivers a higher rate of economic growth" (p. 8). More recently, Henry (2006) finds evidence that opening the capital account leads countries to temporarily invest more and grow faster. See also Edison and others (2004), who provide a review of the literature; and IMF (2007b) on the effects of financial globalization.

[5]See, for example, Smith and Valderrama (2007).

[6]See, for example, Alfaro, Kalemli-Ozcan, and Volosovych (2005).

Box 3.1. Recent Developments with Capital Flows in Emerging Asia and Latin America

Net capital flows to emerging Asia and Latin America are off their highs from a decade ago, even as Central and Eastern Europe are experiencing record net inflows.[1] In 2006, net capital inflows were about 2 percent of GDP in emerging Asia and near zero in Latin America, down from recent highs of about 4 percent. Broad patterns in the respective regions include the following:

• In Asia, gross capital inflows fell dramatically during 1997–98. Since then, gross capital inflows have grown to levels close to their historical highs. However, more recently, gross capital *out*flows from emerging Asia have increased rapidly, exceeding historical levels

Note: Roberto Benelli and Leslie Teo prepared this box.

[1]Net capital inflows are defined as the sum of gross inflows (nonresident investment in the domestic economy) and gross outflows (resident investment abroad).

and thus leading to lower net capital inflows. (These broad features mask differences in the region: China and India continue to receive significant net capital inflows, for instance.)

• In Latin America, gross capital inflows declined from 1998 to 2002 but subsequently remained fairly stable until 2006. Gross inflows remained unchanged as purchases of new claims by nonresidents were offset by repayment of public external debt. At the same time, as in Asia, gross *out*flows from the region increased. Very recently, this pattern has shifted, as gross outflows have declined while a few countries in Latin America— particularly Brazil—have experienced large capital inflows in the first half of 2007. Even if tentative, the recent increase in gross capital outflows reflects financial globalization, liberalization, and a recycling of current account surpluses, especially in Asia. In both regions, home bias has declined and there has

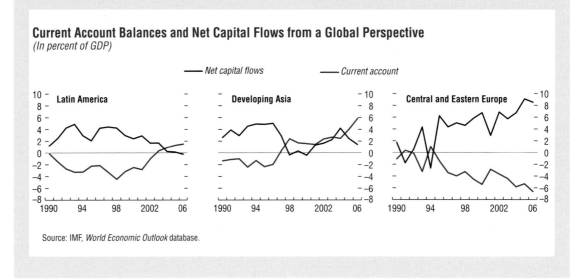

Current Account Balances and Net Capital Flows from a Global Perspective
(In percent of GDP)

Source: IMF, *World Economic Outlook* database.

level and volatility of annual capital inflows.[7] The framework employs a panel specification

[7]In the financial account of the balance of payment statistics, all transactions are recorded on a net change basis (that is, all inflows in a given instrument are netted against all outflows of the same instrument). In this

for 15 developed and 41 emerging market economies. (Annex 3.1 includes a detailed presentation of the data, the specification,

chapter, capital inflows refer to increases in the liabilities of the countries in the group.

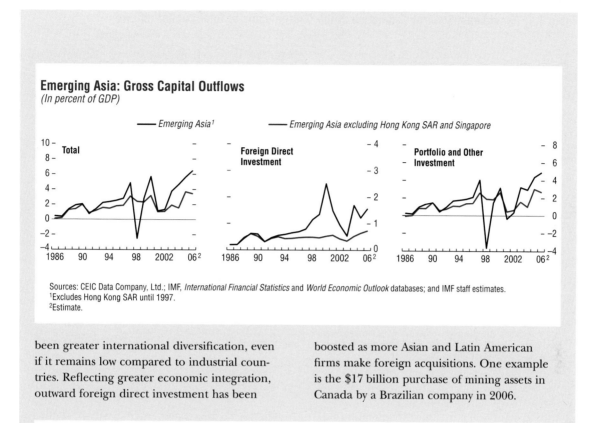

Emerging Asia: Gross Capital Outflows
(In percent of GDP)

Sources: CEIC Data Company, Ltd.; IMF, *International Financial Statistics* and *World Economic Outlook* databases; and IMF staff estimates.
[1]Excludes Hong Kong SAR until 1997.
[2]Estimate.

been greater international diversification, even if it remains low compared to industrial countries. Reflecting greater economic integration, outward foreign direct investment has been boosted as more Asian and Latin American firms make foreign acquisitions. One example is the $17 billion purchase of mining assets in Canada by a Brazilian company in 2006.

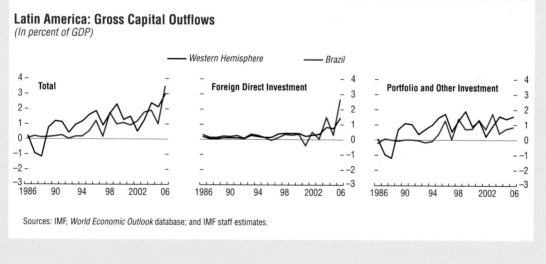

Latin America: Gross Capital Outflows
(In percent of GDP)

Sources: IMF, *World Economic Outlook* database; and IMF staff estimates.

and the estimation results). The estimation utilizes two sets of explanatory variables: equity market liquidity and depth (approximated by equity market turnover and capitalization, respectively); and institutional quality indicators that include financial openness, a de facto measure of corporate governance quality, and accounting standards. We also control for three macroeconomic measures, namely (1) lagged GDP growth as a proxy for domestic growth expectations; (2) a real interest rate spread as a proxy for both risk premia and relative liquidity

Table 3.1. Panel Least-Squares Estimation of the Determinants of Total Capital Inflows

	1977–2006		1998–2006	
	All Countries	Emerging Markets	All Countries	Emerging Markets
Financial Development Indicators				
Equity market turnover	0.127	0.150	0.139	0.216
	[0.002]***	[0.003]***	[0.003]***	[0.001]***
Equity market capitalization	0.027	0.020	0.039	0.018
	[0.292]	[0.512]	[0.312]	[0.739]
Financial openness	1.647	1.550	3.488	3.164
	[0.000]***	[0.000]***	[0.000]***	[0.001]***
Corporate governance quality	. . .	. . .	30.128	16.225
			[0.076]*	[0.290]
Accounting standards	. . .	. . .	0.019	−10.995
			[0.998]	[0.647]
Macroeconomic Factors				
Growth expectation	0.489	0.404	0.668	0.782
	[0.000]***	[0.000]***	[0.000]***	[0.000]***
Interest rate differential	0.043	0.022	0.109	0.086
	[0.030]**	[0.248]	[0.001]***	[0.004]***
Global liquidity	−0.009	−0.003	0.013	−0.036
	[0.849]	[0.948]	[0.863]	[0.353]
Adjusted R^2	0.552	0.510	0.616	0.514

Sources: Bloomberg; Chinn and Ito (2006); Datastream; De Nicolò and others (2006); IMF, *International Financial Statistics* and *World Economic Outlook* databases; Standard and Poor's Emerging Markets Database; and World Federation of Exchanges.

Note: Cross-section fixed-effects estimation. Probability values are in square brackets: *** significant at 1 percent level; ** significant at 5 percent level; and * significant at 10 percent level.

conditions; and (3) a measure of global liquidity conditions.

The estimation results for the full country sample over the 30-year period (1977–2006) suggest that, for a given country, capital inflows increase as market liquidity and financial openness increase. This result is also strong and significant for the emerging market subsample, indicating, for example, that a 1 percent increase in the growth of equity market liquidity relative to GDP is associated, on average, with a 0.15 percent rise in the ratio of capital inflows to GDP (Table 3.1). When estimated for the post-Asian crisis period (1998–2006), equity market liquidity, financial openness, and corporate governance quality indicate an even stronger positive effect on the level of capital inflows for both the full country sample and for emerging markets. As expected, capital inflows increase as economic growth—one of the control variables—strengthens, a result that holds across all country groupings and both sample periods. In view of the potential for feedback effects or reverse causality—i.e., that capital inflows may

influence equity market capitalization—endogeneity is accounted for with a number of statistical techniques to ensure that the parameters were purged of the effects of endogeneity.[8] The estimation results are consistent with the views expressed during our discussions with institutional investors who invest in emerging markets (Box 3.2).

We also examine the effect of financial market development indicators on the level of the different components of capital flows.[9] Here, the

[8]We took one-period lags for all the explanatory variables, except for the institutional quality indicators. We also separately utilized two-period lags and performed two-stage least-squares estimations, but the results did not change significantly in either case. To take dynamics into account, we also performed additional estimations under a different specification, which included one-period lags of the dependent variable in the independent variable set for each equation. These results were not significantly different.

[9]Most studies of capital flows only estimate aggregate flows. There are some studies that investigate the composition of flows, although their focus is on the effects of capital controls and sterilized intervention (see, for example, Montiel and Reinhart, 1999).

findings show that, in addition to the aggregate, (1) the levels of total portfolio, FDI, and the "other" component of capital inflows (primarily comprising bank flows) increase as equity market liquidity rises, and (2) portfolio and FDI flows increase with more financial openness.[10],[11]

[10]In addition to bank lending, the "other" component of capital inflows includes financial derivatives for many countries, for which these data are not classified separately, as well as money market instruments.

[11]Corporate governance quality and accounting standards are not included in the pre-1998 sample because these indicators are not available for the earlier years. A dummy variable, which is included in the 1977–2006 estimations and which has a significant positive sign for

More financial openness is associated with lower capital volatility. For both the full country sample and for emerging markets, the results indicate that in a given country there will be a significant reduction in inflow volatility over time (Table 3.2). Although most of the other factors also show a negative relationship with capital volatility, the coefficients are not statistically significant, except for global liquidity, for

the period 1998–2006, implies that there are factors (such as structural changes) that cannot be captured by the explanatory variables in the full-period sample. The accounting standards indicator is not statistically significant.

Box 3.2. Discussions with Investors into Emerging Markets: Do "Micro" Financial Factors Attract International Capital?

Discussions with private financial institutions that invest in emerging markets suggest that the quality of a country's financial market is a contributing factor in those institutions' decision making as regards asset allocation.[1] However, the relative importance of such domestic "micro" financial factors as the liquidity and depth of the domestic financial market and institutional quality, including transparency, corporate governance, and market infrastructure, varies across types of investors. As expected, on the whole, long-term investors tend to attach higher importance to such factors than do more active investors.

There are a number of metrics that institutional investors use to determine the adequacy of liquidity when considering whether to enter a market. Some investors assess liquidity in an emerging market by the amount of stocks or bonds they can buy and sell within a day, by how big a position they can take with a minimal effect on price, and by how wide the bid/ask spread is. Metrics include the average daily turn-

over of a particular security, how the market has reacted during past periods of stress, and the proportion of the free float of shares. Another important indicator for fixed-income securities is the liquidity of the repo market, because, without it, trades in the cash market need to be funded, which is a disincentive to investment for some types of investors.[2]

Other factors in estimating market liquidity are the size of the national economy and whether there is a broad and diversified group of domestic institutional investors, who generally provide a stabilizing force when foreign investors sell. Thus, the implementation of structural reforms (regarding the pension system or the insurance sector, for example) that are likely to strengthen the role of domestic investors plays an important role. Mexico was mentioned as an example where the average duration of bond investments has increased because of the issuance of long-maturity bonds, on the supply side, and due to the growing demand for securities by local institutional

[1]This box reports on discussions with a broad range of institutional investors, including hedge funds, mutual funds, investment management companies, and banks.

[2]Unfortunately, most of these measures reported by investors are focused on individual securities and are not available on an aggregate basis for many of the countries in our sample over a significant time period.

Box 3.2 *(concluded)*

investors, on the demand side. The Brazilian market's depth is explained in large part by the diversity of domestic investors.

International investors raised the following points regarding the role of institutional quality factors in their asset allocation decisions involving emerging markets:

- *Transparency* is the most important element of institutional quality. Compared with a decade ago, transparency and predictability of information (including timely data) and policies have improved, particularly regarding taxation, accounting standards, and regulations. Together with strengthened macroeconomic fundamentals, this improvement has complemented the "push" factors of global liquidity, and contributed to bringing emerging markets into the mainstream as an asset class.

- In contrast to a decade ago, the recent surge of capital flows can also be partly attributed to improvements in *market infrastructure* in emerging markets across the board. For example, market participants value the sound banking and regulatory system in Brazil and the high level of human capital (e.g., information technology and the knowledge of English) in India.

- Weak *institutional elements* may have a negative influence. For example, although local currency bonds are sufficiently liquid in a particular emerging markets some investors said they would avoid them because they have serious doubts about the independence of the statistical agency and, hence, the reliability of economic data. Other investors reported a large recent sell-off of stocks amid concerns about corporate governance, including minority shareholders' rights in another market. However, a number of the most active hedge funds noted that they are prepared, in most cases, to participate where there is weak governance, if the asset's price reflects an appropriate risk premium.

Views differed among investors on the effectiveness of restrictions on capital inflows. Some investors thought that, under certain circumstances, restrictions could be effective in the short run. Some noted Malaysia as an example where it was possible to prevent offshore trading of a currency without evasion. Other capital restrictions are only partially effective, such as in cases where a wedge develops between the onshore and offshore rates implied by nondeliverable forwards. Investors find ways to gain exposure to a desired emerging market destination despite restrictions, through the use of new vehicles and instruments (see Chapter 1).

---

which there is on average a 1 percent increase relative to GDP with a 0.13 percent decline in inflow volatility.[12]

A broader set of indicators of institutional quality was also found to have a negative relationship with capital flow volatility. The panel estimations discussed above are complemented by plotting a set of six indicators—regulatory quality, rule of law, control of corruption, voice and accountability, political stability, and government effectiveness—against the volatility of capital inflows.[13] As the scatter diagrams suggest, these metrics exhibit a negative correlation with inflow volatility (Figure 3.3).

---

[12]There are a number of possible interpretations as to why these coefficients are not statistically significant. It may be due to the computing method for volatility (e.g., the five-year rolling window), or the low frequency of the data (annual), which does not capture the actual speed with which capital flows may change direction, making statistical significance difficult to obtain. Another computation, using the absolute value of capital flows divided by GDP, obtained similar results.

[13]See Kaufmann, Kraay, and Mastruzzi (2007). These indicators are not included in the panel estimations because they show high correlation coefficients with the institutional quality indicators that are already included in the regressions; and are available for only five years, suggesting that statistical significance would be compromised. The panels in Figure 3.3 show values averaged over these years.

Table 3.2. Panel Generalized Method of Moments Estimation of the Determinants of the Standard Deviation of Total Capital Inflows, 1998–2006

	Standard Deviation of Total Capital Inflows/GDP[1]	
	All countries	Emerging markets
Financial Development Indicators		
Equity market turnover	0.003	−0.009
	[0.881]	[0.784]
Equity market capitalization	−0.015	−0.014
	[0.441]	[0.513]
Financial openness	−2.317	−3.359
	[0.018]**	[0.002]***
Corporate governance quality	5.856	16.530
	[0.704]	[0.420]
Accounting standards	−2.428	−27.769
	[0.916]	[0.395]
Macroeconomic Factors		
Growth expectation	−0.290	−0.133
	[0.196]	[0.568]
Interest rate differential	0.009	0.044
	[0.883]	[0.469]
Global liquidity	−0.079	−0.128
	[0.083]*	[0.053]*
J-statistics[2]	8.206	4.614
	[0.999]	[0.999]
No. of cross-section countries	33	18
No. of observations[3]	254	136
Instrument rank[4]	49	34

Sources: Bloomberg; Chinn and Ito (2006); Datastream; De Nicolò and others (2006); IMF, *International Financial Statistics* and *World Economic Outlook* databases; Standard and Poor's Emerging Markets Database; and World Federation of Exchanges.

[1]Probability values are in square brackets: *** significant at 1 percent level; ** significant at 5 percent level; and * significant at 10 percent level. Cross-section fixed-effects specification with 2SLS instrument weighting matrix.

[2]Test statistics for the null hypothesis that the over-identifying restrictions are valid.

[3]Total number of observations based on the unbalanced panel structure.

[4]Lagged values of independent variables are used as instruments.

Challenges Associated with Capital Inflows and Policy Responses: Case Studies

The empirical work presented in the previous section shows that, over the medium term, deeper and more liquid equity markets and better market infrastructure help attract capital inflows, and that capital volatility is reduced as a country becomes financially more open. Improvements in institutional quality are also associated with reductions in volatility. But mar-

ket development takes time and countries that experience a surge in capital flows are searching for ways to address short-term challenges. This section looks at five country examples—Brazil, India, Romania, South Africa, and Vietnam—and considers whether the challenges associated with large capital inflows and the policy responses vary if countries are at different stages of domestic financial market development.[14]

By way of background, the degree of financial intermediation varies widely across the five countries. Romania has experienced the highest growth rate in private credit during the past five years, and yet remains the country with the lowest credit-to-GDP as well as broad-money-to-GDP ratios (Table 3.3). Vietnam has had the fastest growth in equity market capitalization, but the ratio of that capitalization to GDP in Vietnam was the lowest of the five countries at end-2006. By comparison, South Africa's market capitalization is higher than that of the United Kingdom or the United States, when normalized by GDP, more than doubling in the past five years from a large base; its equity market is also very liquid, far higher than in the other emerging markets. Despite the different degrees of financial intermediation within the group, in recent years the five countries have all experienced a deepening of their internal financial markets and a rise in their market liquidity.

Key Challenges

There are three sets of challenges stemming from a surge of capital inflows.

Macroeconomic

Fundamentally, countries could face a conflict of macroeconomic objectives if they attempt to both target a specific exchange rate or band and, at the same time, maintain control over their domestic monetary policy. This results in

[14]Annex 3.2 presents more detailed information on the challenges facing these countries and the measures they have undertaken. Annex 3.3 provides stylized facts for a larger group of countries.

Figure 3.3. Market Infrastructure and Volatility of Total Capital Inflows[1]

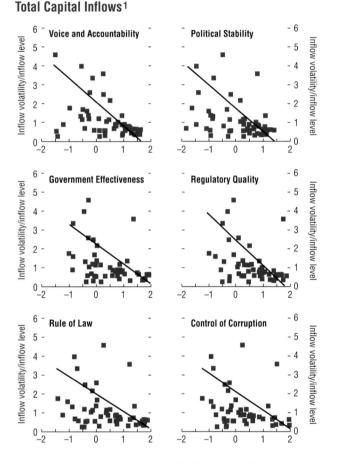

Sources: Kaufmann, Kraay, and Mastruzzi (2007); IMF, *International Financial Statistics*; and IMF staff estimates.
[1]The inflow volatility measure is in absolute values.

common challenges, one of which is the upward exchange market pressure exerted as a result of high levels of capital inflows, possibly raising issues of competitiveness. Ignoring the conflicting macroeconomic objectives, the authorities face the dilemma that intervention to counteract pressure on the currency renders it more attractive to further inflows. Sterilization tends to raise yields, which fosters new capital inflows and further appreciation pressure, thus possibly posing a concern about external competitiveness and potentially setting the stage for financial instability. This conflict appears as a result of both portfolio investment (most notably in Brazil, India, and Vietnam) as well as when capital inflows are channeled through the banking system, as in Romania (Annex 3.2). Even if the authorities are able to prevent nominal exchange rate appreciation, the pressure in many cases will still translate into real exchange rate appreciation through higher domestic inflation.[15]

Domestic Financial System

How, for example, do countries handle rising credit and—in some cases—foreign exchange risk buoyed by large portfolio inflows and external commercial borrowing? In India, although the banking sector as a whole remains healthy, rapid credit growth poses questions regarding credit quality in some banks. In Vietnam, banks' exposure to a booming stock market poses a market risk from their own holdings and indirect credit risk through loans to buy equities for their clients should a correction to the stock market occur. In Romania, although financial soundness indicators suggest that banks enjoy adequate capital and liquidity buffers, banks are exposed to indirect foreign exchange risk stemming from rapidly rising unhedged lending to

[15]This chapter does not expand on the macroeconomic implications of exchange rate policy, but rather focuses on the financial implications of capital inflow surges and the tools to deal with them. For a look at macroeconomic implications, see the discussion of inflow episodes in Chapter 3 of the October 2007 *World Economic Outlook* (IMF, 2007c).

Table 3.3. Indicators for Selected Countries, 2001 and 2006
(In percent)

	Real GDP Growth	Inflation Rate	General Government Balance/ GDP	External Current Account Balance/ GDP	Official Reserves/ Short-Term Debt[1]	Broad Money/ GDP	Credit to Private Sector/ GDP	Equity Market Capitalization/ GDP	Equity Market Turnover/ GDP
Brazil[2]									
2001	1.3	6.8	−3.3	−4.2	55.9	24.1	25.1	33.0	11.5
2006	3.7	4.2	−3.0	1.2	125.6	28.0	30.6	66.5	25.8
India[3]									
2001	3.9	3.8	−9.8	0.3	380.0	59.8	29.7	23.3	52.6
2006	9.7	6.1	−6.0	−1.1	850.0[5]	73.2	47.6	92.3	72.0
Romania[3]									
2001	5.7	30.3	−3.2	−5.5	496.1	25.7	8.7	5.3	0.6
2006	7.7	4.9	−1.7	−10.3	158.8[6]	32.4	27.0	26.9	3.5
South Africa[2]									
2001	2.7	6.5	−1.5	0.3	38.1[7]	59.4	66.1	117.9	58.8
2006	5.0	5.0	0.4	−6.5	150.5[7]	78.1	83.1	280.2	122.4
Vietnam[4]									
2001	6.9	1.9	−2.8	1.6	261.5	52.1	39.3	0.3	0.2
2006	8.2	7.2	−0.7	−0.4	522.7[6]	86.4	71.3	22.7	10.1
Memorandum items:									
Germany[2]									
2001	1.2	1.9	−2.8	0.0	39.7	68.1	118.2	56.6	75.2
2006	2.8	1.8	−1.6	5.0	39.2	72.4	109.9	56.5	94.5
Japan[2]									
2001	0.2	−0.8	−6.3	2.1	136.6	130.0	112.9	55.3	44.8
2006	2.2	0.2	4.1	3.9	229.5	140.3	98.0	109.8	139.1
United Kingdom[2]									
2001	2.4	1.2	0.9	−2.2	1.3	93.8	137.7	150.8	314.9
2006	2.8	2.3	−2.9	−3.7	0.7	114.7	176.1	159.8	319.0
United States[2]									
2001	0.8	2.8	−0.4	−3.8	. . .	74.4	177.7	136.5	219.6
2006	2.9	3.2	−2.3	−6.2	1.4	75.5	200.3	148.3	231.2

Sources: IMF, *World Economic Outlook* and *International Financial Statistics;* U.S. Department of the Treasury; and IMF staff reports.
[1]Ratio for official reserves is to next year's short-term debt, except in 2006 for Japan, the United Kingdom, and the United States, where same-year short-term debt is used.
[2]Independently floating exchange rate.
[3]Managed floating exchange rate.
[4]Conventional peg.
[5]For India, data are for April–March fiscal years. The figure for 2006 is preliminary.
[6]Data for 2006 are preliminary. Short-term external debt plus open forward position.
[7]Short-term external debt plus open forward position.

households. In countries such as India, Vietnam, and Romania, as well as other countries in Central and Eastern Europe, where domestic capital markets are not highly developed, there are concerns about asset price inflation (often in both the stock market and in real estate) in combination with credit growth concentration in certain institutions or sectors. Although financial deepening—typically measured as the ratio of private credit to GDP—is a welcome structural development for these countries over the longer term, the immediate concern is whether it outpaces the speed with which domestic institutions are strengthening.[16] For such countries, in which domestic capital markets are not very liquid or diversified and where a large part of the capital flows is intermediated through the banking system, the challenges tend to be expressed primarily in terms of credit and/or foreign exchange risk.

[16]See Hilbers and others (2005) for a discussion of rapid credit growth buoyed by strong capital inflows with a focus on Central and Eastern Europe.

External

The external challenges to emerging markets involve an abrupt change in global financial conditions and international investor appetite for risk. South Africa, for example, has experienced high volatility of its exchange rate despite a strong macroeconomic performance and a liquid financial market, as evidenced by the May/June 2006 and February/March 2007 episodes when the rand was one of the most affected emerging market currencies; this was probably also due to the large current account deficit and a weakening of commodity prices. As for Brazil, the composition of inflows means that the risk of a sudden withdrawal is high if international investors adjust their portfolios abruptly, since a large part of the inflows is in the form of short-term portfolio flows. However, with strong macroeconomic performance, including an improved debt composition, a well-supervised financial system, and diversified domestic markets, Brazil's external vulnerability is reduced relative to previous episodes of surges and withdrawals of capital flows.

Financial Policies Adopted by the Authorities

In addition to accumulating foreign assets as a financial safety cushion, the five countries discussed here have undertaken a number of reforms that are designed to reduce external vulnerabilities in the long term. Such structural reforms include strengthening the prudential and regulatory framework and market infrastructure, and facilitating a smooth development of domestic capital markets (Annex 3.2). In South Africa, for example, the authorities relaxed restrictions on outward investment in recent years as the economy moves away from exchange controls and toward a system of prudential-based regulations for institutional investors. Brazil removed withholding taxes on income earned by nonresidents from government securities holdings, which, although still at an early stage, appears to have attracted larger investor participation. In addition, limits on the outward investment of Brazilian institutional

asset funds were loosened. The measures taken in the two countries of the group with the more developed capital markets have had the beneficial effects of further enlarging the investor base and allowing for greater risk diversification, and have the potential to reduce currency and inflow volatility.

Other financial measures have been taken with the more immediate aim of reducing the country's short-term vulnerability stemming from capital inflow surges (and potential withdrawals). Some of these policies have had mixed results, while for others it is too early to draw definitive lessons about their effectiveness, since the capital inflow surge is still unfolding. Measures taken include the following:

- Prudential requirements for bank transactions in foreign currency have been tightened (Brazil). On the other hand, a stricter limit to banks' unhedged foreign currency lending introduced in Romania in 2005 was removed in early 2007 because it was no longer effective.
- Banks' reserve requirements were raised (India, Romania, Vietnam) and differentiated between domestic and foreign currency deposits to encourage a switch to domestic currency lending (Romania). Beginning in 2005, Romania also required the separate classification of unhedged foreign currency loans regardless of their repayment performance. It is unclear whether these measures have slowed the growth of unhedged foreign exchange household credit or reduced the currency mismatch on bank balance sheets in Romania.
- Addressing specifically the containment of rapid credit growth, India boosted the risk weights for high-growth areas, such as real estate, to above Basel norms.
- Vietnam took a series of administrative steps to address banks' exposure to the stock market and to contain the strong equity valuation, including tightening the rules for new bank lending for the purchase of stocks, and reregistration and new reporting requirements for foreign investment funds.

Financial Policy Options[17]

There are a number of practices that countries follow to address short-term challenges stemming from capital inflow pressures. These measures can be administrative or market-based, and may include informal official guidance in cases where the weight of the authorities' role relative to that of market forces allows it. Such measures include (1) increasing the cost of central bank credit; (2) raising banks' reserve requirements; (3) varying reserve requirements between domestic and foreign exchange deposits; (4) placing government deposits with the central bank; and (5) introducing taxes to either level out or create a wedge between the yields of domestic and foreign securities. Although market-based measures are preferable to administrative ones, these policies are—either explicitly or implicitly—a tax on the financial system and have the potential to increase interest rates and spur additional inflows. Thus, their cost and potentially distortive side effects ought to be carefully counterbalanced against their effectiveness over time.

As regards prudential measures, they are most effective when they concentrate on what they were intended to achieve, that is, the long-term soundness of the domestic financial system, rather than be stretched to counteract capital inflow pressures. When proposed, their full implications, including possible side effects, need to be carefully considered. Specifically, prudential measures in banking could focus on making sure that banks understand the risks stemming from capital inflows, that the capital structure of banks is appropriate for the type of inflows, and that financial institutions are required to set up proper risk management policies and practices to measure and manage aggregate exposures, including those of offshore exposure of domestic financial institutions. It is important to promote a good understanding of risk among borrowers, in particular for loans in foreign exchange where exchange rate risk for borrowers can easily translate into credit risk for banks.[18]

Prudential measures relating to the capital markets should aim to strengthen corporate governance, including shareholders' rights, listing requirements, and the clearance and settlement system. Margin requirements may be established considering such factors as historical volatility, risks of extreme movements, length of the settlement period, and capital adequacy of brokers. These parameters are most effectively established to promote systemic development and stability in the long run, rather than as a short-term response to capital movements.

Another policy designed to reduce pressures from large capital inflows is the easing of controls on capital outflows. In addition to Brazil, a number of countries—including Chile, China, and Korea—have recently liberalized rules limiting individual or institutional investments abroad. This has led to a rapid increase in portfolio investment outflows, especially in Asia (Box 3.1). It is too early to conclude from the data, however, whether capital outflow liberalization will be effective in relieving inflow pressure over time. More fundamentally, it is difficult to measure the effectiveness of capital outflow liberalization given the possible role of other factors in determining the direction and level of capital flows. There are also indications that in past episodes of capital inflow surges the liberalization of capital outflows was matched by larger inflows (Reinhart and Reinhart, 1998).

In line with the earlier empirical results that suggest that financial openness encourages inflows, capital controls, broadly defined, are usually unhelpful in managing inflows. They pose problems of implementation and circumvention, including governance problems, especially for administrative controls, where one authority possesses the right of discretionary

---

[17]For the purposes of this chapter, the discussion focuses on financial or microeconomic rather than macroeconomic policies.

[18]See Enoch and Ötker-Robe (2007) for a discussion of the use of prudential measures to ensure sound lending practices in cases of rapid credit growth.

decision making.[19] One needs to differentiate between countries that already have capital controls in place (including the accompanying infrastructure and reputation) and delay scheduled liberalization, and countries that impose controls starting from a position of an open capital account regime. In the latter case, capital controls can carry reputational costs, which may be significant if the country meets its financing needs from international capital markets.[20]

If capital controls are used, they best take the form of market-based controls, and should be used only as a transitional measure to provide breathing space while developing an adequate supervisory and regulatory system or strengthening the regulated financial institutions. Other policy adjustments should be undertaken in parallel, as the effectiveness of capital controls tends to diminish over time.[21] Eventually, investors find ways to assume exposure to a desired emerging market destination, thus blunting a country's attempts to relieve pressure on the exchange rate (Box 3.3).[22] In any case, market-based controls, such as unremunerated reserve requirements, would be preferable to administrative measures.

---

[19]This is particularly problematic where transactions or transfers are subject to prior approval by the foreign exchange authority and there are no clear criteria for granting such approval.

[20]To regain monetary policy independence and stabilize short-term capital flows, Malaysia introduced a wide range of direct capital and exchange controls in September 1998. These controls were effective, but, five months later, the costs of weakening investor and market confidence prompted the authorities to loosen them in the form of an exit levy system (Ariyoshi and others, 2000).

[21]To limit short-term capital inflows, Chile introduced capital controls in 1991 in the form of a minimum stay requirement and 20 percent unremunerated reserve requirements (URR). These controls were successful in reducing short-term inflows. However, until 1998, when the measures were eliminated, the rate and coverage of the URR were changed several times in an effort to close the channels that developed to circumvent the controls (Ariyoshi and others, 2000).

[22]Brazil introduced various controls during 1993–97 to lengthen the maturity and change the composition of capital inflows. Since the cost of circumvention declined relative to investors' incentives, the controls gradually lost effectiveness, resulting in additional alteration of them (Ariyoshi and others, 2000).

Key Results and Conclusions

The key results from the estimations presented in this chapter can be summarized as follows:

- Growth and growth prospects are primary domestic determinants of the level of capital inflows.
- Financial market liquidity and financial openness help attract capital inflows.
- More financial openness is associated with lower capital volatility.
- Volatility of capital inflows is partly driven by external factors, such as global financial liquidity, which are outside the control of emerging markets.
- Institutional quality, as expressed by a number of diverse indicators, matters. Specifically, better corporate governance is associated with a higher level of inflows, and a number of institutional quality and market infrastructure indicators, including regulatory quality and the rule of law, are positively associated with a reduction in the volatility of capital inflows.

These results—indicating that the quality of the domestic financial market raises the level and helps reduce the volatility of capital inflows—lend empirical support to conventional wisdom and are consistent with what we learned from discussions with private sector institutional investors, as well as with the findings from the five country examples.

Since the surge in capital inflows is still unfolding, it is hard to draw definitive conclusions on the effectiveness of current financial policies in dealing with the present surges (and possible withdrawals) of capital flows. However, even after the current cycle changes direction, the long-term trend toward increased financial integration is such that countries will need to put themselves in a situation that will make it possible to live with the potential volatility of capital flows. The chapter has provided some clues concerning the longer-term financial policies that will aid countries in this endeavor.

Box 3.3. How Investors Gain Exposure to an Emerging Market in the Presence of Capital Controls: The Case of India

Strong economic performance has increasingly attracted the attention of international investors to India. But direct access to the domestic fixed-income, foreign exchange, and equity markets by international investors is either restricted, through the qualified foreign institutional investor (FII) program, or closed altogether. Several factors constrain investors from entering the Indian market directly. For instance, foreign investors are subject to limits in their holdings of corporate and government securities, cannot participate in the interbank market, and do not have access to local currency instruments for purposes of speculation. In addition, although a level playing field for all investors is welcome, the relatively high withholding and other taxes and the hurdles for opening and operating a domestic settlement account are administratively burdensome for many foreign investors.

Many international investors are able to acquire exposure to Indian markets while avoiding India's regime of restrictions on foreign participation through an increasing number of channels, particularly as derivatives markets have grown. For example, there is a large and relatively liquid offshore market for India's interest rates along the full yield curve—up to 10 years.

The growth of derivatives-related and other transactions opens numerous two-way channels for investors who see India as a desired destination:

- Foreign investors, including hedge funds, can gain entry into the Indian equity market through the purchase of participatory notes offered by registered FIIs. These notes allow offshore participants to gain exposure to Indian equities without registering as an FII.
- The onshore rupee forward market is only available for hedging commercial transactions. Hence, to express an outright currency or interest rate view, foreign investors transact through the nondeliverable forwards and interest rate swaps markets. Liquidity in these markets is provided by foreign banks and offshore Indian accounts.
- A borrowing channel for Indian corporates via foreign currency convertible bonds (FCCBs) gets packaged into structured credit products, such as credit-linked notes and collateralized debt obligations. As a rule, Indian subsidiaries offshore purchase the credit portion, while hedge funds, proprietary desks of investment banks, and other international investors prefer the equity option. Indian corporates indicate that access to low-cost financing through FCCBs is worth this minor dilution in their equity stake. More generally, the credit default market in Indian credits is reasonably active, with offshore subsidiaries of Indian banks providing insurance to international investors, in some cases through structured products. In sum, there are opportunities to gain exposure to Indian credit risk offshore.
- Given the existing restrictions on portfolio ownership by foreign investors, private sector participants can take an increasingly more direct ownership avenue through private equity direct investments. In this context, private equity accounts for a growing share of inflows, much of it targeting real estate-related investments. This development often makes it difficult to distinguish between foreign direct and portfolio investment.

Note: The main contributors to this box are Rebecca McCaughrin and Tao Sun.

In addition to strong macroeconomic fundamentals, including sound fiscal policy and more flexible exchange rates, countries will be better equipped to live with potential capital flow volatility if they either possess or demonstrate progress toward achieving the following long-term structural characteristics:

- Deep and liquid equity markets within a well-regulated system; and
- Strong institutional quality across a broad

range of indicators, including corporate governance, accounting standards, the rule of law, and control of corruption.

Analysis has demonstrated the importance of transparency in relation to both policies (macroeconomic and microfinancial) and data. When this transparency is combined with a strong self-assessment of macro and financial vulnerabilities and with sound risk management systems within financial institutions and the public sector, it improves the ability of countries to deal with capital flows. Private institutional investors have repeatedly expressed the importance of timely and accurate data, as well as a predictable and transparent way of communicating with the investor base, as factors that contribute to the effective management of capital flows.

It is difficult to draw blanket recommendations beyond the ones noted above because policy challenges associated with capital inflows cannot and should not be uniform. Countries differ in their exchange rate regime and the type of capital inflows they experience, and therefore in the challenges they face. They differ also in the depth and diversification of their financial markets and their institutional and regulatory development, which means that they have a different menu of policy options at their disposal.

There are, however, some general guidelines as regards financial sector policies that are aimed at alleviating the pressures arising from large capital inflows:

- Loosening or eliminating restrictions on residents' capital outflows is a tool that can ease pressures from large capital inflows. Outward investment will also lead to internationalization of capital across emerging markets and, therefore, can be a welcome means of risk diversification. More experience will show whether this policy will have a lasting effect.
- Supervisory and prudential measures have a key role to play in addressing the health and stability of the financial system. Ideally, however, they are best used to address prudential considerations such as rapid credit growth or unhedged foreign exchange exposures; that

is, to ensure the soundness of the domestic financial system, rather than as a response designed to alleviate pressures stemming from capital inflow surges. A well-supervised financial system will help provide safeguards that will permit capital flows to enter and exit the financial system without endangering financial stability.

- Capital controls should be used only as a last resort and as part of a package of macroeconomic and prudential measures. They may be able to throw sand in the gears of a surge of short-term speculative inflows under certain circumstances, especially if the infrastructure is already in place. In addition to the challenge of effectiveness, there are reputational costs to be considered. Moreover, the effectiveness of controls can either be circumvented from the start or diminish over time, as financial instruments will likely be found to circumvent them.

Ultimately, however, it is the quality of its domestic financial market—in addition to strong macroeconomic performance—that will put an emerging market in a position to maximize to the fullest extent the benefits of capital inflows and best deal with their potential volatility. Short-term measures intended for an immediate relief of pressure from large capital inflows may have uncertain effectiveness or unintended side effects, or be a distraction from the long-term goal of raising the quality of the domestic market—including depth and liquidity, market infrastructure, supervision, and institutions.

The increasing integration of financial markets—across countries and sectors—witnessed in the past decade has both long-term and cyclical elements. However, even after the current cycle turns, the underlying financial globalization trend is likely to point to continued financial integration, which will affect both advanced and newly arriving emerging markets. Countries, therefore, are best served if their primary response to large capital inflows today is to pursue the longer-term goal of developing their financial markets and building up a resilience to capital volatility rather than making short-term responses to inflow surges. Countries will be better off if flows can both enter and exit freely without disrupting domestic financial stability and the real economy.

Annex 3.1. Estimation Specification and Results

A panel specification is employed to estimate the factors that determine the level of capital inflows for a sample of 56 countries, using an annual sample from 1975 to 2006.[23] The dependent variables used in the estimations comprise total capital flows and four main components, namely portfolio equity, portfolio bonds, FDI, and an "other" category that consists primarily of bank lending and includes financial derivatives for most of the countries that do not report these under a separate category, as well as money market instruments. The variables are normalized by nominal GDP. Total inflows and each of its components are modeled as a function of a set of financial development variables, as well as two macroeconomic measures aiming to control for the effect that these variables may have.

The panel regressions are run on a sample of the following 56 countries:

- *15 developed economies*: Australia, Belgium, Canada, France, Germany, Greece, Italy, Japan, the Netherlands, New Zealand, Spain, Sweden, Switzerland, United Kingdom, and United States.
- *12 emerging market economies—Asia*: China, Hong Kong SAR, India, Indonesia, Korea, Malaysia, Pakistan, the Philippines, Singapore, Sri Lanka, Thailand, and Vietnam.
- *20 emerging market economies—Europe, Middle East, and Africa*: Algeria, Bulgaria, Côte d'Ivoire, Croatia, Czech Republic, Estonia, Hungary, Israel, Jordan, Latvia, Lithuania, Morocco, Nigeria, Poland, Romania, Russia, Saudi Arabia, Slovenia, South Africa, and Turkey.

- *Nine emerging market economies—Latin America*: Argentina, Brazil, Chile, Colombia, Ecuador, Mexico, Panama, Peru, and Venezuela.

We consider two types of factors: macroeconomic factors and financial development indicators.

Macroeconomic Factors

(1) Spread: real interest rate differential measured as the difference between the domestic one-year treasury bill rate and the world rate, calculated as the real GDP-weighted average of each country's one-year rate;

(2) Growth: adaptive expectation for growth measured as real GDP growth rate in the previous year; and

(3) Global liquidity: changes in the sum of money supply (M1) and official reserves in the euro area, Japan, and the United States, a common general proxy for global liquidity.

Financial Development Indicators

(1) Changes in equity market capitalization and equity market turnover, each normalized by nominal GDP;[24]

(2) Financial openness, as reported in Chinn and Ito (2006), which codifies the tabulation of restrictions on cross-border financial transactions reported by the IMF's *Annual Report on Exchange Arrangements and Exchange Restrictions* as an index to measure a country's degree of capital account openness;

(3) Corporate governance quality: a de facto, as opposed to de jure, index comprising a simple average of three indicators constructed from accounting and market data for samples of nonfinancial companies listed in stock markets (De Nicolò, Laeven, and Ueda, 2006); and

(4) Accounting standards: a measure of the amount of accounting information that firms disclose (De Nicolò, Laeven, and Ueda, 2006).

---

[23]Due to the unbalanced structure of the panel data, some countries are dropped from the sample in the estimations.

[24]The sources for these data are the World Federation of Exchanges, Datastream, and Standard and Poor's Emerging Markets Database.

We also performed panel estimations that included in the specification credit market depth (approximated by the change in private credit outstanding normalized by nominal GDP) as an explanatory variable for the level and volatility of capital inflows. However, in most cases, this variable showed the opposite sign and was often not significant. A possible explanation is that domestic bank credit to the private sector works as a substitute for capital inflows, including external bank borrowing, since well-functioning domestic credit markets may raise domestic savings and reduce the need for financing from international markets.

The same specification employed to estimate the factors that determine the level of capital flows is also used for estimating the volatility of inflows measured by their standard deviation computed using a five-year rolling window, also divided by nominal GDP.[25] The generalized method of moments (GMM) estimation is employed with lagged values for independent variables as instruments.[26] To avoid the use

of nonstationary variables and to maintain a relatively large sample, the estimation is limited to the volatility of total capital inflows, which follows a stationary process in the full country sample.

Unit root tests were performed for both panel and individual unit roots. Two tests—Levin, Lin, and Chu (2002), and Breitung (2000)—were conducted to test for the existence of a common unit root process. Three additional tests—Im, Pesaran, and Shin (2003), and Fisher-type tests using the Augmented Dickey-Fuller and the Phillips-Perron tests (Maddala and Wu, 1999; and Choi, 2001)—were conducted to test for unit roots in individual series. The tests indicate that most variables follow a stationary process. Exceptions are for the volatility of portfolio equity, portfolio bonds, and FDI. Similar results hold for the subperiod 1998–2006.

The tables that follow show the descriptive statistics for the variables used in the panel regressions (Table 3.4), and the level estimation results for the 30-year period covering the full country sample and emerging markets (Tables 3.5 and 3.6), and, similarly, for the period 1998–2006 (Tables 3.7. and 3.8.).

---

[25]See Box 2.5 in the April 2007 GFSR for a similar approach (IMF, 2007a).

[26]Since the test results of our volatility measures for serial correlation are mixed, with weakly significant results in some cases, we do not employ lagged values of

dependent variables as instruments, since this would be an improper use of instruments in the GMM framework.

Table 3.4. Descriptive Statistics for Variables Used in Panel Regressions, 1975–2006

	Mean	Median	Standard Deviation	Skewness	Kurtosis	Observations[1]
Dependent Variables[2]						
Level						
Total capital inflows	6.336	4.276	18.439	−0.504	126.707	1,502
Portfolio securities	1.327	0.254	3.207	2.954	43.176	1,470
Equity	0.417	0.000	1.616	12.184	242.222	1,482
Bonds	0.899	0.028	2.602	2.092	60.527	1,486
Foreign direct investment	2.192	1.110	3.237	2.965	19.351	1,506
Other[3]	2.821	1.628	16.832	−0.558	148.527	1,512
Volatility[4]						
Total capital inflows	4.761	2.562	11.514	9.151	98.941	1,279
Portfolio securities	1.143	0.628	1.796	4.668	34.551	1,250
Equity	0.472	0.175	1.049	9.765	147.276	1,262
Bonds	0.905	0.423	1.493	5.013	40.978	1,266
Foreign direct investment	1.024	0.516	1.384	3.329	20.172	1,282
Other[3]	3.950	1.845	11.010	9.353	101.662	1,288
Independent Variables						
Macroeconomic factors						
Interest rate differential[5]	2.955	0.643	17.106	3.884	32.608	1,168
Growth expectation[6]	3.560	3.808	4.196	−0.722	5.580	1,668
Global liquidity[7]	9.269	7.505	8.128	0.380	2.494	1,736
Financial development indicators						
Equity market capitalization[8]	6.007	2.674	20.948	1.405	30.046	1,196
Equity market turnover[8]	5.476	0.766	23.666	2.425	28.604	968
Financial openness[9]	0.571	−0.062	1.650	0.056	1.403	1,474
Corporate governance quality[10]	0.612	0.615	0.076	−0.619	4.495	420
Accounting standards[10]	0.843	0.850	0.041	−1.010	5.362	427

Sources: Bloomberg; Chinn and Ito (2006); Datastream; De Nicolò and others (2006); IMF, *International Financial Statistics* and *World Economic Outlook* databases; Standard and Poor's Emerging Markets Database; and World Federation of Exchanges.

[1]Numbers are different due to differences in time-series and cross-sectional data availabilities for individual countries.

[2]Nominal GDP ratios (in percent).

[3]Consists mainly of bank loans.

[4]The standard deviation of each capital inflow component computed using a five-year rolling window.

[5]One-year real interest rate minus the world rate constructed by the real GDP-weighted average of each rate (in percent).

[6]Measured by the real GDP growth rate in the previous year (i.e., an adaptive expectation).

[7]Growth rate of M1 and official reserves in the euro area, Japan, and the United States.

[8]Changes in stock market capitalization and turnover, respectively, divided by nominal GDP (in percent).

[9]The indicator computed by Chinn and Ito (2006).

[10]The indicators computed by De Nicolò, Laeven, and Ueda (2006).

Table 3.5. Fixed-Effects Panel Least-Squares Estimation of the Determinants of Capital Inflows (All Countries, Full Sample)

	Capital Inflows/GDP[1]					
	Total	Total portfolio	Portfolio equity	Portfolio bonds	Foreign direct investment	Other[2]
Macroeconomic Factors						
Interest rate differential	0.043	−0.009	−0.003	−0.005	0.021	0.031
	[0.030]**	[0.448]	[0.705]	[0.441]	[0.004]***	[0.106]
Growth expectation	0.489	−0.027	−0.034	0.006	0.109	0.406
	[0.000]***	[0.749]	[0.471]	[0.940]	[0.000]***	[0.001]***
Global liquidity	−0.009	0.002	−0.004	0.006	−0.035	0.025
	[0.849]	[0.914]	[0.596]	[0.732]	[0.010]**	[0.452]
Financial Development Indicators						
Equity market capitalization	0.027	0.002	0.004	−0.002	0.019	0.007
	[0.292]	[0.764]	[0.642]	[0.703]	[0.039]**	[0.789]
Equity market turnover	0.127	0.018	0.014	0.004	0.018	0.091
	[0.002]***	[0.002]***	[0.013]**	[0.369]	[0.000]***	[0.013]**
Financial openness	1.647	0.680	0.087	0.590	0.435	0.537
	[0.000]***	[0.000]***	[0.075]*	[0.000]***	[0.000]***	[0.037]**
Other Factors						
Constant	2.294	0.979	0.528	0.454	1.470	−0.198
	[0.010]***	[0.145]	[0.126]	[0.459]	[0.000]***	[0.818]
Dummy for 1998–2006	1.870	1.034	0.292	0.745	1.232	−0.297
	[0.008]***	[0.006]***	[0.034]**	[0.031]**	[0.000]***	[0.577]
Adjusted R[2]	**0.552**	**0.306**	**0.239**	**0.317**	**0.662**	**0.418**
Time-series sample (annual)	1977–2006	1977–2006	1977–2006	1977–2006	1977–2006	1977–2006
No. of cross-section countries	47	47	47	47	47	47
No. of observations[3]	672	665	672	665	672	672

Sources: Bloomberg; Chinn and Ito (2006); Datastream; De Nicolò and others (2006); IMF, *International Financial Statistics* and *World Economic Outlook* databases; Standard and Poor's Emerging Markets Database; and World Federation of Exchanges.

[1]In percent. Probability values are in square brackets (*** significant at 1 percent level; ** significant at 5 percent level; and * significant at 10 percent level). White-type cross-section standard errors and covariance with degree of freedom corrected for robust estimators.

[2]Consists mainly of bank loans.

[3]Total number of observations based on the unbalanced panel structure.

Table 3.6. Fixed-Effects Panel Least-Squares Estimation of the Determinants of Capital Inflows (Emerging Market Economies, Full Sample)

	Capital Inflows/GDP[1]					
	Total	Total portfolio	Portfolio equity	Portfolio bonds	Foreign direct investment	Other[2]
Macroeconomic Factors						
Interest rate differential	0.022	−0.023	−0.011	−0.012	0.020	0.025
	[0.248]	[0.057]*	[0.313]	[0.072]*	[0.010]***	[0.244]
Growth expectation	0.404	−0.115	−0.061	−0.055	0.093	0.421
	[0.000]***	[0.236]	[0.275]	[0.535]	[0.002]***	[0.008]***
Global liquidity	−0.003	−0.007	0.007	−0.014	−0.028	0.032
	[0.948]	[0.656]	[0.442]	[0.254]	[0.054]*	[0.415]
Financial Development Indicators						
Equity market capitalization	0.020	0.000	0.001	0.000	0.021	0.000
	[0.512]	[0.972]	[0.953]	[0.980]	[0.072]*	[0.985]
Equity market turnover	0.150	0.020	0.017	0.002	0.018	0.113
	[0.003]***	[0.017]**	[0.008]***	[0.616]	[0.001]***	[0.010]***
Financial openness	1.550	0.483	0.006	0.475	0.510	0.559
	[0.000]***	[0.001]***	[0.921]	[0.000]***	[0.000]***	[0.027]**
Other Factors						
Constant	3.440	2.200	0.839	1.354	1.827	−0.522
	[0.001]***	[0.013]**	[0.107]	[0.088]*	[0.000]***	[0.670]
Dummy for 1998–2006	−1.260	−0.760	−0.066	−0.676	1.141	−1.679
	[0.062]*	[0.107]	[0.791]	[0.110]	[0.000]***	[0.013]**
Adjusted R[2]	**0.510**	**0.129**	**0.274**	**0.040**	**0.730**	**0.350**
Time-series sample (annual)	1977–2006	1977–2006	1977–2006	1977–2006	1977–2006	1977–2006
No. of cross-section countries	32	32	32	32	32	32
No. of observations[3]	460	453	460	453	460	460

Sources: Bloomberg; Chinn and Ito (2006); Datastream; De Nicolò and others (2006); IMF, *International Financial Statistics* and *World Economic Outlook* databases; Standard and Poor's Emerging Markets Database; and World Federation of Exchanges.

[1]In percent. Probability values are in square brackets (*** significant at 1 percent level; ** significant at 5 percent level; and * significant at 10 percent level). White-type cross-section standard errors and covariance with degree of freedom corrected for robust estimators.

[2]Consists mainly of bank loans.

[3]Total number of observations based on the unbalanced panel structure.

Table 3.7. Fixed-Effects Panel Least-Squares Estimation of the Determinants of Capital Inflows (All Countries, 1998–2006)

| | Capital Inflows/GDP[1] | | | | | |
	Total	Total portfolio	Portfolio equity	Portfolio bonds	Foreign direct investment	Other[2]
Macroeconomic Factors						
Interest rate differential	0.109	−0.027	−0.014	−0.013	0.033	0.103
	[0.001]***	[0.405]	[0.648]	[0.154]	[0.084]*	[0.056]*
Growth expectation	0.668	−0.064	−0.099	0.035	0.175	0.552
	[0.000]***	[0.667]	[0.496]	[0.435]	[0.046]**	[0.016]**
Global liquidity	0.013	0.036	0.001	0.036	−0.060	0.010
	[0.863]	[0.198]	[0.955]	[0.037]**	[0.006]***	[0.785]
Financial Development Indicators						
Equity market capitalization	0.039	0.008	0.009	−0.001	0.023	0.008
	[0.312]	[0.500]	[0.460]	[0.858]	[0.052]*	[0.815]
Equity market turnover	0.139	0.017	0.016	0.001	0.020	0.103
	[0.003]***	[0.003]***	[0.030]**	[0.908]	[0.000]***	[0.025]**
Financial openness	3.488	0.977	0.387	0.559	1.143	1.427
	[0.000]***	[0.002]***	[0.101]	[0.132]	[0.005]***	[0.038]**
Corporate governance quality	30.128	−9.562	−11.948	2.443	−0.849	40.026
	[0.076]*	[0.170]	[0.041]**	[0.257]	[0.895]	[0.000]***
Accounting standards	0.019	3.103	2.788	0.224	−12.126	8.194
	[0.998]	[0.772]	[0.760]	[0.975]	[0.008]***	[0.569]
Other Factors						
Constant	−17.696	5.278	6.019	−0.654	12.635	−34.578
	[0.247]	[0.494]	[0.275]	[0.915]	[0.064]*	[0.001]***
Adjusted R²	**0.616**	**0.485**	**0.221**	**0.607**	**0.653**	**0.469**
Time-series sample (annual)	1998–2006	1998–2006	1998–2006	1998–2006	1998–2006	1998–2006
No. of cross-section countries	34	34	34	34	34	34
No. of observations[3]	277	272	277	272	277	277

Sources: Bloomberg; Chinn and Ito (2006); Datastream; De Nicolò and others (2006); IMF, *International Financial Statistics* and *World Economic Outlook* databases; Standard and Poor's Emerging Markets Database; and World Federation of Exchanges.
    [1]In percent. Probability values are in square brackets (*** significant at 1 percent level; ** significant at 5 percent level; and * significant at 10 percent level). White-type cross-section standard errors and covariance with degree of freedom corrected for robust estimators.
    [2]Consists mainly of bank loans.
    [3]Total number of observations based on the unbalanced panel structure.

Table 3.8. Fixed-Effects Panel Least-Squares Estimation of the Determinants of Capital Inflows (Emerging Market Economies, 1998–2006)

	Capital Inflows/GDP[1]					
	Total	Total portfolio	Portfolio equity	Portfolio bonds	Foreign direct investment	Other[2]
Macroeconomic Factors						
Interest rate differential	0.086	−0.036	−0.030	−0.005	0.033	0.089
	[0.004]***	[0.367]	[0.446]	[0.610]	[0.073]*	[0.130]
Growth expectation	0.782	−0.065	−0.126	0.059	0.158	0.690
	[0.000]***	[0.699]	[0.465]	[0.029]**	[0.046]**	[0.021]**
Global liquidity	−0.036	0.028	0.031	−0.003	−0.055	−0.009
	[0.353]	[0.350]	[0.203]	[0.765]	[0.003]***	[0.831]
Financial Development Indicators						
Equity market capitalization	0.018	0.003	0.003	0.001	0.028	−0.013
	[0.739]	[0.843]	[0.885]	[0.839]	[0.078]*	[0.767]
Equity market turnover	0.216	0.031	0.024	0.006	0.021	0.165
	[0.001]***	[0.008]***	[0.025]**	[0.106]	[0.001]***	[0.003]***
Financial openness	3.164	1.155	0.219	0.900	1.112	0.993
	[0.001]***	[0.001]***	[0.497]	[0.000]***	[0.007]***	[0.226]
Corporate governance quality	16.225	−20.619	−14.584	−5.793	−1.227	36.792
	[0.290]	[0.001]***	[0.018]**	[0.004]***	[0.846]	[0.002]***
Accounting standards	−10.995	2.825	−5.631	8.098	−17.868	4.257
	[0.647]	[0.862]	[0.724]	[0.132]	[0.043]**	[0.784]
Other Factors						
Constant	−1.778	11.322	14.959	−3.463	18.646	−31.190
	[0.914]	[0.325]	[0.188]	[0.500]	[0.004]***	[0.006]***
Adjusted R²	**0.514**	**0.220**	**0.259**	**0.137**	**0.768**	**0.369**
Time-series sample (annual)	1998–2006	1998–2006	1998–2006	1998–2006	1998–2006	1998–2006
No. of cross-section countries	19	19	19	19	19	19
No. of observations[3]	151	146	151	146	151	151

Sources: Bloomberg; Chinn and Ito (2006); Datastream; De Nicolò and others (2006); IMF, *International Financial Statistics* and *World Economic Outlook* databases; Standard and Poor's Emerging Markets Database; and World Federation of Exchanges.

[1]In percent. Probability values are in square brackets (*** significant at 1 percent level; ** significant at 5 percent level; and * significant at 10 percent level). White-type cross-section standard errors and covariance with degree of freedom corrected for robust estimators.

[2]Consists mainly of bank loans.

[3]Total number of observations based on the unbalanced panel structure.

Annex 3.2. Experiences with Recent Capital Inflows: Brazil, India, Romania, South Africa, and Vietnam

Country	Type of Recent Inflows; Policy Framework and Financial System	Challenges Associated with Inflows		Policies Adopted by the Authorities
		Macroeconomic	Financial	
Brazil	Capital inflows exceeded $40 billion during the four quarters through March 2007, compared with negative inflows (i.e., net repayments of liabilities) and outward investment by Brazilian firms during previous quarters. In addition to continued strong FDI inflows, record levels of portfolio inflows—in both equity and debt—are expected in 2007. Foreign investors purchased about two-thirds of Brazilian equity initial public offerings in 2006 and this trend is expected to continue. Short-term inflows have surged as double-digit nominal interest rates and strong economic fundamentals make Brazil an attractive carry-trade destination.	The real appreciated by 5¼ percent in nominal effective terms in the first four months of 2007—more than most other emerging market currencies. In real effective terms, it has appreciated by nearly 40 percent since 2004. Notwithstanding the appreciating currency, following lackluster performance last year, export volume growth has picked up in recent months, but competitiveness could still be adversely affected.	There are risks of a rapid reversal of portfolio inflows should international risk appetite change abruptly.	The exchange rate regime is an independent float, but the authorities have intervened heavily over the past few months in the spot and forward markets.
				Policy interest rates have been cut significantly (by a cumulative 825 basis points since September 2005).
	Both exchange rate and capital account regulations have been liberalized gradually since the early 1990s. However, this process has often not been followed by complementary changes in the overall legislation, which remains complex and ambiguous. For instance, the government still can reintroduce controls on foreign exchange outflows—registration requirements and tax legislation allow for discretionary control over cross-border financial flows.	Yields continue to attract foreign investors, fostering appreciation pressures on the real.		A significant number of reforms, undertaken especially since the crises of the 1990s, have strengthened the financial sector's prudential and regulatory framework. The authorities undertake stress tests on exchange, credit, and interest-rate risk on a regular basis.
		Sterilizing with the sale of real government securities could raise the national debt through higher interest costs.		Prudential requirements for bank transactions in foreign currency were tightened in June 2007.
	Compared with other emerging markets, the financial system is diversified and one of the largest, with a sophisticated derivatives market. It is well regulated and supervised, and, owing to restructuring, has become more streamlined and efficient. Institutionally, the financial sector, dominated by banks, is concentrated: at end-2006, the 10 largest banks accounted for 72 percent of the banking sector's assets. The nonbank financial sector has grown rapidly, from a relatively low base. Assets managed by investment funds, in particular, have increased sharply, from 22 percent of GDP in 2002 to 34 percent in 2006. Activity on the stock market has also increased, but many large companies still prefer to list in New York.			Regulatory restrictions on residents' capital outflows were loosened by allowing mutual funds and other investment funds to invest abroad up to 20 and 10 percent of assets, respectively.
				In early 2007, tariffs were raised on selected imports to the maximum allowed under World Trade Organization rules. Furthermore, subsidized credit lines and tax credits have been extended to exporters in traditional sectors affected by the appreciation of the currency, although these incentives remain small in scale.

India

Capital inflows have surged in recent years to almost 5 percent of GDP. In 2006–07 capital inflows included loans, portfolio bonds, and FDI, notwithstanding the concomitant pickup in outward investment by Indian corporates. Inflows have also reflected an increase in cross-border hedging transactions. Portfolio equity inflows have picked up more recently, in part reflecting large initial public offerings in the first quarter of 2007.

Although gross FDI inflows are poised to exceed portfolio inflows in 2007 for the first time, they remain low relative to many other emerging market economies (Poirson, 2007). While the equity market has deepened, including foreign participation of more than 20 percent of total trading, some segments of other markets, such as the money and corporate securities markets, are illiquid. Recent progress in pension reform is a step toward deepening capital markets and broadening the institutional investor base.

Liquidity conditions remain loose, although some tightening is expected following the lifting of the ceiling on absorption under the reverse repo window, expected to keep the interbank overnight rate higher than its recent lows.

The rupee has appreciated rapidly, although competitiveness does not seem to be a problem to date. Sustained competitiveness, however, will require enhanced infrastructure, lower import tariffs, and an improved business climate (Purfield, 2006).

Rapid credit growth poses concerns regarding credit quality in some banks, although the banking sector as a whole remains healthy.

There is a potential credit or foreign exchange risk associated with rapidly rising corporate credit from abroad and uncertainties over the degree of hedging, although the liquidity/leverage ratios remain comfortable.

Gradually tightened monetary policy by raising the key policy rates several times since September 2004.

The Reserve Bank of India is reported to have intervened in the foreign exchange market to slow the pace of rupee appreciation every month since November 2006, thus partially interfering with sterilization.

Recently, conducted a series of increases in the reserve requirement ratio by a total of 1 percent in four consecutive months aimed at absorbing excess liquidity in the system.

Raised the ceiling for issuance of market sterilization bonds.

Raised general provisioning requirements and boosted risk weights on high-growth areas, such as real estate, to above Basel norms to contain rapid credit growth.

Gradual liberalization of capital flows continues. Although there are controls, including procedural hurdles and approval requirements, recent reforms include liberalization of overseas investments/FDI in some sectors and relaxation of controls on external commercial borrowing. A roadmap to capital account convertibility (the Tarapore report), produced by a committee of external experts established by the Reserve Bank of India, presents a hierarchy of preferences for liberalizing capital inflows; rupee-denominated debt in preference to foreign currency debt; medium- and long-term debt to short-term debt; and direct investment to portfolio flows.

The Reserve Bank of India has initiated banking reforms aimed at increasing public sector banks' autonomy and expanding foreign banks' presence by allowing foreign banks since 2005 to establish subsidiaries (they currently account for about 7 percent of total assets of the banking system).

Annex 3.2 (continued)

Country	Type of Recent Inflows; Policy Framework and Financial System	Challenges Associated with Inflows		Policies Adopted by the Authorities
		Macroeconomic	Financial	
Romania	Strong capital inflows have financed a widening current account deficit and have led to marked appreciation of the leu, raising concerns about the potential loss of competitiveness. Capital inflows have increased markedly since 2004 with the opening of the capital account and with prospects of European Union membership. Nondebt-creating inflows are estimated to have covered 91 percent of the current account deficit in 2006, although this coverage is expected to be lower in 2007 as privatization inflows are expected to decline.

In the absence of well-developed capital markets, capital inflows have been channeled predominantly through the banking system. High spreads between domestic and foreign interest rates elicited rapid credit growth, increasing vulnerabilities in the banking sector through indirect foreign exchange risk and a potentially deteriorating loan portfolio. Private sector external borrowing increased by 28 percent from 2005 to 2006, reaching 11 percent of GDP. | Widening current account deficit driven by domestic demand.

Government's budget under pressure (pressing expenditure needs, wage increases in the public sector, low revenue ratio, recently approved sharp pension increases), which may add to the economy overheating.

Monetary policy faces a dilemma as tightening would foster new capital inflows and exchange rate appreciation, thus raising concerns about external competitiveness.

Overheating housing market; asset price increases. | Financial soundness indicators suggest that the banking sector enjoys adequate capital and liquidity buffers.

Significant bank exposure to indirect foreign exchange risk (unhedged consumer lending is reported to be one of the highest in the region).

Credit risk may be a concern. Increasing competition may have led banks to target less creditworthy customers. Despite the favorable operating environment, the nonperforming loan ratio has remained broadly unchanged (8 percent on a gross basis, including loss, doubtful, and substandard; moreover, classification criteria and provisioning requirements are conservative). The loan-loss provision coverage ratio is low due to the use of collateral as a mitigating factor, but collateral recovery may prove difficult during times of stress.

Vulnerable to world interest rate movements and shifts in global risk appetite. | Inflation targeting was introduced in 2005 after abolishing restrictions on short-term capital inflows; the monetary authority is still in the process of establishing its prioritization of inflation targeting over exchange rate policy, in the eyes of financial markets.

Several changes to the level and base of banks' reserve requirements were implemented to encourage a switch away from foreign currency lending (currently, reserve requirements are 40 and 20 percent on foreign currency and domestic liabilities, respectively).

Limits to household lending were tightened, with a debt-service ceiling relating to the net monthly income of the borrower (August 2005), but eliminated in March 2007. A requirement for a 25 percent down payment for mortgage loans was also eliminated.

A limit was introduced to banks' unhedged foreign currency lending to three times their own capital. This limit, established in September 2005, was removed at the beginning of 2007 because it lost effectiveness. The limit had a short-term impact of an increased demand for leu loans.

In 2005, banks were required to classify unhedged foreign currency lending as "watch" regardless of the loans' repayment performance.

Cross-country cooperation has been enhanced (memoranda of understanding have been signed with foreign regulatory and supervisory authorities of countries with a bank presence in Romania). |

South Africa

In recent years, South Africa received significant amounts of net capital inflows—primarily portfolio—turning from negative levels in 2001 to over 8 percent of GDP in 2006, of which portfolio equity investment accounted for almost 5 percent of GDP.

Since 1995, exchange controls on nonresidents have been eliminated and capital transactions by residents have been relaxed, with the main remaining restrictions on the latter comprising certain controls on FDI, ceilings on portfolio outflows by corporations, and ceilings on individuals' offshore investments. The banking system is deep, and the insurance sector has the highest penetration (in terms of premia to GDP) among emerging markets, close to the UK level. The banking sector is adequately capitalized and profitable, with high asset growth and low levels of nonperforming assets. Local capital markets, including derivatives, are well developed, and securitization is growing rapidly, albeit from a low base.

Despite strong fundamentals, including low external debt and a solid financial system, the external current account deficit has been widening in the last few years, largely reflecting strong domestic demand. It reached 6.5 percent of GDP in 2006 and is projected to remain at that level in 2007 and to decline gradually in subsequent years.

Despite strong macroeconomic performance, vulnerabilities exist, as evidenced by the February/March 2007 and May/June 2006 turbulence when the rand was one of the most affected emerging market currencies. Inflows of capital, however, did not appear to be significantly affected. The official "growth diagnostics" exercise carried out by the government lists exchange rate volatility as a constraint on economic growth in South Africa. However, the official position on this matter is to reduce volatility by strengthening international reserves and continuing to pursue sound macroeconomic policies.

While household sector debt rose markedly, household debt service remains moderate at about 9 percent of disposable income as of March 2007, although potential pockets of weakness might be hidden in these average figures. Nonperforming loan rates are low at present.

Vulnerable to world interest rate movements and shifts in global risk appetite. Vulnerable to commodity price declines.

The fiscal position is strong, which helps to strengthen the country's resilience to shocks and sudden stops, and supports financial market confidence.

Monetary policy tightened in late 2006 and again in mid-2007, in response to a deterioration of the inflation outlook.

Limits on outward FDI have been relaxed in recent years. The authorities' strategy is to move away from outward exchange controls toward a system of prudential regulations for institutional investors.

Annex 3.2 *(concluded)*

Country	Type of Recent Inflows; Policy Framework and Financial System	Challenges Associated with Inflows		Policies Adopted by the Authorities
		Macroeconomic	Financial	
Vietnam	Total portfolio inflows—comprised primarily of portfolio equity—were estimated at $1.9 billion in 2006, with foreign investors accounting for as much as 30 to 50 percent of daily equity trading. This has led to an unprecedented boom of the stock market, whose index rose by 145 percent in 2006, and by another 25 percent through July 27, 2007.

The banking system is dominated by a few state-owned banks, especially for foreign exchange transactions, and the nonbank financial sector is at an early stage of development. The Bank for Foreign Trade handles 30 to 40 percent of foreign exchange transactions. Growing confidence in the dong and the local banking system, coupled with capital inflows, led to an annual 31 percent deposit increase in the past few years and a rapid growth of bank credit. The capital market regulatory and supervisory structure, trading infrastructure, and information systems are at early stages of development. The bond market is fragmented and the secondary market is inactive, as most investors buy and hold to maturity. | Monetary policy could lead to extensive intervention in support of the de facto peg to the U.S. dollar. If such policy were to become untenable, allowing the dong to appreciate could pose competitiveness issues for the export sector.

Wealth effect of the stock market boom could lead to a consumption or investment-led import surge and reemergence of a large current account deficit. | Indicators point to a large overvaluation of the stock market. The price-earnings ratio of the largest 20 listed firms—accounting for 99 percent of market capitalization—is estimated at 30.

Large bank exposure to the stock market poses a significant credit risk.

Vulnerable to world interest rate movements and shifts in global risk appetite. | The authorities have followed a policy mix of extensive reserve accumulation toward comfortably meeting balance of payments needs in the event of a portfolio inflow reversal accompanied by sterilization operations and a recent move toward a more flexible exchange rate regime.

Steps were taken recently to tighten stock market regulation and supervision, with plans to further strengthen prudential requirements in the future.

The rules for new bank lending for the purchase of stocks were tightened to limit potential spillover effects from a stock market correction to the banking system.

Securities companies and investment fund managers have been requested to provide information on their recent stock market operations.

Representative offices of foreign investment funds are required to reregister with the State Securities Commission. |

Note: L. Effie Psalida prepared this annex with input from Turgut Kisinbay, Annamaria Kokenyne, Gillian Nkhata, Seiichi Shimizu, Judit Vadasz, and area departments.

Annex 3.3. Experiences with Recent Capital Inflows: Selected Countries

Country	Exchange Rate Regime (de facto)	Predominant Types of Capital Inflows[1]	Challenges Associated with Capital Inflows	Policies Adopted by the Authorities
China	Crawling peg	Foreign direct investment (FDI) Portfolio equity	Rapid credit growth Inflation pressures	Monetary tightening by raising the benchmark lending rate and reserve requirements ratio Administrative controls and lending guidance to restrain credit growth Gradual liberalization of exchange controls (market reforms, liberalization of capital outflows)
Colombia	Managed floating with no predetermined path for the exchange rate	Bank lending FDI Portfolio equity	Inflation pressures Appreciation pressures Rapid growth of domestic demand	Capital controls (unremunerated reserve requirements) Foreign exchange intervention
Egypt	Conventional fixed peg (against U.S. dollar)	FDI Portfolio equity and bonds Workers' remittances (broad concept)	Appreciation pressures Inflation pressures	Monetary tightening by raising policy rate Interventions against exchange rate appreciation Structural reforms, including privatization to attract FDI
Hungary	Pegged exchange rate with horizontal bands	FDI Portfolio bond (sovereign) Bank lending (short-term)	Inflation pressures Appreciation pressures Rapid credit growth (household credits and foreign currency loans) Risk of flow reversals due to global external factors	Fiscal consolidation Strengthening inflation targeting Administrative measures to increase borrowers' awareness of exchange rate risk
Iceland	Independently floating	Portfolio bond (banks issuing)	Inflation pressure Risk of flow reversal (sudden depreciation)	Monetary tightening by raising policy rate
Indonesia	Managed floating with no predetermined path for the exchange rate	FDI Portfolio bond Portfolio equity	Risk of flow reversal due to global factors	Monetary tightening by rising policy rates Authorities sought swap agreements with China and Japan under the Chiang Mai Initiative
Kazakhstan	Managed floating with no predetermined path for the exchange rate	Total inflows (energy export revenues) Bank lending FDI	Appreciation pressures Rapid credit growth	Monetary tightening Prudential measures to limit bank borrowing and credit boom

Annex 3.3. *(continued)*

Country	Exchange Rate Regime (de facto)	Predominant Types of Capital Inflows[1]	Challenges Associated with Capital Inflows	Policies Adopted by the Authorities
Korea	Independently floating	FDI Financial derivatives	Rapid credit growth to households and small and medium-sized enterprise (SME) sector (with decline in corporate profitability, especially SMEs)	Macroeconomic/monetary policy measures Liberalization of outflows Move to risk-based supervision
New Zealand	Independently floating	Portfolio bond (domestic banks and corporates)	Inflation pressures (medium-term) Risk of flow reversal (sudden depreciation)	Monetary tightening by raising policy rate Foreign exchange interventions (June 2007, for the first time since 1985)
Pakistan	Conventional fixed peg (against U.S. dollar)	FDI Portfolio bond (sovereign)	Inflation pressures Rapid credit growth Risk of flow reversals due to global external factors	Reserve accumulation
Peru	Managed floating with no predetermined path for the exchange rate	FDI Portfolio equity	Appreciation pressures Risk of flow reversals due to global external factors	Reserve accumulation Fiscal consolidation Strengthening prudential framework
Philippines	Independently floating	Workers' remittances (broad concept) FDI	Appreciation pressures (loss of competitiveness) Inadequate financial sector risk management	Reserve accumulation Shift toward domestic budget financing Liberalization of foreign exchange system
Poland	Independently floating	FDI Portfolio bond Portfolio equity Bank lending	Appreciation pressures Inflation pressures Rapid credit growth in both domestic and foreign currency Risk of flow reversals due to global external factors	Fiscal tightening (European Union convergence) Free float of currency Liberalization of capital account Strengthening regulatory and prudential framework in line with EU accession requirements Tightening risk management and disclosure standards related to foreign-currency-denominated lending

Annex 3.3. *(concluded)*

Country	Exchange Rate Regime (de facto)	Predominant Types of Capital Inflows[1]	Challenges Associated with Capital Inflows	Policies Adopted by the Authorities
Russia	Managed floating with no predetermined path for the exchange rate	Total inflows (energy export revenues) Bank lending (corporates), including carry trade FDI	Inflation pressures Appreciation pressures Rapid credit growth Asset price boom	Monetary tightening Increased exchange rate flexibility Partial capital account liberalization, including elimination of special accounts and unremunerated reserve requirements to control capital flows Strengthening prudential regulation and supervision
Thailand	Managed floating with no predetermined path for the exchange rate	FDI Portfolio Bank-related flows	Appreciation pressures (concerns over competitiveness) and volatility	Interventions on the foreign exchange market and moral suasion Introduction of capital controls in the form of unremunerated reserve requirements Partial liberalization of outflows
Turkey	Independently floating	Portfolio bond Portfolio equity Bank lending FDI	Appreciation pressures Rapid credit growth Corporate exchange rate risk exposure	Allow currency to appreciate Raise capital adequacy ratio Increase provisioning requirements Measures introduced to improve liquidity management
Uruguay	Managed floating with no predetermined path for the exchange rate	Portfolio bond Portfolio equity	Appreciation pressures	Interventions in the foreign exchange market to build up reserves and slow down appreciation

Note: Annamaria Kokenyne, Turgut Kisinbay, Gillian Nkhata, Seiichi Shimizu, and Judit Vadasz prepared this annex.

[1]Capital inflows are noted according to the broad balance of payments classification.

References

Alfaro, Laura, Sebnem Kalemli-Ozcan, and Vadym Volosovych, 2005, "Capital Flows in a Globalized World: The Role of Policies and Institutions," NBER Working Paper No. 11696 (Cambridge, Massachusetts: National Bureau of Economic Research).

Ariyoshi, Akira, Karl Habermeier, Bernard Laurens, Inci Ötker-Robe, Jorge Canales-Kriljenko, and Andrei Kirilenko, 2000, *Capital Controls: Country Experiences with Their Use and Liberalization*, IMF Occasional Paper No. 190 (Washington: International Monetary Fund).

Breitung, Jörg, 2000, "The Local Power of Some Unit Root Tests for Panel Data," in *Nonstationary Panels, Panel Cointegration, and Dynamic Panels*, Advances in Econometrics, Vol. 15, ed. by Badi H. Baltagi (New York: Elsevier Science), pp. 161–78.

Chinn, Menzie, and Hiro Ito, 2006, "What Matters for Financial Development? Capital Controls, Institutions, and Interactions," *Journal of Development Economics*, Vol. 81 (October), pp. 163–92.

Choi, In, 2001, "Unit Root Tests for Panel Data," *Journal of International Money and Finance*, Vol. 20 (April), pp. 249–72.

De Nicolò, Gianni, Luc Laeven, and Kenichi Ueda, 2006, "Corporate Governance Quality: Trends and Real Effects," IMF Working Paper 06/293 (Washington: International Monetary Fund).

Edison, Hali J., Michael W. Klein, Luca Antonio Ricci, and Torsten Sløk, 2004, "Capital Account Liberalization and Economic Performance: Survey and Synthesis," *IMF Staff Papers*, Vol. 51, No. 2, pp. 220–56.

Eichengreen, Barry J., 2001, "Capital Account Liberalization: What Do Cross-Country Studies Tell Us?" *World Bank Economic Review*, Vol. 15, No. 3, pp. 341–65.

Enoch, Charles, and Inci Ötker-Robe, eds., 2007, *Rapid Credit Growth in Central and Eastern Europe: Endless Boom or Early Warning* (New York: Palgrave Macmillan).

Henry, Peter Blair, 2006, "Capital Account Liberalization: Theory, Evidence, and Speculation," NBER Working Paper No. 12698 (Cambridge, Massachusetts: National Bureau of Economic Research).

Hilbers, Paul, Inci Ötker-Robe, Ceyla Pazarbasioglu, and Gudrun Johnsen, 2005, "Assessing and Managing Rapid Credit Growth and the Role of Supervisory and Prudential Policies," IMF Working Paper 151/05 (Washington: International Monetary Fund).

Im, Kyung So, M. Hashem Pesaran, and Yongcheol Shin, 2003, "Testing for Unit Roots in Heterogeneous Panels," *Journal of Econometrics*, Vol. 115 (July), pp. 53–74.

International Monetary Fund (IMF), 2007a, *Global Financial Stability Report*, World Economic and Financial Surveys (Washington, April). Available via the Internet: http://www.imf.org/External/Pubs/FT/GFSR/2007/01/index.htm.

——, 2007b, "Reaping the Benefits of Financial Globalization," IMF Discussion Paper. Available via the Internet: http://www.imf.org/external/np/res/docs/2007/0607.htm.

——, 2007c, "Managing Large Capital Inflows," in *World Economic Outlook*, World Economic and Financial Surveys (Washington, October).

Kaufmann, Daniel, Aart Kraay, and Massimo Mastruzzi, 2007, "Governance Matters IV: Governance Indicators for 1996–2006," Policy Research Working Paper No. 4280 (Washington: World Bank).

Levin, Andrew, Chien-Fu Lin, and James Chia-Shang Chu, 2002, "Unit Root Tests in Panel Data: Asymptotic and Finite-Sample Properties," *Journal of Econometrics*, Vol. 108 (May), pp. 1–24.

Maddala, G.S., and Shaowen Wu, 1999, "A Comparative Study of Unit Root Tests with Panel Data and A New Simple Test," *Oxford Bulletin of Economics and Statistics*, Vol. 61 (November), pp. 631–52.

Montiel, Peter, and Carmen M. Reinhart, 1999, "Do Capital Controls and Macroeconomic Policies Influence the Volume and Composition of Capital Flows? Evidence from the 1990s," *Journal of International Money and Finance*, Vol. 18 (August), pp. 619–35.

Poirson, Hélène, 2007, "Country Study: India," *IMF Research Bulletin*, Vol. 8 (June), pp. 6–8.

Prasad, Eswar, Kenneth Rogoff, Shang-Jin Wei, and Ayhan Kose, 2003, *Effects of Financial Globalization on Developing Countries: Some Empirical Evidence*, IMF Occasional Paper No. 220 (Washington: International Monetary Fund).

Purfield, Catriona, 2006, "Maintaining Competitiveness in the Global Economy" in *India Goes Global: Its Expanding Role in the World Economy*, ed. by C. Purfield and J. Schiff (Washington: International Monetary Fund).

Reinhart, Carmen M., and Vincent R. Reinhart, 1998, "Some Lessons for Policy Makers Who Deal with the Mixed Blessing of Capital Inflows," in *Capital Flows and Financial Crises*, ed. by M. Kahler (Ithaca, New York: Cornell University Press).

Smith, Katherine A., and Diego Valderrama, 2007, "The Composition of Capital Inflows When Emerging Market Firms Face Financing Constraints,"

FRBSF Working Paper No. 2007-13, (San Francisco, California: Federal Reserve Bank of San Francisco).

World Bank, 2007, "Financial Flows to Developing Countries: Recent Trends and Prospects," in *Global Development Finance 2007: The Globalization of Corporate Finance in Developing Countries* (Washington: World Bank).

GLOSSARY

ABX	An index of credit default swaps referencing 20 bonds collateralized by subprime mortgages.
Asset-backed commercial paper (ABCP)	Commercial paper collateralized by loans, leases, receivables or asset-backed securities.
Asset-backed security (ABS)	A security that is collateralized by the cash flows from a pool of underlying loans, leases, receivables, installment contracts on personal property, or on real estate. Often, when the security is collateralized by real estate, it is called a mortgage-backed security (MBS), although in principle an MBS is a type of ABS.
Assets under management (AUM)	Assets managed by an investment company on behalf of investors.
Call (put) option	A financial contract that gives the buyer the right, but not the obligation, to buy (sell) a financial instrument at a set price on or before a given date.
Capital-to-risk-weighted assets ratio	A measure that represents an institution's capacity to cope with credit risk. It is often calculated as a ratio of categories of capital to assets, which are weighted for riskiness.
Carry trade	A leveraged transaction in which borrowed funds are used to take a position in which the expected return exceeds the cost of the borrowed funds. The "cost of carry" or "carry" is the difference between the yield on the investment and the financing cost (e.g., in a "positive carry" the yield exceeds the financing cost).
Cash securitization	The creation of securities from a pool of preexisting assets and receivables that are placed under the legal control of investors through a special intermediary created for this purpose. This compares with a "synthetic" securitization where the generic securities are created out of derivative instruments.
CAT (catastrophe) bonds	A type of insurance-linked security whereby investors bear risk if a specified catastrophic event occurs in return for an interest premium.
Collateralized debt obligation (CDO)	A structured credit security backed by a pool of securities, loans, or credit default swaps, and where securitized interests in the security are divided into tranches with differing repayment and interest earning streams.

Collateralized loan obligation (CLO)	A structured vehicle backed by whole commercial loans, revolving credit facilities, letters of credit, or other asset-backed securities.
Commercial paper	A private unsecured promissory note with short maturity. It need not be registered with the Securities and Exchange Commission provided the maturity is within 270 days, and it is typically rolled over such that new issues finance maturing ones.
Corporate governance	The governing relationships between all the stakeholders in a company—including the shareholders, directors, and management—as defined by the corporate charter, bylaws, formal policy, and rule of law.
Credit default swap (CDS)	A default-triggered credit derivative. Most CDS settlements are "physical," whereby the protection seller buys a defaulted reference asset from the protection buyer at its face value. "Cash" settlement involves a net payment to the protection buyer equal to the difference between the reference asset face value and the price of the defaulted asset.
Credit derivative	A financial contract under which an agent buys or sells risk protection against the credit risk associated with a specific reference entity (or specific entities). For a periodic fee, the protection seller agrees to make a contingent payment to the buyer on the occurrence of a credit event (default in the case of a credit default swap).
Credit-linked note (CLN)	A security that is bundled with an embedded credit default swap and is intended to transfer a specific credit risk to investors. CLNs are usually backed by highly rated collateral.
Credit risk indicator	An indicator that measures the probability of multiple defaults among the firms in selected portfolios.
Credit spread	The spread between benchmark securities and other debt securities that are comparable in all respects except for credit quality (e.g., the difference between yields on U.S. treasuries and those on single A-rated corporate bonds of a certain term to maturity).
Derivatives	Financial contracts whose value derives from underlying securities prices, interest rates, foreign exchange rates, commodity prices, and market or other indices.
EBITDA	Earnings before interest, taxes, depreciation, and amortization.
Economic risk capital (ERC)	An assessment of the amount of capital a financial institution requires to absorb losses from extremely unlikely events over long time horizons with a given degree of certainty. ERC calculations make provision not just for market risk, but also for credit and operational risks, and may also take account of liquidity, legal, and reputational risks.

EMBIG	JP Morgan's Emerging Market Bond Index Global, which tracks the total returns for traded external debt instruments in 34 emerging market economies with weights roughly proportional to the market supply of debt.
Emerging markets	Developing countries' financial markets that are less than fully developed, but are nonetheless broadly accessible to foreign investors.
Expected default frequency	An estimate of a firm's probability of default over a specific time horizon constructed using balance sheet and equity price data according to a Merton-type model.
Expected shortfall	The average expected portfolio loss, conditional on the loss exceeding the value-at-risk threshold.
Foreign direct investment (FDI)	The acquisition abroad (i.e., outside the home country) of physical assets, such as plant and equipment, or of a controlling stake in a company (usually greater than 10 percent of shareholdings).
Generalized method of moments (GMM)	A generalized statistical method—used primarily in econometrics—for obtaining estimates of parameters of statistical models; many common estimators in econometrics, such as ordinary least squares, are special cases of the GMM. The GMM estimator is robust in that it does not require information on the exact distribution of the disturbances.
Hedge funds	Investment pools, typically organized as private partnerships and often resident offshore for tax and regulatory purposes. These funds face few restrictions on their portfolios and transactions. Consequently, they are free to use a variety of investment techniques—including short positions, transactions in derivatives, and leverage—to raise returns and cushion risk.
Hedging	Offsetting an existing risk exposure by taking an opposite position in the same or a similar risk, for example, by buying derivatives contracts.
Home-equity loan/Home-equity line of credit (HEL/HELOC)	Loans or lines of credit drawn against the equity in a home, calculated as the current market value less the value of the first mortgage. When originating a HEL or HELOC, the lending institution generally secures a second lien on the home, i.e., a claim that is subordinate to the first mortgage (if it exists).
Implied volatility	The expected volatility of a security's price as implied by the price of options or swaptions (options to enter into swaps) traded on that security. Implied volatility is computed as the expected standard deviation that must be imputed to investors to satisfy risk neutral arbitrage conditions, and is calculated with the use of an options pricing model such as Black-Scholes. A rise in implied volatility suggests the market is willing to pay more to insure against the risk of higher volatility, and hence implied volatility is sometimes used as a measure of risk

appetite (with higher risk appetite being associated with lower implied volatility). One of the most widely quoted measures of implied volatility is the VIX, an index of implied volatility on the S&P 500 index of U.S. stocks.

Institutional investor	A bank, insurance company, pension fund, mutual fund, hedge fund, brokerage, or other financial group that takes large investments from clients or invests on its own behalf.
Interest rate swap	An agreement between counterparties to exchange periodic interest payments on some predetermined dollar principal, which is called the notional principal amount. For example, one party will make fixed-rate and receive variable-rate interest payments.
Intermediation	The process of transferring funds from the ultimate source to the ultimate user. A financial institution, such as a bank, intermediates credit when it obtains money from depositors or other lenders and on-lends it to borrowers.
Investment-grade obligation	A bond or loan is considered investment grade if it is assigned a credit rating in the top four categories. S&P and Fitch classify investment-grade obligations as BBB- or higher, and Moody's classifies investment grade bonds as Baa3 or higher.
Large complex financial institution (LCFI)	A major financial institution frequently operating in multiple sectors and often with an international scope.
Leverage	The proportion of debt to equity. Leverage can be built up by borrowing (on-balance-sheet leverage, commonly measured by debt-to-equity ratios) or by using off-balance-sheet transactions.
Leveraged buyout (LBO)	Acquisition of a company using a significant level of borrowing (through bonds or loans) to meet the cost of acquisition. Usually, the assets of the company being acquired are used as collateral for the loans.
Leveraged loans	Bank loans that are rated below investment grade (BB+ and lower by S&P or Fitch, and Baa1 and lower by Moody's) to firms with a sizable debt-to-EBITDA ratio, or trade at wide spreads over LIBOR (e.g., more than 150 basis points).
LIBOR	London Interbank Offered Rate.
Liquidity-adjusted value-at-risk (L-VaR)	A value-at-risk calculation that makes an adjustment for the trading liquidity of the assets that constitute the assessed portfolio. This can either be limits on trading positions in the portfolio linked to the assets' underlying turnover or adjustments made to the VaR's volatility and correlation structures to take account of illiquidity risk in extreme circumstances.

Mark-to-market	The valuation of a position or portfolio by reference to the most recent price at which a financial instrument can be bought or sold in normal volumes. The mark-to-market value might equal the current market value—as opposed to historic accounting or book value—or the present value of expected future cash flows.
Mezzanine capital	Unsecured, high-yield, subordinated debt, or preferred stock that represents a claim on a company's assets that is senior only to that of a company's shareholders.
Mortgage-backed security (MBS)	A security that derives its cash flows from principal and interest payments on pooled mortgage loans. An MBS can be backed by residential mortgage loans or loans on commercial properties.
Nonperforming loans	Loans that are in default or close to being in default (i.e., typically past due for 90 days or more).
Payment-in-kind toggle note	A note (or loan) feature that gives the borrower the option to defer the interest due on existing debt or to make payment using new debt, and in the process pay an effectively higher interest rate.
Primary market	The market in which a newly issued security is first offered/sold to investors.
Private equity	Shares in companies that are not listed on a public stock exchange.
Private equity funds	Pools of capital invested by private equity partnerships. Investments can include leveraged buyouts, as well as mezzanine and venture capital. In addition to the sponsoring private equity firm, other qualified investors can include pension funds, financial institutions, and wealthy individuals.
Put (call) option	A financial contract that gives the buyer the right, but not the obligation, to sell (buy) a financial instrument at a set price on or before a given date.
Risk aversion	The degree to which an investor who, when faced with two investments with the same expected return but different risk, prefers the one with the lower risk. That is, it measures an investor's aversion to uncertain outcomes or payoffs.
Risk premium	The extra expected return on an asset that investors demand in exchange for accepting the risk associated with the asset.
Secondary markets	Markets in which securities are traded after they are initially offered/sold in the primary market.
Securitization	The creation of securities from a pool of preexisting assets and receivables that are placed under the legal control of investors through a special intermediary created for this purpose (a "special-purpose

vehicle" [SPV] or "special-purpose entity" [SPE]). With a "synthetic" securitization the securities are created out of a portfolio of derivative instruments.

Security arbitrage conduit	A conduit (a vehicle that issues ABCP only) that is formed specifically for the purpose of investing in assets using relatively cheap financing. The mix of assets can change over time.
Sovereign wealth fund (SWF)	A special investment fund created/owned by government to hold assets for long-term purposes; it is typically funded from reserves or other foreign currency sources and predominantly owns, or has significant ownership of, foreign currency claims on nonresidents.
Spread	See "credit spread" (the word credit is sometimes omitted). Other definitions include (1) the gap between bid and ask prices of a financial instrument; and (2) the difference between the price at which an underwriter buys an issue from the issuer and the price at which the underwriter sells it to the public.
Structured investment vehicle (SIV)	A legal entity, whose assets consist of asset-backed securities and various types of loans and receivables. An SIV's liabilities are usually tranched and include debt that matures in less than one year and must be rolled over.
Sub-investment-grade obligation	An obligation rated below investment-grade, sometimes referred to as "high-yield" or "junk."
Subprime mortgages	Mortgages to borrowers with impaired or limited credit histories, who typically have low credit scores.
Swaps	An agreement between counterparties to exchange periodic interest payments based on different references on a predetermined notional amount. For example, in an interest rate swap, one party will make fixed-rate and receive variable-rate interest payments.
Syndicated loans	Large loans made jointly by a group of banks to one borrower. Usually, one lead bank takes a small percentage of the loan and partitions (syndicates) the rest to other banks.
Value-at-risk (VaR)	An estimate of the loss, over a given horizon, that is statistically unlikely to be exceeded at a given probability level.
Yield curve	A chart that plots the yield to maturity at a specific point in time for debt securities having equal credit risk but different maturity dates.

SUMMING UP BY THE ACTING CHAIR

The following remarks by the Acting Chair were made at the conclusion of the Executive Board's discussion of the Global Financial Stability Report *on September 14, 2007.*

Assessing Global Financial Stability Risks

Directors noted that global financial stability has endured a difficult period since the publication of the April 2007 *Global Financial Stability Report* (GFSR). Overall, financial risks have risen and markets are continuing to experience bouts of turbulence. Directors agreed with staff that, while there has been some calming in certain respects, markets generally remain unsettled, and credit conditions may not normalize soon.

Against this background, Directors welcomed the GFSR as providing a clear, well-focused, and timely analysis of the recent market turbulence. They broadly concurred with the report's insights regarding the causes and consequences of the recent episode of turmoil, and felt that the report presents a balanced assessment of the primary areas of concern and the potential policy responses. Directors continued to view the staff's use of the global financial stability map as useful, allowing them to track the deterioration in risks and conditions more concretely.

Directors noted that the threat to financial stability has been most evident in the money markets that provide short-term financing. At the heart of the difficulties in these markets was a funding mismatch whereby medium-term, illiquid, hard-to-value assets, such as structured credit securities, had been financed by short-term money market securities—often asset-backed commercial paper. When these asset values were threatened by a rise in delinquencies and ratings declined, short-term funding for those holding these assets became more difficult to obtain. For some entities, especially some conduits and special investment vehicles, inves-

tors became uncomfortable holding the commercial paper that was supporting these illiquid, hard-to-value assets. For others, such as hedge funds, this forced a deleveraging process, once their prime brokers balked at providing additional funding and insisted that more collateral be posted at lower values.

Directors noted that, in the recent situation of market turbulence, various central banks had moved quickly to provide liquidity—both in the overnight market, but also at longer maturities. Despite significant injections of liquidity, market participants remain uncertain about their counterparties' condition, and are thus reluctant to onlend.

Directors agreed with staff that there are potentially a number of other reasons why funding markets had not functioned normally—including the possibility that large banks have experienced an increase in their balance sheets in the form of structured credit securities or loans associated with leveraged buyouts. In such circumstances, it remains to be seen how effective lower interest rates will be in stemming pressures in money markets, and how policymakers will balance medium-term inflation objectives against nearer-term threats to financial stability. Some Directors cautioned that care will be needed to avoid moral hazard, including by ensuring that central banks focus on addressing general disorderly markets, rather than taking on credit risk or favoring certain institutions.

Directors commended the staff for its analysis of the various issues raised by the turbulence, including the implications of the potential losses, their distribution, and their wider impact on the financial system of developments in U.S.

mortgage markets. Many Directors cautioned that the difficult conditions in the U.S. subprime mortgage market may continue, calling for continued vigilance. Directors also noted that the continued work on leveraged buyout activity has aided understanding of why major banks may be unwilling to provide liquidity to others—including the likelihood that they may be holding the excess liquidity in anticipation of leveraged loans arriving on their balance sheets.

Directors noted that, so far, the financial market turbulence has not had a large adverse effect on emerging market and low-income countries. As a whole, these countries' very favorable growth performance over the last several years has encouraged both residents and nonresidents to invest in local markets and in private sector assets. Several Directors noted, however, that the risks for emerging markets may be finely balanced, and cautioned that the turmoil in mature markets may yet spill over to emerging market countries. The deterioration in financial market confidence seen in mature markets could be expected to begin to affect some emerging market countries going forward, particularly those that have been experiencing rapid credit growth. This concern is heightened in countries where credit extension has been primarily supported by external funding, or where other vulnerabilities—such as large current account or fiscal deficits—are present. Against this background, Directors underscored the need for strengthened vigilance and surveillance in emerging markets—in addition to mature markets—to ensure credit discipline and sound development of financial markets.

On the use of synthetic rate and structured credit products by investors in emerging market countries, Directors noted that, as the growth of these instruments has been associated with a period of benign volatility, some investors are likely to see losses with the reversal of this environment. The reversal of carry-trade-style external borrowing by emerging market firms could also be detrimental to investors. Directors advised that monitoring systems for these types of exposures of domestic corporations and

financial institutions be strengthened so that risks can be better managed.

Directors considered that the current episode of turbulence should not be viewed as having ended, and with this awareness, broadly endorsed the initial set of policy conclusions reached in the report. Directors recognized that the development of financial markets in recent years has resulted in many benefits and useful innovations, and underscored the importance of not rushing to judgment about the causes of the current turmoil or the implications for financial sector policies. At the same time, they noted that much remains to be done to improve transparency and disclosure, starting with the complex structured products that have proliferated across large parts of the global financial system. More information about how they are valued and the underlying assumptions—as well as how they are distributed across investors—would remove much of the uncertainty that underlies the current concerns of market participants. Directors also viewed better transparency and disclosure regarding financial institutions, and their various conduits and special investment vehicles, as particularly important. Directors also generally considered that the recent episode suggests that the "originate and distribute" business model used by many financial institutions to securitize and redistribute risks may need to be reevaluated to ensure that the supply chain has adequate incentives to evaluate the credit quality of the loans being repackaged.

Many Directors noted concerns about the ratings agencies' conflict of interest, as they both rate and help design complex securities for issuers requesting the rating. Some Directors noted that this is a longstanding conflict, and that ratings agencies still perform a useful and fundamental role in rating credit risks that will need to be retained. It was also suggested that ratings agencies should review the quality of their methodologies. At the same time, most Directors agreed that investors, for their part, must also take responsibility for their own analysis of such products, particularly given that the risks are not confined to credit risk, but also entail market and liquidity risks.

Many Directors viewed the recent episode as a reminder to regulators and supervisors that there remain gaps in their oversight of financial institutions that would likely require further attention and examination. Directors noted that some financial institutions' risk management systems and their disclosures—even to supervisors—make it difficult to detect the off-balance sheet risks being undertaken, and that this would need to be rectified going forward. At the same time, Directors acknowledged that the experience to date does not point to a need for a substantial overhaul of regulatory frameworks. Any revisions would have to be carefully considered, and unintended consequences anticipated.

Do Market Risk Management Techniques Amplify Systemic Risks?

Directors welcomed the improvements in market risk management systems in recent years. At the same time, they welcomed the staff analysis of certain weaknesses in these systems as a timely and relevant reminder that no risk management system is perfect. In particular, Directors noted that risk management practices and models—including the popular value-at-risk (VaR) measures—have the potential to exacerbate volatility and to lead to systemic risks if followed mechanistically.

Some Directors observed that it would be difficult to avoid the trend toward greater uniformity in the approaches that firms use in risk management modeling, as the desire to attain "best practices" is encouraged by many aspects of risk management—including through supervisory guidance and capital requirements, peer pressure, and similarly-trained risk managers. Nonetheless, Directors generally acknowledged that financial institutions should aim to analyze the risks specific to their organization, by developing their own models and rigorously stress-testing their positions to assure the institutions' viability during a time of stress.

Directors noted that recent events point to the potentially negative influence of some risk management practices—such as margin requirements—that have added to "fire sales" of some assets used as collateral. However, if margin requirements are initially set more conservatively and are less risk sensitive, market dynamics would be more stable. Further, it was noted that a diversity of positions and types of trading strategies could help contain amplifying effects. Directors also believed that better disclosure of how risks are managed could allow institutions and supervisors to better anticipate the negative effects during stressful events.

The Quality of Domestic Financial Markets and Capital Inflows

Given the rapid capital inflows experienced by several emerging market countries, Directors welcomed the renewed focus on the challenges—and related policy responses—associated with surges in capital inflows. They observed that, while macroeconomic performance and growth prospects are the dominant influences on capital flows, equity market liquidity and financial openness also help attract capital inflows. Most Directors concurred with the empirical analysis that more financial openness is associated with lower capital inflow volatility. Also, improved institutional quality in the financial sector is shown to lower the volatility of capital inflows. While Directors agreed with the main results of the study, several Directors noted that its recommendation—to improve financial market infrastructure and depth—represents a medium-term challenge.

Directors recognized that large capital inflows in different country circumstances call for different policy responses. Good regulation and supervision, as well as strong risk management practices, are important for mitigating the potentially destabilizing effects of a reversal of inflows. In this context, many Directors questioned the usefulness and effectiveness of capital controls for managing capital inflows—especially given the difficulties in their sustained implementation and the associated reputational costs. Some Directors, however, recognized the usefulness of capital controls in the short term in stemming large, speculative capital inflows. It was noted that, if capital controls are used, they should preferably be market-based, have a fixed horizon, and be considered as part of a consistent set of macroeconomic and prudential measures. Several Directors also noted that concerns related to rapid and risky credit expansion are best dealt with through prudential measures, rather than by attempts to impede the inflow of capital.

Directors welcomed the analysis of Sovereign Wealth Funds (SWFs) contained in the report. Some Directors observed that some SWFs have adopted best practices in financial management. Moreover, SWFs can play a positive role in enhancing market liquidity and financial resource allocation. Several Directors suggested that SWFs warrant further study, given their macroeconomic role, potential size, and implications for global capital flows and asset prices. They called on staff to engage in further research on the objectives and characteristics of SWFs, including their asset management strategies, institutional and governance arrangements, and disclosure practices.

Finally, Directors commented on the broader question of the IMF's role as an international monetary institution in situations such as the recent market turmoil. A key aspect of this role entails working closely—and exchanging views and information—with national regulators, central banks, and other international institutions, both bilaterally and through established fora such as the Financial Stability Forum. Several Directors underscored that the IMF should be able to act in a timely and proactive fashion in sharing its perspectives with, and providing its advice to, national authorities, drawing on its unique insights gained from financial surveillance of its virtually universal membership. To this end, continued work to broaden and deepen the IMF's financial market expertise—including with respect to emerging markets with increasingly globalized financial systems—will be important. Given the crucial need for timely and accurate information in assessing and responding to financial market turbulence, several Directors also highlighted the important contribution that the IMF can make to filling information gaps by virtue of its access to financial sector information in its surveillance activities. Overall, Directors saw a role for the IMF in facilitating appropriate responses to the current situation, and more broadly in promoting global financial stability.

STATISTICAL APPENDIX

This statistical appendix presents data on financial developments in key financial centers and emerging markets. It is designed to complement the analysis in the text by providing additional data that describe key aspects of financial market developments. These data are derived from a number of sources external to the IMF, including banks, commercial data providers, and official sources, and are presented for information purposes only; the IMF does not, however, guarantee the accuracy of the data from external sources.

Presenting financial market data in one location and in a fixed set of tables and charts, in this and future issues of the GFSR, is intended to give the reader an overview of developments in global financial markets. Unless otherwise noted, the statistical appendix reflects information available up to July 27, 2007.

Mirroring the structure of the chapters of the report, the appendix presents data separately for key financial centers and emerging market countries. Specifically, it is organized into three sections:

• Figures 1–14 and Tables 1–9 contain information on market developments in key financial centers. This includes data on global capital flows, and on markets for foreign exchange, bonds, equities, and derivatives as well as sectoral balance sheet data for the United States, Japan, and Europe.

• Figures 15 and 16, and Tables 10–21 present information on financial developments in emerging markets, including data on equity, foreign exchange, and bond markets, as well as data on emerging market financing flows.

• Tables 22–27 report key financial soundness indicators for selected countries, including bank profitability, asset quality, and capital adequacy.

List of Tables and Figures

Key Financial Centers

Figures

Tables

Emerging Markets

Figures

Tables

Financial Soundness Indicators

Figure 1. Major Net Exporters and Importers of Capital in 2006

Countries That Export Capital[1]

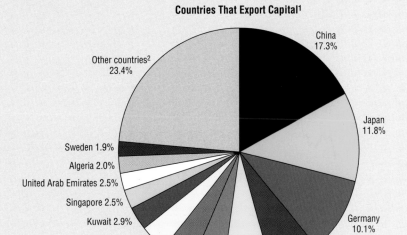

Other countries[2]
23.4%

China
17.3%

Japan
11.8%

Germany
10.1%

Saudi Arabia
6.6%

Russia
6.6%

Switzerland
4.6%

Netherlands 4.0%

Norway 3.8%

Kuwait 2.9%

Singapore 2.5%

United Arab Emirates 2.5%

Algeria 2.0%

Sweden 1.9%

Countries That Import Capital[3]

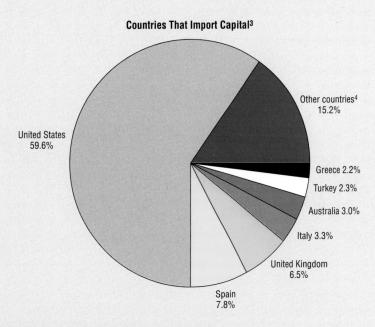

United States
59.6%

Other countries[4]
15.2%

Greece 2.2%

Turkey 2.3%

Australia 3.0%

Italy 3.3%

United Kingdom
6.5%

Spain
7.8%

Source: IMF, *World Economic Outlook* database, as of August 21, 2007.

[1]As measured by countries' current account surplus (assuming errors and omissions are part of the capital and financial accounts).

[2]Other countries include all countries with shares of total surplus less than 1.9 percent.

[3]As measured by countries' current account deficit (assuming errors and omissions are part of the capital and financial accounts).

[4]Other countries include all countries with shares of total deficit less than 2.2 percent.

Figure 2. Exchange Rates: Selected Major Industrial Countries
(Weekly data)

——— Bilateral exchange rate (left scale)[1]
——— Nominal effective exchange rate (right scale)[2]

Sources: Bloomberg L.P.; and the IMF Global Data System.
Note: In each panel, the effective and bilateral exchange rates are scaled so that an upward movement implies an appreciation of the respective local currency.
[1]Local currency units per U.S. dollar except for the euro area and the United Kingdom, for which data are shown as U.S. dollars per local currency.
[2]2000 = 100; constructed using 1999–2001 trade weights.

Figure 3. United States: Yields on Corporate and Treasury Bonds
(Monthly data)

Yields
(In percent)

Baa

Merrill Lynch high-yield bond index

10-year treasury bond

Aaa

1978 80 82 84 86 88 90 92 94 96 98 2000 02 04 06

20 18 16 14 12 10 8 6 4 2 0

Yield Differentials with 10-Year U.S. Treasury Bond
(In basis points)

Merrill Lynch high-yield bond index

Baa

Aaa

1978 80 82 84 86 88 90 92 94 96 98 2000 02 04 06

1200 1000 800 600 400 200 0 −200

Sources: Bloomberg L.P.; and Merrill Lynch.

Figure 4. Selected Spreads
(In basis points; monthly data)

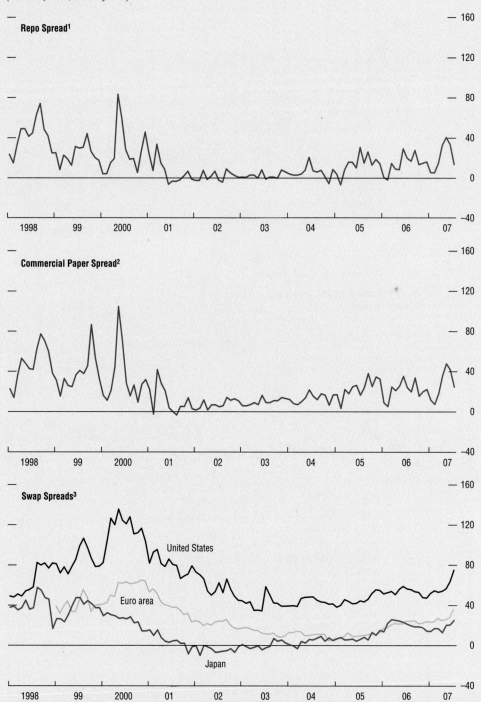

Sources: Bloomberg L.P.; and Merrill Lynch.
[1]Spread between yields on three-month U.S. treasury repo and on three-month U.S. treasury bill.
[2]Spread between yields on 90-day investment-grade commercial paper and on three-month U.S. treasury bill.
[3]Spread over 10-year government bond.

Figure 5. Nonfinancial Corporate Credit Spreads
(In basis points; monthly data)

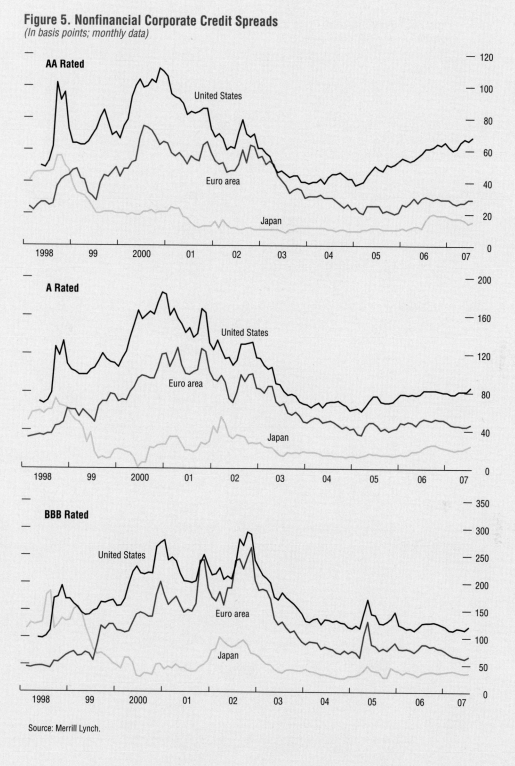

Source: Merrill Lynch.

Figure 6. Equity Markets: Price Indices
(January 1, 1990 = 100; weekly data)

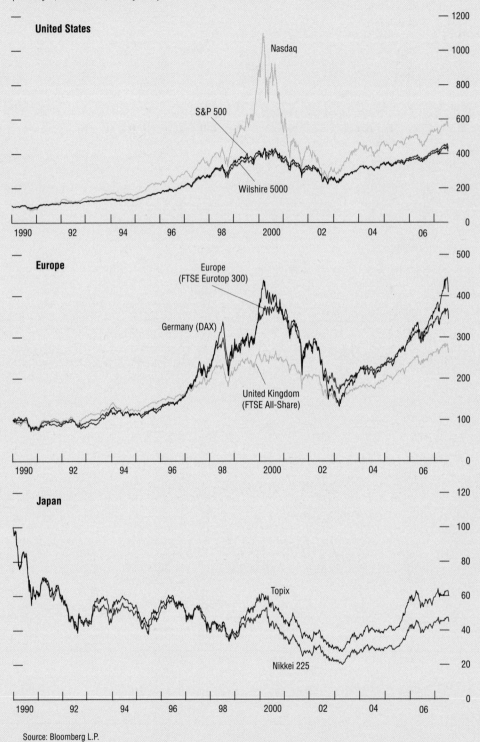

Source: Bloomberg L.P.

Figure 7. Implied and Historical Volatility in Equity Markets
(Weekly data)

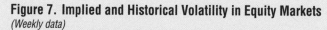

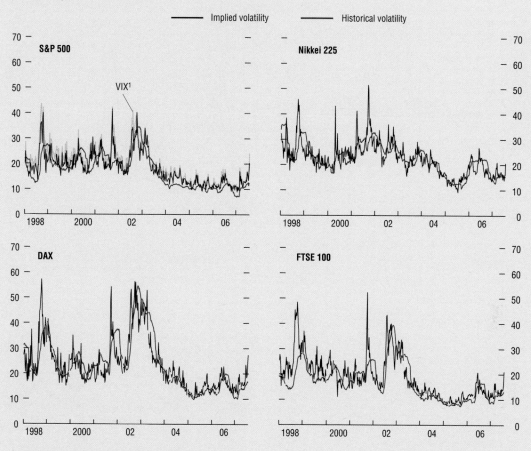

Sources: Bloomberg L.P.; and IMF staff estimates.

Note: Implied volatility is a measure of the equity price variability implied by the market prices of call options on equity futures. Historical volatility is calculated as a rolling 100-day annualized standard deviation of equity price changes. Volatilities are expressed in percent rate of change.

[1]VIX is the Chicago Board Options Exchange volatility index. This index is calculated by taking a weighted average of implied volatility for the eight S&P 500 calls and puts.

Figure 8. Historical Volatility of Government Bond Yields and Bond Returns for Selected Countries[1]
(Weekly data)

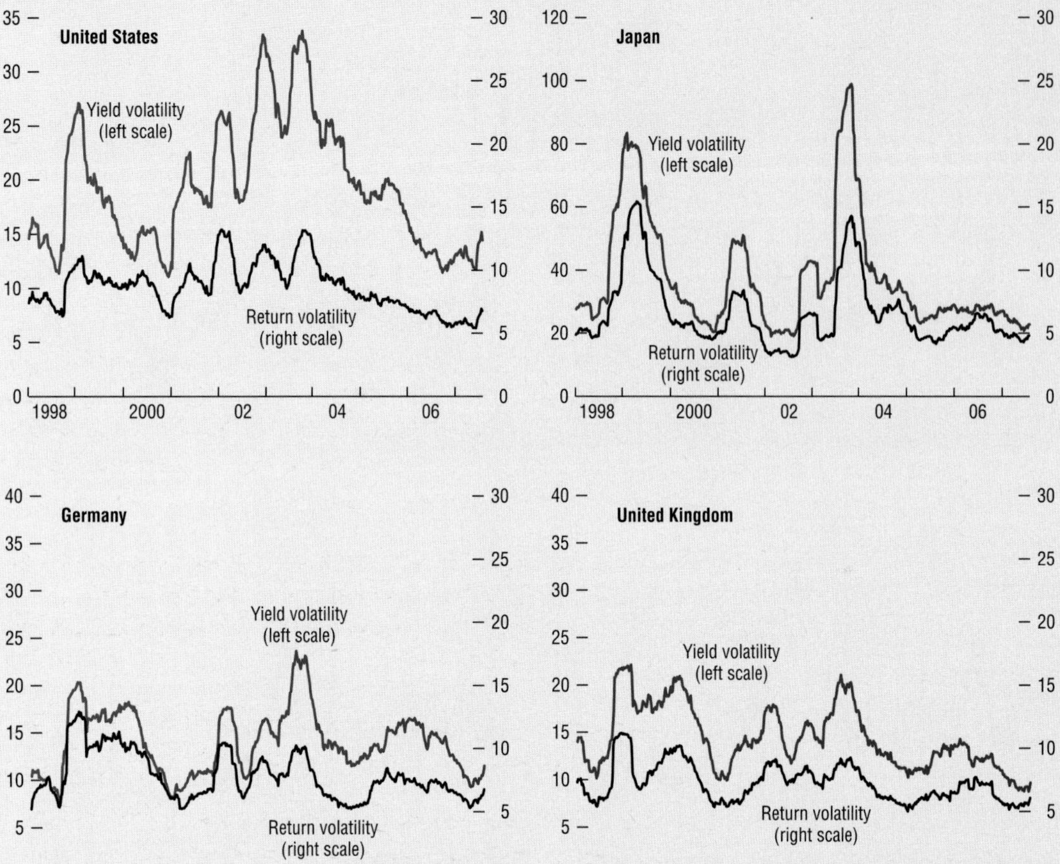

Sources: Bloomberg L.P.; and Datastream.
[1]Volatility calculated as a rolling 100-day annualized standard deviation of changes in yield and returns on 10-year government bonds. Returns are based on 10-plus year government bond indices.

Figure 9. Twelve-Month Forward Price/Earnings Ratios

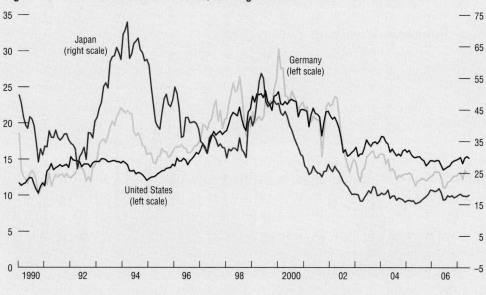

Source: I/B/E/S.

Figure 10. Flows into U.S.-Based Equity Funds

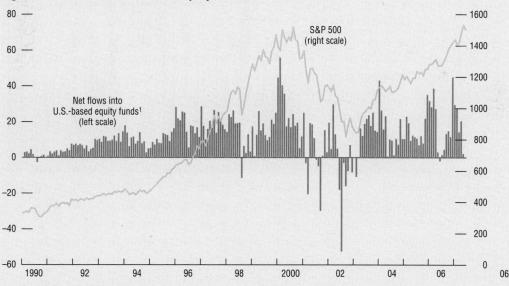

Sources: Investment Company Institute; and Datastream.
[1]In billions of U.S. dollars.

Figure 11. United States: Corporate Bond Market

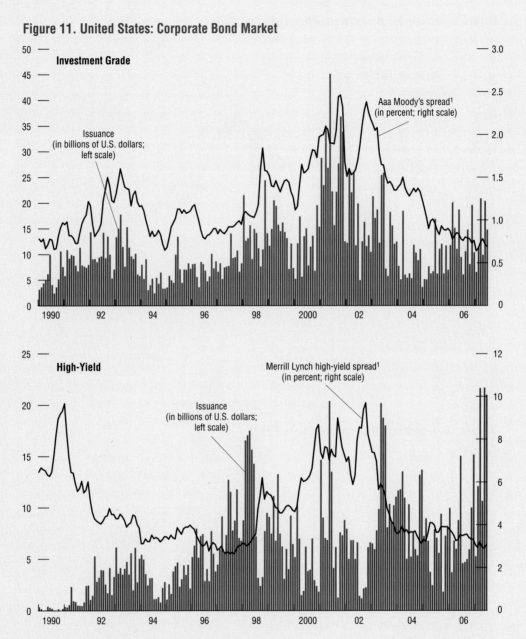

Sources: Board of Governors of the Federal Reserve System; and Bloomberg L.P.
[1]Spread against yield on 10-year U.S. government bonds.

Figure 12. Europe: Corporate Bond Market[1]

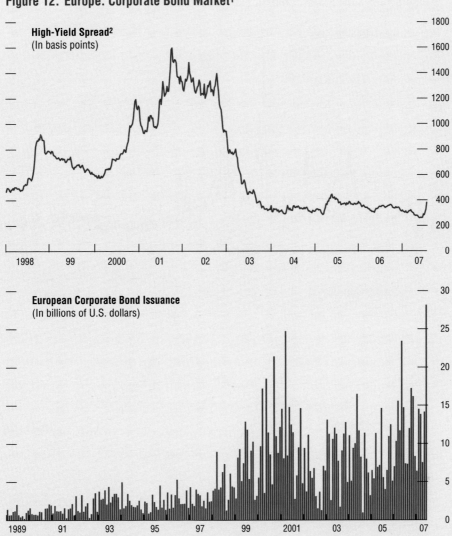

Sources: Bondware; and Datastream.
[1]Nonfinancial corporate bonds.
[2]Spread between yields on a Merrill Lynch High-Yield European Issuers Index bond and a 10-year German government benchmark bond.

Figure 13. United States: Commercial Paper Market[1]

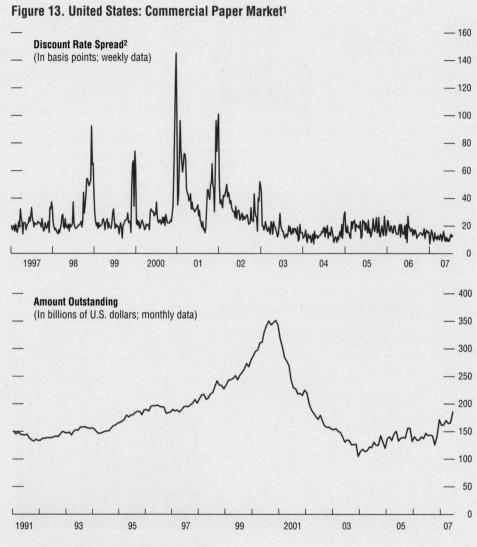

Discount Rate Spread[2]
(In basis points; weekly data)

Amount Outstanding
(In billions of U.S. dollars; monthly data)

Source: Board of Governors of the Federal Reserve System.
[1]Nonfinancial commercial paper.
[2]Difference between 30-day A2/P2 and AA commercial paper.

Figure 14. United States: Asset-Backed Securities

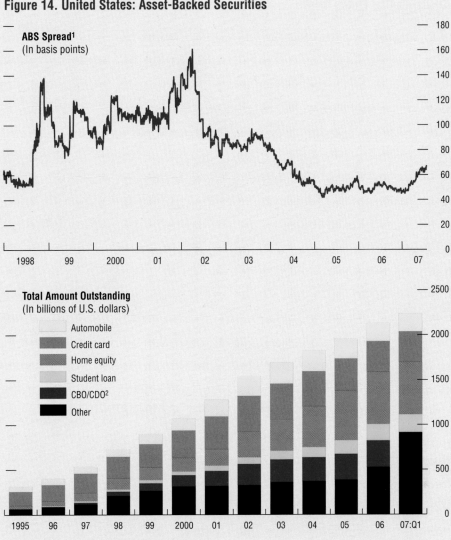

ABS Spread[1]
(In basis points)

Total Amount Outstanding
(In billions of U.S. dollars)

- Automobile
- Credit card
- Home equity
- Student loan
- CBO/CDO[2]
- Other

Sources: Merrill Lynch; Datastream; and the Bond Market Association.
[1]Merrill Lynch AAA Asset-Backed Master Index (fixed rate) option-adjusted spread.
[2]Collateralized bond/debt obligations; for 2007 Q1, CBO/CDO amount outstanding is included in Other.

Table 1. Global Capital Flows: Inflows and Outflows[1]
(In billions of U.S. dollars)

	Inflows										
	1996	1997	1998	1999	2000	2001	2002	2003	2004	2005	2006
United States											
Direct investment	86.5	105.6	179.0	289.4	321.3	167.0	84.4	63.8	145.8	109.0	180.6
Portfolio investment	332.8	333.1	187.6	285.6	436.6	428.3	427.6	550.2	867.3	832.0	1,017.4
Other investment	131.8	268.1	57.0	165.2	289.0	187.5	285.8	250.4	448.6	263.2	661.6
Reserve assets	n.a.	n.a.	n.a.	n.a.	n.a.	n.a.	n.a.	n.a.	n.a.	n.a.	n.a.
Total capital flows	551.1	706.8	423.6	740.2	1,046.9	782.9	797.8	864.4	1,461.8	1,204.2	1,859.6
Canada											
Direct investment	9.6	11.5	22.7	24.8	66.1	27.7	22.1	7.2	−0.7	29.1	69.1
Portfolio investment	13.7	11.7	16.6	2.7	10.3	24.2	11.9	14.1	42.0	7.9	28.7
Other investment	15.7	28.0	5.4	−10.8	0.8	7.8	5.1	12.3	−3.9	27.0	28.2
Reserve assets	n.a.	n.a.	n.a.	n.a.	n.a.	n.a.	n.a.	n.a.	n.a.	n.a.	n.a.
Total capital flows	39.1	51.2	44.8	16.6	77.2	59.7	39.0	33.6	37.4	64.1	126.0
Japan											
Direct investment	0.2	3.2	3.3	12.3	8.2	6.2	9.1	6.2	7.8	3.2	−6.8
Portfolio investment	66.8	79.2	56.1	126.9	47.4	60.5	−20.0	81.2	196.7	183.1	198.6
Other investment	31.1	68.0	−93.3	−265.1	−10.2	−17.6	26.6	34.1	68.3	45.9	−89.1
Reserve assets	n.a.	n.a.	n.a.	n.a.	n.a.	n.a.	n.a.	n.a.	n.a.	n.a.	n.a.
Total capital flows	98.1	150.4	−34.0	−125.9	45.4	49.1	15.7	121.5	272.8	232.3	102.6
United Kingdom											
Direct investment	27.4	37.5	74.7	89.3	122.2	53.8	25.5	27.6	77.9	195.6	139.7
Portfolio investment	68.0	43.7	35.2	183.9	255.6	69.6	76.2	155.6	159.9	240.3	288.8
Other investment	251.8	322.2	110.5	90.0	414.6	327.0	109.1	396.7	741.2	936.2	817.7
Reserve assets	n.a.	n.a.	n.a.	n.a.	n.a.	n.a.	n.a.	n.a.	n.a.	n.a.	n.a.
Total capital flows	347.2	403.4	220.3	363.3	792.4	450.5	210.8	579.9	979.0	1,372.1	1,246.3
Euro Area											
Direct investment	...	...	...	216.3	416.3	199.8	185.0	151.3	116.0	113.0	198.5
Portfolio investment	...	...	...	305.1	268.1	318.3	298.4	399.6	520.1	697.7	941.8
Other investment	...	...	...	198.4	340.3	238.1	59.9	198.0	354.6	816.2	963.8
Reserve assets	n.a.	n.a.	n.a.	n.a.	n.a.	n.a.	n.a.	n.a.	n.a.	n.a.	n.a.
Total capital flows	...	...	...	719.8	1,024.7	756.3	543.2	748.9	990.7	1,626.9	2,104.1
Emerging Markets and Developing Countries[2]											
Direct investment	148.4	191.5	187.4	213.1	211.7	225.5	182.2	199.6	272.8	361.2	422.3
Portfolio investment	174.7	147.0	32.2	102.8	93.3	11.7	−10.3	91.2	141.3	214.1	211.9
Other investment	95.4	141.1	−119.6	−77.7	−8.8	−61.6	1.8	124.7	200.5	146.3	358.9
Reserve assets	n.a.	n.a.	n.a.	n.a.	n.a.	n.a.	n.a.	n.a.	n.a.	n.a.	n.a.
Total capital flows	418.5	479.6	100.1	238.2	296.1	175.5	173.7	415.5	614.5	721.7	993.2

Sources: International Monetary Fund, *International Financial Statistics* and *World Economic Outlook* database as of August 21, 2007.

[1]The total net capital flows are the sum of direct investment, portfolio investment, other investment flows, and reserve assets. "Other investment" includes bank loans and deposits.

[2]This aggregate comprises the group of Other Emerging Market and Developing Countries defined in the *World Economic Outlook,* together with Hong Kong SAR, Israel, Korea, Singapore, and Taiwan Province of China.

					Outflows					
1996	1997	1998	1999	2000	2001	2002	2003	2004	2005	2006
−91.9	−104.8	−142.6	−224.9	−159.2	−142.4	−154.5	−149.6	−279.1	7.7	−235.4
−149.3	−116.9	−130.2	−122.2	−127.9	−90.6	−48.6	−123.1	−153.4	−203.4	−426.1
−178.9	−262.8	−74.2	−165.6	−273.1	−144.7	−87.9	−54.3	−475.4	−245.2	−396.1
6.7	−1.0	−6.7	8.7	−0.3	−4.9	−3.7	1.5	2.8	14.1	2.4
−413.4	−485.5	−353.8	−504.1	−560.5	−382.6	−294.7	−325.4	−905.0	−426.9	−1,055.2
−13.1	−23.1	−34.1	−17.3	−44.5	−36.2	−26.8	−23.6	−43.0	−33.6	−45.4
−14.2	−8.6	−15.1	−15.6	−43.0	−24.4	−18.6	−13.8	−18.9	−44.1	−69.4
−21.1	−16.2	9.4	10.2	−4.2	−10.7	−7.9	−14.2	−7.0	−16.6	−30.4
−5.5	2.4	−5.0	−5.9	−3.7	−2.2	0.2	3.3	2.8	−1.3	−0.8
−53.9	−45.4	−44.8	−28.5	−95.4	−73.4	−53.2	−48.4	−66.1	−95.6	−146.0
−23.4	−26.1	−24.6	−22.3	−31.5	−38.5	−32.0	−28.8	−31.0	−45.4	−50.2
−100.6	−47.1	−95.2	−154.4	−83.4	−106.8	−85.9	−176.3	−173.8	−196.4	−71.0
5.2	−192.0	37.9	266.3	−4.1	46.6	36.4	149.9	−48.0	−106.6	−86.2
−35.1	−6.6	6.2	−76.3	−49.0	−40.5	−46.1	−187.2	−160.9	−22.3	−32.0
−154.0	−271.6	−75.8	13.4	−168.0	−139.2	−127.7	−242.3	−413.6	−370.8	−239.4
−36.7	−60.9	−122.8	−202.5	−246.3	−61.8	−50.3	−65.6	−98.2	−91.7	−128.7
−93.4	−85.0	−53.2	−34.3	−97.2	−124.7	1.2	−58.4	−259.2	−291.5	−368.1
−214.7	−277.8	−22.9	−97.1	−426.8	−255.5	−151.0	−415.6	−596.9	−931.6	−702.8
0.7	3.9	0.3	1.0	−5.3	4.5	0.6	2.6	−0.4	−1.7	1.3
−344.1	−419.8	−198.6	−332.9	−775.6	−437.6	−199.5	−537.1	−954.7	−1,316.5	−1,198.3
...	...	...	−348.8	−413.7	−298.0	−163.8	−165.0	−202.4	−372.0	−396.1
...	...	...	−341.7	−385.3	−255.0	−163.2	−316.2	−427.1	−512.0	−594.3
...	...	...	−30.2	−165.8	−243.6	−220.7	−284.1	−392.5	−715.6	−945.9
...	...	...	11.6	16.2	16.4	−3.0	32.8	15.6	22.9	−5.2
...	...	...	−709.2	−948.7	−780.1	−550.7	−732.5	−1,006.5	−1,576.7	−1,941.4
−31.6	−41.2	−26.6	−34.8	−43.0	−42.5	−33.4	−34.7	−82.4	−106.8	−194.0
−85.9	−110.2	−8.7	−46.7	−105.8	−105.1	−91.0	−137.7	−157.5	−257.8	−414.5
−93.0	−128.2	35.6	−65.0	−127.7	46.5	31.4	−120.2	−194.3	−241.2	−368.8
−103.5	−88.0	−29.0	−97.3	−132.0	−120.8	−199.5	−360.4	−508.5	−592.4	−746.6
−313.9	−367.7	−28.7	−243.8	−408.5	−221.8	−292.5	−653.0	−942.6	−1,198.2	−1,723.8

Table 2. Global Capital Flows: Amounts Outstanding and Net Issues of International Debt Securities by Currency of Issue and Announced International Syndicated Credit Facilities by Nationality of Borrower
(In billions of U.S. dollars)

	2001	2002	2003	2004	2005	2006	2007 Q1
Amounts outstanding of international debt securities by currency of issue							
U.S. dollar	3,700.4	4,123.9	4,537.8	4,906.7	5,382.1	6,400.9	6,712.7
Japanese yen	411.4	433.2	488.0	530.5	472.1	487.4	497.2
Pound sterling	505.6	618.2	776.3	981.0	1,062.6	1,450.5	1,521.9
Canadian dollar	47.6	51.6	79.5	112.6	146.7	178.0	196.9
Swedish krona	8.2	11.1	15.8	20.9	23.2	34.3	34.6
Swiss franc	123.6	159.2	195.6	227.9	208.6	253.7	264.4
Euro	2,289.8	3,283.2	4,826.6	6,211.8	6,309.5	8,313.2	8,814.5
Other	110.4	152.0	216.7	285.4	355.2	455.8	506.1
Total	7,196.9	8,832.3	11,136.2	13,276.6	13,960.0	17,573.9	18,548.4
Net issues of international debt securities by currency of issue							
U.S. dollar	668.8	423.5	413.9	368.9	475.4	1,018.9	311.7
Japanese yen	18.5	−17.5	3.7	26.9	3.9	19.4	6.5
Pound sterling	65.1	52.4	84.5	133.2	197.6	223.7	74.0
Canadian dollar	−1.1	3.6	15.6	25.5	29.4	32.1	16.9
Swedish krona	1.4	1.1	2.0	3.4	6.2	7.0	1.1
Swiss franc	−5.2	8.0	15.8	12.7	13.1	28.1	10.5
Euro	622.8	492.0	779.0	917.8	987.0	1,208.6	401.3
Other	19.3	30.7	38.0	52.6	87.3	79.8	44.1
Total	1,389.6	993.8	1,352.3	1,540.9	1,800.0	2,617.7	866.0
Announced international syndicated credit facilities by nationality of borrower							
All countries	1,381.4	1,296.9	1,241.4	1,806.7	2,232.3	2,121.2	451.6
Industrial countries	1,270.3	1,199.9	1,131.0	1,636.7	1,990.9	1,822.3	358.2
Of which:							
United States	845.2	739.7	606.6	897.5	978.5	848.0	195.5
Japan	23.8	19.5	18.2	27.5	19.3	42.9	20.0
Germany	36.5	84.4	97.6	116.3	132.1	170.8	4.3
France	50.3	64.1	65.9	150.9	171.8	119.3	33.1
Italy	35.9	22.8	45.3	22.3	74.0	26.0	7.1
United Kingdom	106.0	109.8	103.9	150.3	178.6	136.3	33.5
Canada	39.2	34.9	30.4	38.7	71.2	73.9	8.3

Source: Bank for International Settlements.

Table 3. Selected Indicators on the Size of the Capital Markets, 2006

(In billions of U.S. dollars unless noted otherwise)

| | GDP | Total Reserves Minus Gold[1] | Stock Market Capitalization | Debt Securities | | | Bank Assets[2] | Bonds, Equities, and Bank Assets[3] | Bonds, Equities and Bank Assets[2] *(In percent of GDP)* |
				Public	Private	Total			
World	48,204.4	5,091.5	50,826.6	25,634.7	43,099.7	68,734.4	70,860.5	190,421.5	395.0
European Union	13,644.4	252.7	13,068.8	7,695.0	15,507.7	23,202.7	36,642.0	72,913.5	534.4
Euro area	10,588.9	157.5	8,419.1	6,582.2	12,186.1	18,768.3	25,837.6	53,268.8	503.1
North America	14,470.0	89.8	21,269.7	6,936.0	21,135.5	28,071.6	12,122.6	61,463.9	424.8
Canada	1,275.3	35.0	1,700.7	702.4	633.4	1,335.8	1,917.9	4,954.5	388.5
United States	13,194.7	54.9	19,569.0	6,233.6	20,502.1	26,735.8	10,204.7	56,509.4	428.3
Japan	4,366.2	879.7	4,795.8	6,750.6	1,968.7	8,719.3	6,415.4	19,930.5	456.5
Memorandum items:									
EU countries									
Austria	323.8	7.0	192.8	187.7	334.9	522.6	419.7	1,135.0	350.5
Belgium	394.5	8.8	335.1	424.3	404.3	828.6	1,837.2	3,000.9	760.7
Denmark	276.4	29.7	239.5	95.9	484.2	580.1	795.2	1,614.7	584.2
Finland	209.8	6.5	309.5	122.1	102.5	224.5	243.8	777.7	370.8
France	2,252.0	42.7	2,312.8	1,241.1	2,254.2	3,495.3	7,637.3	13,445.5	597.1
Germany	2,899.4	41.7	1,637.6	1,479.1	3,371.7	4,850.9	4,413.0	10,901.4	376.0
Greece	308.7	0.6	208.3	364.3	97.5	461.8	351.7	1,021.7	330.9
Ireland	219.4	0.7	163.3	41.8	378.2	420.0	1,246.3	1,829.6	834.0
Italy	1,852.6	25.7	1,026.5	1,759.0	1,732.0	3,491.0	3,627.4	8,144.9	439.6
Luxembourg	41.5	0.2	79.5	0.0	96.5	96.5	708.2	884.2	2,130.4
Netherlands	666.6	10.8	725.1	286.1	1,414.2	1,700.3	3,097.6	5,523.0	828.6
Portugal	194.9	2.1	105.8	155.9	206.3	362.2	203.9	671.9	344.7
Spain	1,225.8	10.8	1,322.9	520.8	1,793.8	2,314.6	2,295.4	5,933.0	484.0
Sweden	384.4	24.8	615.9	175.5	381.2	556.7	552.8	1,725.4	448.9
United Kingdom	2,394.7	40.7	3,794.3	841.5	2,456.2	3,297.7	9,212.6	16,304.6	680.9
Emerging market countries[4]	14,078.5	1,932.0	11,692.4	3,876.1	2,180.3	6,056.4	11,271.3	29,020.1	206.1
Of which:									
Asia	6,259.5	1,248.9	6,857.0	2,024.5	1,493.1	3,517.5	7,487.1	17,861.6	285.4
Latin America	2,941.8	195.5	1,454.2	1,098.8	458.0	1,556.8	1,433.7	4,444.6	151.1
Middle East	1,326.1	149.5	657.4	37.9	61.0	98.9	873.7	1,630.1	122.9
Africa	920.2	91.5	850.9	83.5	57.4	140.9	500.4	1,492.2	162.2
Europe	2,631.0	246.6	1,872.8	631.5	110.8	742.3	976.5	3,591.6	136.5

Sources: World Federation of Exchanges; Bank for International Settlements; International Monetary Fund, *International Financial Statistics (IFS)* and *World Economic Outlook* database as of August 21, 2007; ©2003 Bureau van Dijk Electronic Publishing-Bankscope; and Standard & Poor's Emerging Market Database.

[1]Data are from IFS.

[2]Assets of commercial banks.

[3]Sum of the stock market capitalization, debt securities, and bank assets.

[4]This aggregate comprises the group of Other Emerging Market and Developing Countries defined in the *World Economic Outlook,* together with Hong Kong SAR, Israel, Korea, Singapore, and Taiwan Province of China.

Table 4. Global Over-the-Counter Derivatives Markets: Notional Amounts and Gross Market Values of Outstanding Contracts[1]
(In billions of U.S. dollars)

	Notional Amounts					Gross Market Values				
	End-Dec. 2004	End-June 2005	End-Dec. 2005	End-June 2006	End-Dec. 2006	End-Dec. 2004	End-June 2005	End-Dec. 2005	End-June 2006	End-Dec. 2006
Total	**257,894**	**281,493**	**297,670**	**369,507**	**415,183**	**9,377**	**10,605**	**9,749**	**9,936**	**9,695**
Foreign exchange	**29,289**	**31,081**	**31,364**	**38,091**	**40,179**	**1,546**	**1,141**	**997**	**1,134**	**1,262**
Forwards and forex swaps	14,951	15,801	15,873	19,396	19,828	643	464	406	435	467
Currency swaps	8,223	8,236	8,504	9,669	10,772	745	549	453	533	600
Options	6,115	7,045	6,987	9,027	9,579	158	129	138	166	196
Interest rate[2]	**190,502**	**204,795**	**211,971**	**261,960**	**291,987**	**5,417**	**6,699**	**5,397**	**5,436**	**4,834**
Forward rate agreements	12,789	13,973	14,269	18,117	18,689	22	31	22	25	31
Swaps	150,631	163,749	169,106	207,043	229,780	4,903	6,077	4,778	4,831	4,166
Options	27,082	27,073	28,596	36,800	43,518	492	592	597	579	636
Equity-linked	**4,385**	**4,551**	**5,793**	**6,782**	**7,485**	**498**	**382**	**582**	**671**	**851**
Forwards and swaps	756	1,086	1,177	1,431	1,764	76	88	112	147	165
Options	3,629	3,465	4,617	5,351	5,721	422	294	470	523	687
Commodity[3]	**1,443**	**2,940**	**5,435**	**6,394**	**6,938**	**169**	**376**	**871**	**718**	**668**
Gold	369	288	334	456	463	32	24	51	77	56
Other	1,074	2,652	5,100	5,938	6,475	137	351	820	641	611
Forwards and swaps	559	1,748	1,909	2,188	2,813	...	...	...	...	...
Options	516	904	3,191	3,750	3,663	...	...	...	...	...
Credit default swaps	**6,396**	**10,211**	**13,908**	**20,352**	**28,838**	**134**	**188**	**243**	**294**	**470**
Single-name instruments	5,117	7,310	10,432	13,873	18,885	112	136	171	186	289
Multi-name instruments	1,279	2,901	3,476	6,479	9,953	22	52	72	109	181
Unallocated	**25,879**	**27,915**	**29,199**	**35,928**	**39,755**	**1,613**	**1,818**	**1,659**	**1,683**	**1,610**
Memorandum items:										
Gross credit exposure[4]	n.a.	n.a.	n.a.	n.a.	n.a.	2,075	1,897	1,900	2,029	2,045
Exchange-traded derivatives	29,289	31,081	31,364	38,091	40,179	...	...	...	...	...

Source: Bank for International Settlements.

[1]All figures are adjusted for double-counting. Notional amounts outstanding have been adjusted by halving positions vis-à-vis other reporting dealers. Gross market values have been calculated as the sum of the total gross positive market value of contracts and the absolute value of the gross negative market value of contracts with non-reporting counterparties.

[2]Single-currency contracts only.

[3]Adjustments for double-counting are estimated.

[4]Gross market values after taking into account legally enforceable bilateral netting agreements.

Table 5. Global Over-the-Counter Derivatives Markets: Notional Amounts and Gross Market Values of Outstanding Contracts by Counterparty, Remaining Maturity, and Currency[1]

(In billions of U.S. dollars)

	Notional Amounts					Gross Market Values				
	End-Dec. 2004	End-June 2005	End-Dec. 2005	End-June 2006	End-Dec. 2006	End-Dec. 2004	End-June 2005	End-Dec. 2005	End-June 2006	End-Dec. 2006
Total	**257,894**	**281,493**	**297,670**	**369,507**	**415,183**	**9,377**	**10,605**	**9,749**	**9,936**	**9,695**
Foreign exchange	**29,289**	**31,081**	**31,364**	**38,091**	**40,179**	**1,546**	**1,141**	**997**	**1,134**	**1,262**
By counterparty										
With other reporting dealers	11,668	12,179	12,161	15,278	15,597	486	377	323	367	437
With other financial institutions	11,417	12,334	12,721	15,118	15,878	648	471	412	471	520
With nonfinancial customers	6,204	6,568	6,482	7,695	8,704	413	294	261	296	306
By remaining maturity[2]										
Up to one year	22,834	24,256	23,910	29,563	30,228	...	...	...	...	...
One to five years	4,386	4,729	5,165	5,837	6,658	...	...	...	...	...
Over five years	2,069	2,097	2,289	2,691	3,293	...	...	...	...	...
By major currency[3]										
U.S. dollar	25,726	27,585	26,297	31,756	33,775	1,408	1,024	867	967	1,066
Euro	11,900	12,405	12,857	15,340	15,907	752	512	397	472	508
Japanese yen	7,076	6,907	7,578	9,504	9,548	258	220	256	242	323
Pound sterling	4,331	4,273	4,424	5,217	6,128	220	150	121	148	197
Other	9,545	10,994	11,572	14,365	15,000	455	377	354	439	431
Interest rate[4]	**190,502**	**204,795**	**211,971**	**261,960**	**291,987**	**5,417**	**6,699**	**5,397**	**5,436**	**4,834**
By counterparty										
With other reporting dealers	82,258	87,049	91,541	114,465	126,445	2,155	2,598	2,096	2,215	1,954
With other financial institutions	85,729	92,092	95,321	114,865	127,215	2,631	3,265	2,625	2,515	2,252
With nonfinancial customers	22,516	25,655	25,109	32,630	38,327	631	837	676	706	628
By remaining maturity[2]										
Up to one year	62,659	66,681	69,378	90,585	104,207	...	...	...	...	...
One to five years	77,929	82,341	86,550	101,608	110,417	...	...	...	...	...
Over five years	49,915	55,773	56,042	69,767	77,362	...	...	...	...	...
By major currency										
U.S. dollar	61,103	72,558	74,441	88,022	97,612	1,535	1,826	1,515	2,117	1,665
Euro	76,162	76,426	81,442	103,429	112,116	2,986	3,692	2,965	2,298	2,306
Japanese yen	24,209	25,224	25,605	32,146	37,954	352	454	295	457	295
Pound sterling	15,289	16,621	15,060	19,066	22,274	240	372	344	291	311
Other	13,740	13,966	15,422	19,296	22,031	305	356	279	273	257
Equity-linked	**4,385**	**4,551**	**5,793**	**6,782**	**7,485**	**498**	**382**	**582**	**671**	**851**
Commodity[5]	**1,443**	**2,940**	**5,435**	**6,394**	**6,938**	**169**	**376**	**871**	**718**	**668**
Credit default swaps	**6,396**	**10,211**	**13,908**	**20,352**	**28,838**	**134**	**188**	**243**	**294**	**470**
Unallocated	**25,879**	**27,915**	**29,199**	**35,928**	**39,755**	**1,613**	**1,818**	**1,659**	**1,683**	**1,610**

Source: Bank for International Settlements.

[1]All figures are adjusted for double-counting. Notional amounts outstanding have been adjusted by halving positions vis-à-vis other reporting dealers. Gross market values have been calculated as the sum of the total gross positive market value of contracts and the absolute value of the gross negative market value of contracts with non-reporting counterparties.

[2]Residual maturity.

[3]Counting both currency sides of each foreign exchange transaction means that the currency breakdown sums to twice the aggregate.

[4]Single-currency contracts only.

[5]Adjustments for double-counting are estimated.

Table 6. Exchange-Traded Derivative Financial Instruments: Notional Principal Amounts Outstanding and Annual Turnover

	1993	1994	1995	1996	1997	1998	1999
	(In billions of U.S. dollars)						
Notional principal amounts outstanding							
Interest rate futures	4,960.4	5,807.6	5,876.2	5,979.0	7,586.7	8,031.4	7,924.8
Interest rate options	2,361.4	2,623.2	2,741.8	3,277.8	3,639.8	4,623.5	3,755.5
Currency futures	34.7	40.4	33.8	37.7	42.3	31.7	36.7
Currency options	75.9	55.7	120.4	133.4	118.6	49.2	22.4
Stock market index futures	110.0	127.7	172.2	195.9	210.9	291.6	346.9
Stock market index options	231.6	242.7	337.7	394.5	808.7	947.4	1,510.3
Total	7,774.1	8,897.2	9,282.0	10,018.2	12,407.1	13,974.8	13,596.6
North America	4,359.9	4,823.4	4,852.3	4,841.2	6,347.9	7,395.1	6,930.6
Europe	1,777.9	1,831.8	2,241.2	2,828.0	3,587.3	4,397.1	4,008.5
Asia-Pacific	1,606.0	2,171.8	1,990.1	2,154.0	2,235.7	1,882.5	2,407.8
Other	30.3	70.3	198.4	195.0	236.2	300.1	249.7
	(In millions of contracts traded)						
Annual turnover							
Interest rate futures	427.0	628.5	561.0	612.2	701.6	760.1	672.7
Interest rate options	82.9	116.6	225.5	151.1	116.8	129.7	118.0
Currency futures	39.0	69.8	99.6	73.7	73.6	54.5	37.1
Currency options	23.7	21.3	23.3	26.3	21.1	12.1	6.8
Stock market index futures	71.2	109.0	114.8	93.8	115.9	178.0	204.9
Stock market index options	144.1	197.6	187.3	172.3	178.2	195.0	322.5
Total	787.9	1,142.9	1,211.5	1,129.4	1,207.1	1,329.3	1,362.0
North America	382.4	513.5	455.0	428.3	463.5	530.0	462.8
Europe	263.4	398.1	354.8	391.7	482.8	525.9	604.7
Asia-Pacific	98.5	131.7	126.4	115.9	126.9	170.9	207.7
Other	43.6	99.6	275.5	193.4	134.0	102.5	86.8

Source: Bank for International Settlements.

	2000	2001	2002	2003	2004	2005	2006	2007 Q1
	(In billions of U.S. dollars)							
	7,907.8	9,269.5	9,955.6	13,123.7	18,164.9	20,708.8	24,478.3	28,737.5
	4,734.2	12,492.8	11,759.5	20,793.7	24,604.1	31,588.3	38,173.7	48,533.5
	74.4	65.6	47.0	79.9	103.5	107.6	178.5	423.9
	21.4	27.4	27.4	37.9	60.7	66.1	78.6	82.8
	377.5	344.2	365.5	549.3	635.2	793.5	1,048.5	1,191.6
	1,148.4	1,574.9	1,700.8	2,202.4	3,023.8	4,532.1	6,564.0	8,054.0
	14,263.8	23,774.4	23,855.8	36,786.8	46,592.3	57,796.4	70,521.6	87,023.2
	8,168.0	16,203.2	13,719.8	19,504.0	27,608.3	36,383.7	42,550.1	52,596.5
	4,197.9	6,141.6	8,800.8	15,406.4	16,307.8	17,973.1	23,275.0	28,883.3
	1,611.8	1,318.4	1,206.0	1,659.9	2,426.9	3,014.1	4,069.8	4,830.1
	286.2	111.2	129.1	216.5	249.3	425.5	626.7	713.3
	(In millions of contracts traded)							
	781.2	1,057.5	1,152.1	1,576.8	1,902.6	2,110.4	2,621.2	736.8
	107.7	199.6	240.3	302.3	361.0	430.8	566.7	151.4
	43.5	49.0	42.6	58.8	83.7	143.0	231.1	76.1
	7.0	10.5	16.1	14.3	13.0	19.4	24.3	7.7
	225.2	337.1	530.3	725.6	804.4	918.7	1,233.6	412.9
	481.5	1,148.2	2,235.5	3,233.9	2,980.1	3,139.8	3,177.5	946.2
	1,646.0	2,801.9	4,216.8	5,911.6	6,144.8	6,762.0	7,854.4	2,331.1
	461.3	675.6	912.2	1,279.8	1,633.6	1,926.8	2,541.8	704.5
	718.6	957.7	1,074.8	1,346.3	1,412.6	1,592.8	1,947.3	609.2
	331.3	985.1	2,073.1	3,111.6	2,847.6	2,932.4	2,957.1	882.9
	134.9	183.4	156.7	174.0	251.0	310.0	408.2	134.5

Table 7. United States: Sectoral Balance Sheets
(In percent)

	2001	2002	2003	2004	2005	2006
Corporate sector						
Debt/net worth	50.8	49.7	47.6	44.3	42.0	40.7
Short-term debt/total debt	33.3	30.0	27.1	26.9	27.4	27.1
Interest burden[1]	17.7	14.4	11.8	8.7	8.1	8.4
Household sector						
Net worth/assets	82.8	80.2	92.4	89.2	80.9	80.7
Equity/total assets	26.8	20.6	27.3	26.5	23.3	23.8
Equity/financial assets	41.7	34.3	38.7	39.1	38.4	39.0
Net worth/disposable personal income	539.4	495.7	538.7	552.5	560.4	583.4
Home mortgage debt/total assets	10.9	12.3	14.4	14.5	13.9	14.1
Consumer credit/total assets	3.9	4.2	4.4	4.1	3.6	3.5
Total debt/financial assets	25.5	30.2	29.2	30.2	31.4	31.6
Debt-service burden[2]	13.1	13.4	13.5	13.5	14.1	14.4
Banking sector[3]						
Credit quality						
Nonperforming loans[4]/total loans	1.4	1.5	1.2	0.9	0.8	0.8
Net loan losses/average total loans	1.0	1.1	0.9	0.7	0.6	0.4
Loan-loss reserve/total loans	1.9	1.9	1.8	1.5	1.3	1.2
Net charge-offs/total loans	1.0	1.1	0.9	0.6	0.6	0.4
Capital ratios						
Total risk-based capital	12.7	12.8	12.8	12.6	12.3	13.0
Tier 1 risk-based capital	9.9	10.0	10.1	10.0	9.9	10.5
Equity capital/total assets	9.0	9.2	9.2	10.1	10.3	10.5
Core capital (leverage ratio)	7.8	7.8	7.9	7.8	7.9	7.9
Profitability measures						
Return on average assets (ROA)	1.2	1.3	1.4	1.3	1.3	1.4
Return on average equity (ROE)	13.2	14.5	15.3	13.7	13.3	13.5
Net interest margin	3.9	4.1	3.8	3.6	3.6	3.4
Efficiency ratio[5]	57.7	55.8	56.5	58.0	57.2	57.1

Sources: Board of Governors of the Federal Reserve System, *Flow of Funds;* Department of Commerce, Bureau of Economic Analysis; Federal Deposit Insurance Corporation; and Federal Reserve Bank of St. Louis.

[1]Ratio of net interest payments to pre-tax income.

[2]Ratio of debt payments to disposable personal income.

[3]FDIC-insured commercial banks.

[4]Loans past due 90+ days and nonaccrual.

[5]Noninterest expense less amortization of intangible assets as a percent of net interest income plus noninterest income.

Table 8. Japan: Sectoral Balance Sheets[1]

(In percent)

	FY2000	FY2001	FY2002	FY2003	FY2004	FY2005	FY2006
Corporate sector							
Debt/shareholders' equity (book value)	156.8	156.0	146.1	121.3	121.5	101.7	98.2
Short-term debt/total debt	37.7	36.8	39.0	37.8	36.8	36.4	35.3
Interest burden[2]	28.4	32.3	27.8	22.0	18.4	15.6	15.2
Debt/operating profits	1,229.3	1,480.0	1,370.0	1,079.2	965.9	839.9	820.4
Memorandum item:							
Total debt/GDP[3]	103.9	102.0	100.9	90.9	96.5	85.7	89.9
Household sector							
Net worth/assets	84.7	84.5	84.4	84.5	84.6	85.1	...
Equity	4.7	3.6	3.5	4.9	5.7	8.8	...
Real estate	36.6	35.7	34.6	32.9	31.4	29.7	...
Net worth/net disposable income	752.2	744.9	725.2	728.5	723.0	746.0	...
Interest burden[4]	5.4	5.2	5.1	4.9	4.8	4.7	...
Memorandum item:							
Debt/equity	324.5	427.2	448.2	317.6	268.4	169.4	...
Debt/real estate	41.7	43.2	45.1	47.1	49.0	50.3	...
Debt/net disposable income	135.4	136.1	134.2	133.2	131.5	131.1	...
Debt/net worth	18.0	18.3	18.5	18.3	18.2	17.6	...
Equity/net worth	5.5	4.3	4.1	5.8	6.8	10.4	...
Real estate/net worth	43.2	42.3	41.0	38.9	37.1	35.0	...
Total debt/GDP[3]	80.3	80.2	79.4	77.5	76.1	75.6	...
Banking sector							
Credit quality							
Nonperforming loans[5]/total loans	6.3	8.4	7.4	5.8	4.0	2.9	2.5
Capital ratio							
Stockholders' equity/assets	4.6	3.9	3.3	3.9	4.2	4.9	5.3
Profitability measures							
Return on equity (ROE)[6]	−0.5	−14.3	−19.5	−2.7	4.1	11.3	8.5

Sources: Ministry of Finance, *Financial Statements of Corporations by Industries;* Cabinet Office, Economic and Social Research Institute, *Annual Report on National Accounts;* Japanese Bankers Association, *Financial Statements of All Banks;* and Financial Services Agency, *The Status of Nonperforming Loans.*

[1]Data are fiscal year beginning April 1. Stock data on households are only available through FY2005.
[2]Interest payments as a percent of operating profits.
[3]Revised due to the change in GDP figures.
[4]Interest payments as a percent of disposable income.
[5]Nonperforming loans are based on figures reported under the Financial Reconstruction Law.
[6]Net income as a percentage of stockholders' equity (no adjustment for preferred stocks, etc.).

Table 9. Europe: Sectoral Balance Sheets[1]

(In percent)

	2000	2001	2002	2003	2004	2005	2006
Corporate sector							
Debt/equity[2]	68.0	72.5	75.9	73.1	71.7	73.8	77.3
Short-term debt/total debt	37.4	36.8	35.2	35.1	35.0	37.1	39.0
Interest burden[3]	18.3	19.4	18.4	17.1	17.4	18.1	19.8
Debt/operating profits	315.7	321.6	338.7	327.9	326.2	348.3	381.2
Memorandum items:							
Financial assets/equity	1.5	1.5	1.4	1.4	1.4	1.5	1.5
Liquid assets/short-term debt	73.6	76.6	77.0	83.3	91.0	95.6	93.7
Household sector							
Net worth/assets	84.5	83.9	83.9	84.0	84.1	84.6	84.9
Equity/net worth	15.5	13.5	10.8	11.4	11.4	12.0	11.9
Equity/net financial assets	39.8	36.5	31.8	33.1	33.3	34.1	33.8
Interest burden[4]	6.5	6.2	6.1	6.0	5.7	5.7	5.8
Memorandum items:							
Nonfinancial assets/net worth	59.7	61.7	65.7	65.6	65.9	64.6	64.7
Debt/net financial assets	46.1	48.4	53.3	51.6	51.6	47.6	47.0
Debt/income	94.6	94.8	98.2	100.8	105.6	106.9	110.6
Banking sector[5]							
Credit quality							
Nonperforming loans/total loans	3.0	2.9	2.5	2.3	2.4	2.2	2.2
Loan-loss reserve/nonperforming loans	82.1	80.8	81.5	73.0	67.8	74.6	67.8
Loan-loss reserve/total loans	2.5	2.4	2.4	2.4	1.9	1.6	1.5
Capital ratios							
Equity capital/total assets	4.3	3.3	3.1	2.9	3.5	3.5	3.5
Capital funds/liabilities	6.9	6.8	5.4	5.0	5.7	5.6	5.7
Profitability measures							
Return on assets (after tax)	0.8	0.5	0.4	0.5	0.5	0.5	0.6
Return on equity (after tax)	18.3	11.2	9.0	11.3	13.7	15.0	16.7
Net interest margin	1.5	1.4	1.6	1.5	1.1	1.0	0.9
Efficiency ratio[6]	66.4	68.2	69.0	73.1	64.3	62.6	60.2

Sources: ©2003 Bureau van Dijk Electronic Publishing-Bankscope; European Central Bank, *Monthly Bulletin;* and IMF staff estimates.
[1]GDP-weighted average for France, Germany, and the United Kingdom, unless otherwise noted.
[2]Corporate equity adjusted for changes in asset valuation.
[3]Interest payments as a percent of gross operating profits.
[4]Interest payments as percent of disposable income.
[5]Fifty largest European banks. Data availability may restrict coverage to less than 50 banks for specific indicators.
[6]Cost-to-income ratio.

Figure 15. Emerging Market Volatility Measures

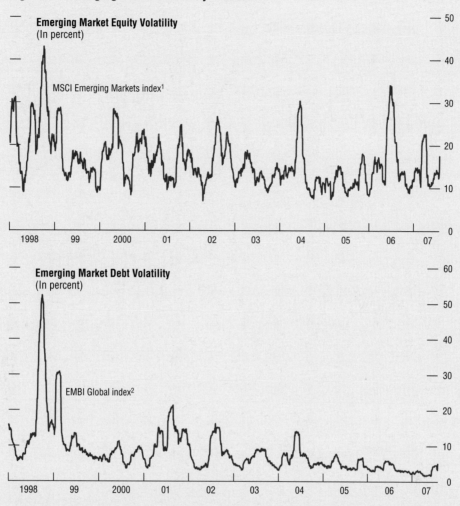

Sources: For "Emerging Market Equity Volatility," Morgan Stanley Capital International (MSCI); and IMF staff estimates. For "Emerging Market Debt Volatility," JPMorgan Chase & Co.; and IMF staff estimates.
[1]Data utilize the MSCI Emerging Markets index in U.S. dollars to calculate 30-day rolling volatilities.
[2]Data utilize the EMBI Global total return index in U.S. dollars to calculate 30-day rolling volatilities.

Figure 16. Emerging Market Debt Cross-Correlation Measures

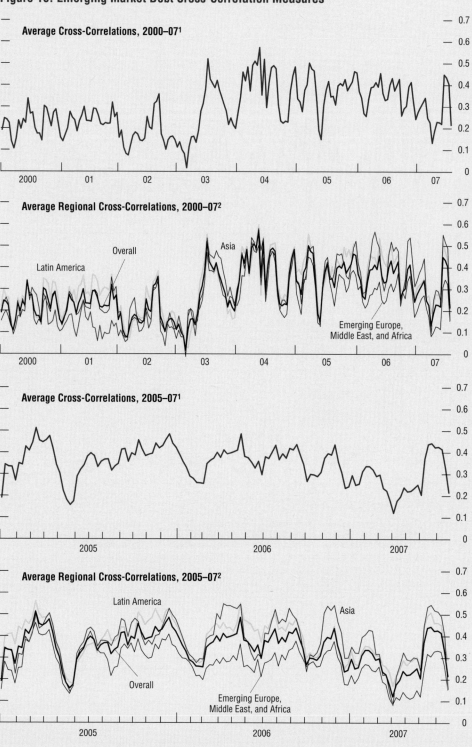

Average Cross-Correlations, 2000–07[1]

Average Regional Cross-Correlations, 2000–07[2]

Latin America

Overall

Asia

Emerging Europe,
Middle East, and Africa

Average Cross-Correlations, 2005–07[1]

Average Regional Cross-Correlations, 2005–07[2]

Latin America

Asia

Overall

Emerging Europe,
Middle East, and Africa

Sources: JPMorgan Chase & Co.; and IMF staff estimates.
[1]Thirty-day moving simple average across all pair-wise return correlations of 20 constituents included in the EMBI Global.
[2]Simple average of all pair-wise correlations of all markets in a given region with all other bond markets, regardless of region.

Table 10. Equity Market Indices

	2007 End of Period Q1	Q2	2006 End of Period Q1	Q2	Q3	Q4	End of Period 2002	2003	2004	2005	2006	12-Month High	12-Month Low	All-Time High[1]	All-Time Low[1]
World	**1,514.2**	**1,602.4**	**1,335.1**	**1,319.9**	**1,373.4**	**1,483.6**	**792.2**	**1,036.3**	**1,169.3**	**1,257.8**	**1,483.6**	**1,630.1**	**1,261.0**	**1,630.1**	**423.1**
Emerging Markets	**929.0**	**1,059.7**	**787.8**	**747.5**	**778.2**	**912.7**	**292.1**	**442.8**	**542.2**	**706.5**	**912.7**	**1,067.0**	**710.3**	**1,067.0**	**175.3**
Latin America	**3,163.2**	**3,754.2**	**2,469.4**	**2,368.2**	**2,473.1**	**2,995.7**	**658.9**	**1,100.9**	**1,483.6**	**2,150.0**	**2,995.7**	**3,838.6**	**2,237.7**	**3,838.6**	**185.6**
Argentina	3,014.6	3,188.6	2,370.3	2,473.9	2,307.7	3,084.1	470.3	933.6	1,163.0	1,857.1	3,084.1	3,342.8	2,227.6	3,342.8	152.6
Brazil	2,325.9	2,857.3	1,886.2	1,821.9	1,790.8	2,205.4	395.4	802.0	1,046.6	1,569.4	2,205.4	2,921.6	1,673.8	2,921.6	84.1
Chile	1,592.6	1,891.2	1,263.7	1,169.3	1,262.8	1,492.4	445.5	800.6	997.3	1,180.7	1,492.4	1,891.2	1,111.7	1,891.2	183.0
Colombia	516.9	604.2	580.4	395.3	470.7	549.8	68.3	108.6	245.0	495.7	549.8	627.4	385.9	627.4	41.2
Mexico	5,802.9	6,497.0	4,216.0	4,016.0	4,645.1	5,483.3	1,442.8	1,873.1	2,715.6	3,943.6	5,483.3	6,764.2	3,877.5	6,764.2	308.9
Peru	828.2	1,089.4	483.5	543.7	598.7	671.4	182.7	344.1	343.4	441.3	671.4	1,091.6	522.2	1,091.6	73.5
Venezuela	154.3	178.6	161.1	151.4	156.2	174.1	77.7	103.8	151.0	107.4	174.1	202.5	103.9	278.4	56.1
Asia	**370.1**	**435.6**	**311.9**	**303.7**	**322.9**	**371.5**	**140.4**	**206.4**	**231.6**	**286.2**	**371.5**	**440.6**	**286.6**	**440.6**	**104.1**
China	51.3	63.2	35.6	35.7	38.6	52.3	14.1	25.5	25.3	29.3	52.3	64.1	34.8	136.9	12.9
India	530.6	598.6	459.2	427.5	501.4	560.8	148.8	246.2	273.1	382.9	560.8	598.6	402.8	598.6	77.7
Indonesia	2,433.2	2,757.2	1,831.5	1,808.8	2,108.2	2,449.0	519.6	831.1	1,324.0	1,579.8	2,449.0	2,761.5	1,755.7	2,761.5	280.0
Korea	404.8	469.6	386.0	365.3	384.0	395.2	184.7	246.0	256.4	386.3	395.2	489.4	346.3	489.4	59.5
Malaysia	471.7	508.1	345.9	338.5	356.8	408.8	244.0	300.4	335.9	329.0	408.8	523.5	332.7	523.5	88.3
Pakistan	381.2	462.6	407.3	335.8	355.4	333.7	146.0	188.2	211.7	333.3	333.7	462.6	322.0	462.6	54.4
Philippines	660.3	762.0	460.4	445.6	531.1	620.2	210.1	303.7	381.1	431.9	620.2	780.7	444.7	917.3	132.6
Taiwan Province of China	312.8	352.2	279.7	279.5	286.2	318.3	189.5	259.1	257.7	275.8	318.3	355.2	258.5	483.5	103.9
Thailand	272.9	312.8	293.5	271.3	280.7	274.9	130.2	280.5	263.9	292.0	274.9	315.4	246.4	669.4	72.0
Europe, Middle East, & Africa	**376.1**	**391.4**	**342.6**	**306.5**	**306.3**	**364.4**	**108.4**	**163.9**	**222.7**	**300.3**	**364.4**	**396.9**	**291.3**	**396.9**	**80.8**
Czech Republic	436.6	490.2	394.5	357.7	369.8	408.3	116.2	152.9	234.8	371.5	408.3	490.2	337.7	490.2	62.8
Egypt	1,431.5	1,553.6	1,320.0	960.0	1,266.1	1,389.3	97.4	234.6	505.3	1,215.7	1,389.3	1,588.2	967.9	1,588.2	89.9
Hungary	1,594.7	1,965.5	1,586.2	1,450.7	1,446.0	1,690.0	535.5	646.9	1,057.0	1,447.0	1,690.0	2,008.1	1,396.0	2,008.1	77.1
Israel	213.1	232.9	201.4	176.4	187.7	194.4	90.8	141.4	167.4	209.3	194.4	242.1	165.7	242.1	67.6
Jordan	481.5	445.6	554.4	486.0	482.2	439.6	153.5	238.3	379.2	650.6	439.6	515.3	422.7	760.7	103.1
Morocco	424.4	418.6	315.3	303.6	333.5	342.9	138.5	171.4	189.1	231.3	342.9	461.7	294.5	461.7	99.6
Poland	2,451.5	2,594.7	1,980.2	1,953.5	1,979.1	2,253.2	861.0	1,118.3	1,419.3	1,867.4	2,253.2	2,627.4	1,933.3	2,627.4	99.6
Russia	1,212.7	1,202.4	1,043.6	1,065.0	1,067.4	1,250.3	270.7	461.1	479.9	813.4	1,250.3	1,252.3	993.9	1,252.3	30.6
South Africa	699.5	695.4	561.3	548.3	553.3	641.3	272.7	296.8	352.4	492.0	641.3	742.7	516.9	742.7	99.7
Turkey	686,668	731,869	682,935	558,350	581,504	614,409	169,900	319,808	425,008	645,739	614,409	755,480	509,075	777,492	426
Sectors															
Energy	723.4	807.1	680.6	680.6	654.5	760.0	163.1	287.4	349.0	548.6	760.0	807.1	619.3	807.1	81.7
Materials	496.6	559.8	374.6	382.2	374.5	442.1	182.8	250.1	265.0	325.4	442.1	572.5	362.5	572.5	98.5
Industrials	229.1	294.4	175.0	166.8	181.5	210.7	61.8	98.9	128.0	156.1	210.7	294.4	158.5	294.4	52.6
Consumer discretionary	441.2	479.7	398.4	352.5	370.3	422.6	138.8	233.8	292.3	381.1	422.6	484.0	327.6	484.0	74.1
Consumer staple	269.3	301.1	225.1	211.4	226.1	266.2	88.2	118.6	147.0	197.0	266.2	309.8	206.0	309.8	80.4
Health care	382.2	420.8	405.5	328.0	350.5	356.3	169.8	272.5	290.8	393.3	356.3	420.8	308.8	433.8	83.3
Financials	330.6	372.4	269.1	250.3	266.0	328.8	98.6	138.8	187.9	240.6	328.8	376.8	237.2	376.8	74.6
Information technology	220.0	243.4	212.9	202.6	216.4	231.8	103.9	149.6	161.5	209.1	231.8	247.0	187.8	300.0	73.1
Telecommunications	226.6	259.9	169.7	158.4	180.7	218.0	72.7	100.8	131.6	158.9	218.0	260.7	152.8	260.7	62.9
Utilities	288.0	342.8	229.6	217.8	232.2	282.1	72.4	127.2	149.8	197.0	282.1	342.8	206.8	342.8	63.1

Table 10 *(continued)*

	2007 End of period		2006 End of period				End of period				
	Q1	Q2	Q1	Q2	Q3	Q4	2002	2003	2004	2005	2006
World	**24.0**	**5.8**	**6.1**	**−1.1**	**4.0**	**8.0**	**−21.1**	**30.8**	**12.8**	**7.6**	**18.0**
Emerging Markets	**1.8**	**14.1**	**11.5**	**−5.1**	**4.1**	**17.3**	**−8.0**	**51.6**	**22.4**	**30.3**	**29.2**
Latin America	**5.6**	**18.7**	**14.9**	**−4.1**	**4.4**	**21.1**	**−24.8**	**67.1**	**34.8**	**44.9**	**39.3**
Argentina	−2.3	5.8	27.6	4.4	−6.7	33.6	−51.0	98.5	24.6	59.7	66.1
Brazil	5.5	22.8	20.2	−3.4	−1.7	23.2	−33.8	102.9	30.5	50.0	40.5
Chile	6.7	18.8	7.0	−7.5	8.0	18.2	−21.7	79.7	24.6	18.4	26.4
Colombia	−6.0	16.9	17.1	−31.9	19.1	16.8	18.3	59.0	125.7	102.3	10.9
Mexico	5.8	12.0	6.9	−4.7	15.7	18.0	−15.0	29.8	45.0	45.2	39.0
Peru	23.4	31.5	9.6	12.4	10.1	12.1	26.8	88.4	−0.2	28.5	52.1
Venezuela	−11.4	15.8	50.0	−6.0	3.1	11.5	−18.6	33.6	45.4	−28.9	62.2
Asia	**−0.4**	**17.7**	**9.0**	**−2.6**	**6.3**	**15.0**	**−6.2**	**47.1**	**12.2**	**23.5**	**29.8**
China	−1.8	23.0	21.5	0.3	8.2	35.4	−16.0	80.3	−0.7	15.6	78.7
India	−5.4	12.8	19.9	−6.9	17.3	11.8	5.3	65.5	11.0	40.2	46.5
Indonesia	−0.6	13.3	15.9	−1.2	16.6	16.2	18.9	60.0	59.3	19.3	55.0
Korea	2.4	16.0	−0.1	−5.4	5.1	2.9	−3.0	33.2	4.2	50.6	2.3
Malaysia	15.4	7.7	5.1	−2.1	5.4	14.6	−2.7	23.1	11.8	−2.1	24.2
Pakistan	14.2	21.3	22.2	−17.5	5.8	−6.1	116.7	28.9	12.5	57.5	0.1
Philippines	6.5	15.4	6.6	−3.2	19.2	16.8	−28.1	44.5	25.5	13.3	43.6
Taiwan Province of China	−1.7	12.6	1.4	−0.1	2.4	11.2	−25.8	36.7	−0.6	7.0	15.4
Thailand	−0.7	14.6	0.5	−7.6	3.5	−2.1	21.1	115.4	−5.9	10.6	−5.9
Europe, Middle East, & Africa	**3.2**	**4.1**	**14.1**	**−10.5**	**−0.1**	**19.0**	**4.7**	**51.2**	**35.8**	**34.9**	**21.3**
Czech Republic	6.9	12.3	6.2	−9.3	3.4	10.4	19.2	31.6	53.6	58.2	9.9
Egypt	3.0	8.5	8.6	−27.3	31.9	9.7	−4.4	140.8	115.4	140.6	14.3
Hungary	−5.6	23.3	9.6	−8.5	−0.3	16.9	5.4	20.8	63.4	36.9	16.8
Israel	9.7	9.3	−3.8	−12.4	6.4	3.6	−31.6	55.7	18.4	25.0	−7.1
Jordan	9.5	−7.4	−14.8	−12.3	−0.8	−8.8	2.6	55.3	59.1	71.6	−32.4
Morocco	23.8	−1.4	36.3	−3.7	9.9	2.8	−23.1	23.8	10.4	22.3	48.3
Poland	8.8	5.8	6.0	−1.4	1.3	13.9	−3.5	29.9	26.9	31.6	20.7
Russia	−3.0	−0.8	28.3	2.0	0.2	17.1	13.9	70.3	4.1	69.5	53.7
South Africa	9.1	−0.6	14.1	−2.3	0.9	15.9	−11.8	8.8	18.7	39.6	30.3
Turkey	11.8	6.6	5.8	−18.2	4.1	5.7	−27.5	88.2	32.9	51.9	−4.9
Sectors											
Energy	−4.8	11.6	24.0	0.0	−3.8	16.1	0.6	76.2	21.4	57.2	38.5
Materials	12.3	12.7	15.1	2.0	−2.0	18.1	5.2	36.8	6.0	22.8	35.9
Industrials	8.7	28.5	12.1	−4.7	8.8	16.1	−3.2	60.1	29.5	22.0	35.0
Consumer discretionary	4.4	8.7	4.5	−11.5	5.0	14.1	6.3	68.4	25.0	30.4	10.9
Consumer staple	1.2	11.8	14.2	−6.1	6.9	17.8	−6.7	34.4	24.0	34.0	35.1
Health care	7.3	10.1	3.1	−19.1	6.9	1.6	15.9	60.5	6.7	35.2	−9.4
Financials	0.5	12.6	11.8	−7.0	6.2	23.6	−8.4	40.7	35.4	28.1	36.7
Information technology	−5.1	10.6	1.8	−4.8	6.8	7.1	−22.6	43.9	8.0	29.5	10.9
Telecommunications	3.9	14.7	6.8	−6.6	14.0	20.7	−20.9	38.7	30.5	20.8	37.2
Utilities	2.1	19.0	16.5	−5.1	6.6	21.5	−20.9	75.7	17.8	31.5	43.2

Period on Period Percent Change

Table 10 *(concluded)*

	2007 End of Period		2006 End of Period				End of Period					12-Month High	12-Month Low	All-Time High[1]	All-Time Low[1]
	Q1	Q2	Q1	Q2	Q3	Q4	2002	2003	2004	2005	2006				
Developed Markets															
Australia	1,200.5	1,254.1	1,036.4	1,025.2	1,037.9	1,135.1	604.4	655.5	797.9	959.6	1,135.1	1,279.1	986.5	1,279.1	250.2
Austria	331.6	339.7	290.3	266.1	277.3	316.6	91.8	118.0	185.3	262.7	316.6	348.9	256.1	348.9	79.7
Belgium	116.3	117.4	102.0	95.5	106.8	113.0	55.3	60.1	77.9	94.8	113.0	121.0	92.9	121.0	35.4
Canada	1,659.0	1,750.7	1,518.8	1,448.9	1,464.4	1,628.3	818.3	1,019.7	1,139.3	1,406.8	1,628.3	1,786.3	1,426.2	1,786.3	338.3
Denmark	3,884.7	4,066.3	3,161.1	2,997.2	3,285.4	3,662.6	1,448.8	1,772.7	2,115.9	2,994.0	3,662.6	4,198.4	2,898.5	4,198.4	556.5
Finland	151.6	170.6	141.2	129.6	132.4	140.3	100.3	97.4	93.9	123.4	140.3	176.3	121.6	383.1	22.9
France	149.8	159.3	137.8	131.3	138.9	147.1	81.3	93.2	100.6	124.9	147.1	162.9	125.1	178.6	42.9
Germany	123.5	138.8	108.8	100.6	106.4	116.9	56.0	74.6	79.2	98.2	116.9	140.3	95.3	163.6	41.4
Greece	133.2	136.7	121.1	109.1	115.7	127.3	46.8	63.6	83.3	108.1	127.3	142.4	103.5	197.2	38.2
Hong Kong SAR	10,223.1	10,681.2	8,556.6	8,438.1	8,940.4	10,152.8	4,808.4	6,341.3	7,668.5	8,016.2	10,152.8	. . .	. . .	. . .	. . .
Ireland	117.3	119.0	104.2	97.9	107.0	120.3	56.8	65.9	85.2	93.5	120.3	126.8	93.2	126.8	40.5
Italy	121.3	121.4	112.3	107.7	113.5	121.4	69.6	78.1	93.2	106.0	121.4	128.7	104.2	132.1	39.5
Japan	1,081.6	1,123.3	1,061.4	980.5	1,001.1	1,060.2	524.3	637.3	699.1	999.3	1,060.2	1,146.6	912.5	1,655.3	462.1
Netherlands	107.7	113.5	95.9	88.9	98.6	101.3	66.0	68.4	69.3	88.3	101.3	115.0	85.5	134.9	38.5
New Zealand	136.0	141.0	135.7	124.5	123.7	138.2	90.0	107.6	127.0	130.0	138.2	145.2	117.3	145.2	56.7
Norway	3,094.2	3,368.7	2,710.5	2,499.8	2,454.9	2,951.8	898.3	1,240.9	1,690.3	2,267.7	2,951.8	3,368.7	2,330.6	3,368.7	455.9
Portugal	109.2	123.9	97.1	90.1	97.5	105.5	57.0	66.1	74.7	82.2	105.5	124.4	88.8	128.0	35.2
Singapore	1,850.2	2,033.2	1,398.8	1,352.4	1,431.3	1,696.1	764.9	1,005.1	1,148.1	1,295.4	1,696.1	2,089.9	1,282.4	2,089.9	508.2
Spain	162.8	166.2	133.4	129.4	144.9	158.2	69.9	89.6	104.3	122.1	158.2	173.0	124.9	173.0	27.4
Sweden	9,624.1	10,011.1	8,366.7	7,434.4	8,083.7	9,047.5	3,517.4	4,675.2	5,785.4	7,489.8	9,047.5	10,338.8	6,914.6	12,250.4	787.2
Switzerland	1,183.9	1,215.0	1,052.8	1,005.2	1,104.4	1,159.5	603.2	714.3	747.1	994.6	1,159.5	1,256.8	978.4	1,256.8	158.1
United Kingdom	1,897.2	1,978.1	1,785.9	1,742.6	1,782.6	1,865.6	1,179.2	1,348.7	1,453.0	1,685.3	1,865.6	2,016.6	1,692.4	2,016.6	585.4
United States	1,344.0	1,420.3	1,224.1	1,199.3	1,257.9	1,336.3	824.6	1,045.4	1,137.4	1,180.6	1,336.3	1,454.5	1,162.9	1,493.0	273.7

Period on Period Percent Change

	Q1	Q2	Q1	Q2	Q3	Q4	2002	2003	2004	2005	2006				
Developed Markets															
Australia	5.8	4.5	8.0	−1.1	1.2	9.4	−12.5	8.5	21.7	20.3	18.3	. . .	. . .	. . .	. . .
Austria	4.7	2.5	10.5	−8.3	4.2	14.2	−3.0	28.5	57.0	41.7	20.5	. . .	. . .	. . .	. . .
Belgium	2.9	1.0	7.7	−6.4	11.9	5.7	−29.7	8.7	29.5	21.7	19.2	. . .	. . .	. . .	. . .
Canada	1.9	5.5	8.0	−4.6	1.1	11.2	−15.3	24.6	11.7	23.5	15.7	. . .	. . .	. . .	. . .
Denmark	6.1	4.7	5.6	−5.2	9.6	11.5	−29.7	22.4	19.4	41.5	22.3	. . .	. . .	. . .	. . .
Finland	8.0	12.6	14.4	−8.2	2.2	6.0	−41.6	−2.9	−3.6	31.4	13.7	. . .	. . .	. . .	. . .
France	1.8	6.4	10.4	−4.7	5.8	5.9	−34.0	14.6	7.9	24.2	17.8	. . .	. . .	. . .	. . .
Germany	5.6	12.5	10.7	−7.5	5.8	9.9	−44.0	33.2	6.1	24.1	19.0	. . .	. . .	. . .	. . .
Greece	4.6	2.7	12.0	−9.9	6.1	10.0	−39.1	35.8	31.1	29.8	17.7	. . .	. . .	. . .	. . .
Hong Kong SAR	0.7	4.5	6.7	−1.4	6.0	13.6	−20.6	31.9	20.9	4.5	26.7	. . .	. . .	. . .	. . .
Ireland	−2.5	1.5	11.4	−6.0	9.3	12.4	−39.0	16.0	29.2	9.8	28.7	. . .	. . .	. . .	. . .
Italy	−0.1	0.0	6.0	−4.1	5.4	6.9	−23.6	12.2	19.3	13.8	14.6	. . .	. . .	. . .	. . .
Japan	2.0	3.9	6.2	−7.6	2.1	5.9	−19.4	21.6	9.7	42.9	6.1	. . .	. . .	. . .	. . .
Netherlands	6.4	5.3	8.6	−7.3	10.9	2.7	−34.3	3.6	1.3	27.5	14.7	. . .	. . .	. . .	. . .
New Zealand	−1.5	3.7	4.4	−8.3	−0.6	11.7	−4.4	19.6	18.0	2.4	6.3	. . .	. . .	. . .	. . .
Norway	4.8	8.9	19.5	−7.8	−1.8	20.2	−29.7	38.1	36.2	34.2	30.2	. . .	. . .	. . .	. . .
Portugal	3.6	13.4	18.2	−7.3	8.2	8.2	−28.3	15.9	13.1	10.0	28.3	. . .	. . .	. . .	. . .
Singapore	9.1	9.9	8.0	−3.3	5.8	18.5	−18.4	31.4	14.2	12.8	30.9	. . .	. . .	. . .	. . .
Spain	2.9	2.1	9.2	−3.0	12.0	9.1	−29.5	28.3	16.4	17.0	29.5	. . .	. . .	. . .	. . .
Sweden	6.4	4.0	11.7	−11.1	8.7	11.9	−43.1	32.9	23.7	29.5	20.8	. . .	. . .	. . .	. . .
Switzerland	2.1	2.6	5.8	−4.5	9.9	5.0	−25.8	18.4	4.6	33.1	16.6	. . .	. . .	. . .	. . .
United Kingdom	1.7	4.3	6.0	−2.4	2.3	4.7	−25.7	14.4	7.7	16.0	10.7	. . .	. . .	. . .	. . .
United States	0.6	5.7	3.7	−2.0	4.9	6.2	−24.0	26.8	8.8	3.8	13.2	. . .	. . .	. . .	. . .

Source: Data are provided by Morgan Stanley Capital International. Regional and sectoral compositions conform to Morgan Stanley Capital International Definitions.
[1]From 1990 or initiation of the index.

Table 11. Foreign Exchange Rates

(Units per U.S. dollar)

	2007 End of Period		2006 End of Period				End of Period					12-Month High[1]	12-Month Low[1]	All-Time High[1]	All-Time Low[1]
	Q1	Q2	Q1	Q2	Q3	Q4	2002	2003	2004	2005	2006				
Emerging Markets															
Latin America															
Argentina	3.10	3.09	3.08	3.09	3.10	3.06	3.36	2.93	2.97	3.03	3.06	3.05	3.11	0.98	3.86
Brazil	2.06	1.93	2.16	2.17	2.17	2.14	3.54	2.89	2.66	2.34	2.14	1.90	2.22	0.00	3.95
Chile	539	528	526	539	535	533	720	593	556	512	533	517	549	295	760
Colombia	2,203	1,975	2,291	2,574	2,398	2,240	2,867	2,780	2,355	2,287	2,240	1,872	2,421	689	2,980
Mexico	11.04	10.81	10.87	11.34	10.98	10.82	10.37	11.23	11.15	10.63	10.82	10.72	11.21	2.68	11.67
Peru	3.18	3.17	3.37	3.26	3.25	3.20	3.51	3.46	3.28	3.42	3.20	3.16	3.25	1.28	3.65
Venezuela	2,147	2,147	2,147	2,147	2,147	2,147	1,389	1,598	1,918	2,147	2,147	2,147	2,147	45	2,148
Asia															
China	7.73	7.61	8.02	7.99	7.90	7.81	8.28	8.28	8.28	8.07	7.81	7.61	7.94	4.73	8.73
India	43.47	40.70	44.62	46.04	45.93	44.26	47.98	45.63	43.46	45.05	44.26	40.49	46.08	16.92	49.05
Indonesia	9,121	9,025	9,070	9,263	9,223	8,994	8,950	8,420	9,270	9,830	8,994	8,670	9,250	1,977	16,650
Korea	941	924	972	949	947	930	1,186	1,192	1,035	1,010	930	914	964	684	1,963
Malaysia	3.46	3.45	3.68	3.67	3.69	3.53	3.80	3.80	3.80	3.78	3.53	3.38	3.70	2.44	4.71
Pakistan	60.74	60.47	60.12	60.21	60.55	60.88	58.25	57.25	59.43	59.79	60.88	60.47	61.00	21.18	64.35
Philippines	48.27	46.20	51.06	53.14	50.25	49.01	53.60	55.54	56.23	53.09	49.01	45.64	50.36	23.10	56.46
Taiwan Province of China	33.06	32.85	32.46	32.38	33.10	32.59	34.64	33.96	31.74	32.83	32.59	32.29	33.44	24.48	35.19
Thailand	32.40	31.70	38.88	38.12	37.57	35.45	43.11	39.62	38.92	41.03	35.45	31.44	37.77	23.15	55.50
Europe, Middle East, & Africa															
Czech Republic	20.97	21.24	23.50	22.27	22.32	20.83	30.07	25.71	22.42	24.55	20.83	20.55	22.60	20.55	42.17
Egypt	5.70	5.69	5.75	5.76	5.74	5.71	4.62	6.17	6.09	5.74	5.71	5.68	5.74	3.29	6.25
Hungary	185.64	182.21	217.88	221.39	215.30	190.29	224.48	208.70	181.02	212.97	190.29	179.95	217.00	90.20	317.56
Israel	4.16	4.25	4.66	4.43	4.30	4.22	4.74	4.39	4.32	4.61	4.22	3.94	4.35	1.96	5.01
Jordan	0.71	0.71	0.71	0.71	0.71	0.71	0.71	0.71	0.71	0.71	0.71	0.71	0.71	0.64	0.72
Morocco	11.40	10.60	11.48	11.34	11.42	11.70	9.80	10.08	11.09	11.94	11.70	10.60	11.83	7.75	12.06
Poland	2.89	2.78	3.24	3.18	3.13	2.90	3.83	3.73	3.01	3.25	2.90	2.75	3.14	1.72	4.71
Russia	25.99	25.74	27.70	26.85	26.80	26.33	31.96	29.24	27.72	28.74	26.33	25.68	26.98	0.98	31.96
South Africa	7.26	7.04	6.18	7.17	7.77	7.01	8.57	6.68	5.67	6.33	7.01	6.89	7.88	2.50	12.45
Turkey	1.39	1.31	1.35	1.59	1.51	1.42	1.66	1.41	1.34	1.35	1.42	1.30	1.53	—	1.77
Developed Markets															
Australia[2]	0.81	0.85	0.72	0.74	0.75	0.79	0.56	0.75	0.78	0.73	0.79	0.74	0.85	0.85	0.48
Canada	1.15	1.07	1.17	1.12	1.12	1.17	1.57	1.30	1.20	1.16	1.17	1.06	1.18	1.06	1.61
Denmark	5.58	5.50	6.16	5.83	5.88	5.65	7.08	5.91	5.49	6.30	5.65	5.46	5.96	5.34	9.00
Euro area[2]	1.34	1.35	1.21	1.28	1.27	1.32	1.05	1.26	1.36	1.18	1.32	1.25	1.37	1.37	0.83
Hong Kong SAR	7.81	7.82	7.76	7.77	7.79	7.78	7.80	7.76	7.77	7.75	7.78	7.77	7.82	7.70	7.82
Japan	117.83	123.18	117.78	114.42	118.18	119.07	118.79	107.22	102.63	117.75	119.07	114.90	123.90	80.63	159.90
New Zealand[2]	0.71	0.77	0.62	0.61	0.65	0.70	0.52	0.66	0.72	0.68	0.70	0.65	0.77	0.77	0.39
Norway	6.08	5.89	6.55	6.22	6.53	6.24	6.94	6.67	6.08	6.74	6.24	5.89	6.78	5.51	9.58
Singapore	1.52	1.53	1.62	1.58	1.59	1.53	1.73	1.70	1.63	1.66	1.53	1.51	1.59	1.39	1.91
Sweden	6.98	6.83	7.80	7.20	7.33	6.85	8.69	7.19	6.66	7.94	6.85	6.69	7.41	5.09	11.03
Switzerland	1.22	1.22	1.30	1.22	1.25	1.22	1.38	1.24	1.14	1.31	1.22	1.19	1.27	1.12	1.82
United Kingdom[2]	1.97	2.01	1.74	1.85	1.87	1.96	1.61	1.79	1.92	1.72	1.96	1.85	2.01	2.01	1.37

Table 11 *(concluded)*

	2007 End of period		2006 End of period				End of period				
	Q1	Q2	Q1	Q2	Q3	Q4	2002	2003	2004	2005	2006
Emerging Markets											
Latin America											
Argentina	−1.2	0.3	−1.7	−0.1	−0.6	1.4	−70.2	14.7	−1.4	−1.9	−1.0
Brazil	3.7	6.7	7.9	0.0	−0.2	1.6	−34.7	22.4	8.9	13.7	9.4
Chile	−1.1	2.2	−2.7	−2.3	0.7	0.3	−8.2	21.5	6.7	8.5	−4.0
Colombia	1.7	11.5	−0.2	−11.0	7.4	7.0	−20.6	3.1	18.1	3.0	2.1
Mexico	−2.0	2.2	−2.2	−4.1	3.2	1.5	−11.7	−7.6	0.7	4.8	−1.7
Peru	0.4	0.5	1.5	3.3	0.4	1.7	−2.0	1.5	5.6	−4.1	7.1
Venezuela	0.0	0.0	0.0	0.0	0.0	0.0	−45.5	−13.1	−16.7	−10.7	0.0
Asia											
China	1.0	1.5	0.7	0.3	1.1	1.3	0.0	0.0	0.0	2.6	3.4
India	1.8	6.8	1.0	−3.1	0.3	3.8	0.6	5.2	5.0	−3.5	1.8
Indonesia	−1.4	1.1	8.4	−2.1	0.4	2.5	16.2	6.3	−9.2	−5.7	9.3
Korea	−1.1	1.8	3.9	2.4	0.2	1.8	10.8	−0.5	15.2	2.5	8.6
Malaysia	2.0	0.1	2.6	0.2	−0.4	4.5	0.0	0.0	0.0	0.5	7.1
Pakistan	0.2	0.4	−0.5	−0.1	−0.6	−0.5	2.8	1.7	−3.7	−0.6	−1.8
Philippines	1.5	4.5	4.0	−3.9	5.7	2.5	−3.7	−3.5	−1.2	5.9	8.3
Taiwan Province of China	−1.4	0.6	1.1	0.2	−2.2	1.6	0.9	2.0	7.0	−3.3	0.7
Thailand	9.4	2.2	5.5	2.0	1.5	6.0	2.6	8.8	1.8	−5.1	15.7
Europe, Middle East, & Africa											
Czech Republic	−0.7	−1.3	4.5	5.5	−0.2	7.2	18.4	16.9	14.7	−8.7	17.9
Egypt	0.3	0.1	−0.2	−0.1	0.3	0.5	−0.9	−25.1	1.3	6.1	0.5
Hungary	2.5	1.9	−2.3	−1.6	2.8	13.1	22.4	7.6	15.3	−15.0	11.9
Israel	1.4	−2.2	−1.2	5.3	2.9	2.1	−7.3	8.0	1.6	−6.1	9.2
Jordan	0.0	0.1	0.0	0.0	0.0	−0.1	−0.1	0.1	0.0	0.1	−0.1
Morocco	2.7	7.5	4.0	1.3	−0.7	−2.5	−1.9	−2.7	−9.2	−7.1	2.0
Poland	0.3	4.0	0.3	1.8	1.5	7.9	3.5	2.6	24.0	−7.2	11.8
Russia	1.3	1.0	3.7	3.2	0.2	1.8	−4.5	9.3	5.5	−3.6	9.2
South Africa	−3.4	3.0	2.5	−13.9	−7.7	10.9	39.6	28.2	18.0	−10.5	−9.7
Turkey	2.0	5.8	0.2	−15.0	4.9	6.7	−12.4	17.7	4.7	−0.6	−4.7
Developed Markets											
Australia	2.5	5.0	−2.2	3.6	0.5	5.7	10.2	33.9	3.8	−6.1	7.6
Canada	1.0	8.3	−0.6	4.7	−0.2	−4.1	1.3	21.2	7.9	3.4	−0.3
Denmark	1.3	1.5	2.3	5.6	−0.9	4.1	17.9	19.8	7.8	−12.9	11.5
Euro area	1.2	1.4	2.3	5.5	−0.9	4.1	18.0	20.0	7.6	−12.6	11.4
Hong Kong SAR	−0.5	−0.1	−0.1	−0.1	−0.3	0.2	0.0	0.4	−0.1	0.2	−0.3
Japan	1.1	−4.3	0.0	2.9	−3.2	−0.7	10.8	10.8	4.5	−12.8	−1.1
New Zealand	1.5	8.1	−9.9	−1.2	7.3	7.8	25.9	25.0	9.5	−4.8	3.0
Norway	2.5	3.2	2.9	5.3	−4.8	4.8	29.2	4.1	9.6	−9.8	8.1
Singapore	1.1	−0.9	2.9	2.1	−0.3	3.5	6.4	2.1	4.2	−1.9	8.4
Sweden	−1.9	2.2	1.8	8.3	−1.9	7.1	20.6	20.9	8.0	−16.2	15.9
Switzerland	0.3	−0.5	0.7	6.6	−2.2	2.6	20.0	11.7	8.7	−13.2	7.7
United Kingdom	0.5	2.1	0.8	6.4	1.3	4.6	10.7	10.9	7.4	−10.2	13.7

Source: Bloomberg L.P.

[1]High value indicates value of greatest appreciation against the U.S. dollar; low value indicates value of greatest depreciation against the U.S. dollar. "All-Time" refers to the period since 1990 or initiation of the currency.

[2]U.S. dollars per unit.

Table 12. Emerging Market Bond Index: EMBI Global Total Returns Index

	2007 End of Period		2006 End of Period				End of Period					12-Month High	12-Month Low	All-Time High	All-Time Low
	Q1	Q2	Q1	Q2	Q3	Q4	2002	2003	2004	2005	2006				
EMBI Global	**394**	**388**	**355**	**348**	**370**	**384**	**225**	**283**	**316**	**350**	**384**	**398**	**348**	**398**	**63**
Latin America															
Argentina	130	108	98	92	106	126	57	67	81	83	126	131	91	194	47
Brazil	603	598	522	516	555	580	230	390	446	505	580	617	515	617	68
Chile	188	187	176	175	182	185	150	162	172	177	185	190	175	190	98
Colombia	291	296	264	252	271	283	169	201	228	256	283	299	252	299	70
Dominican Republic	189	191	164	162	176	184	117	99	126	156	184	195	162	195	83
Ecuador	696	668	702	687	681	561	230	464	562	636	561	750	522	750	61
El Salvador	156	157	137	134	145	152	98	110	123	134	152	...	...	...	...
Mexico	359	358	327	322	343	353	254	284	308	333	353	366	324	366	58
Panama	648	650	583	558	610	637	395	452	511	567	637	664	559	664	56
Peru	603	599	519	528	565	591	341	431	485	514	591	616	527	616	52
Uruguay	181	182	156	146	162	177	62	97	129	151	177	188	146	188	38
Venezuela	635	570	595	571	602	634	281	393	484	562	634	638	570	638	59
Asia															
China	276	274	256	256	267	271	230	241	253	260	271	278	255	278	98
Indonesia	155	154	136	136	146	154	...	...	121	133	154	158	135	158	98
Malaysia	227	226	211	209	219	224	175	194	207	215	224	229	208	229	64
Philippines	398	397	349	342	368	394	230	261	280	337	394	406	342	406	81
Vietnam	113	111	102	100	106	112	...	...	...	101	112	114	99	114	98
Europe, Middle East, & Africa															
Bulgaria	688	682	635	622	662	676	525	578	630	643	676	697	622	697	80
Côte d'Ivoire	99	127	95	95	90	84	43	58	65	79	84	135	84	135	29
Egypt	164	165	152	151	157	161	122	140	150	155	161	165	151	165	87
Hungary	156	154	144	142	150	153	137	142	144	148	153	157	142	157	97
Iraq	105	101	100	101	102	102	...	...	...	...	102	106	98	106	98
Lebanon	225	226	217	218	216	215	148	177	195	212	215	226	202	226	99
Morocco	...	...	288	292	296	299	237	262	268	285	299	299	293	299	73
Nigeria	778	778	731	739	758	760	376	586	656	727	760	787	736	787	66
Pakistan	124	124	113	110	117	123	160	160	107	112	123	125	110	160	91
Poland	346	342	321	319	335	340	280	290	312	327	340	348	318	348	71
Russia	577	569	531	523	554	568	348	426	475	538	568	582	522	582	26
Serbia[1]	120	121	110	102	110	117	...	...	...	108	117	122	102	122	99
South Africa	359	357	334	327	344	349	271	297	323	337	349	363	327	363	99
Tunisia	152	152	141	139	147	149	112	127	138	143	149	154	139	154	98
Turkey	363	367	339	314	340	356	213	279	307	336	356	371	316	371	91
Ukraine	364	365	330	325	342	353	241	289	310	334	353	369	324	369	100
Latin America	**364**	**356**	**324**	**318**	**340**	**354**	**189**	**252**	**285**	**316**	**354**	**369**	**318**	**369**	**62**
Non-Latin America	**451**	**450**	**414**	**404**	**428**	**443**	**291**	**342**	**374**	**413**	**443**	**456**	**404**	**456**	**72**

Table 12 *(concluded)*

| | Period on Period Percent Change | | | | | | | | | | |
| | 2007 End of period | | 2006 End of period | | | | End of period | | | | |
	Q1	Q2	Q1	Q2	Q3	Q4	2002	2003	2004	2005	2006
EMBI Global	**2.4**	**−1.4**	**1.5**	**−2.1**	**6.6**	**3.8**	**13.1**	**25.7**	**11.7**	**10.7**	**9.9**
Latin America											
Argentina	3.7	−17.0	17.9	−6.0	14.8	19.0	−6.4	19.1	19.8	2.7	51.3
Brazil	4.0	−0.9	3.4	−1.2	7.6	4.4	−3.6	69.8	14.3	13.2	14.8
Chile	1.8	−0.6	−0.9	−0.4	3.9	1.5	15.8	8.3	6.0	3.2	4.1
Colombia	2.5	1.7	3.1	−4.3	7.2	4.7	13.3	19.4	13.2	12.4	10.7
Dominican Republic	2.6	1.3	5.3	−1.3	8.6	4.6	13.9	−15.3	27.2	24.1	18.0
Ecuador	24.1	−4.1	10.4	−2.2	−0.9	−17.6	−4.7	101.5	21.1	13.2	−11.8
El Salvador	2.3	0.8	2.9	−2.8	8.7	5.0	. . .	11.9	11.5	8.8	14.1
Mexico	1.9	−0.4	−1.7	−1.4	6.4	2.8	16.1	11.6	8.6	8.1	6.0
Panama	1.7	0.4	2.8	−4.3	9.3	4.4	11.9	14.4	13.0	11.1	12.3
Peru	2.0	−0.5	0.9	1.8	7.0	4.5	10.8	26.6	12.6	6.0	14.8
Uruguay	2.3	0.9	3.8	−6.7	11.2	8.8	−40.6	55.6	34.0	16.3	17.3
Venezuela	0.3	−10.4	5.9	−3.9	5.3	5.3	18.9	39.9	23.2	16.1	12.8
Asia											
China	1.8	−0.5	−1.5	−0.1	4.2	1.6	13.6	4.5	5.1	3.0	4.1
Indonesia	0.8	−0.8	2.0	0.1	7.4	5.7	. . .	. . .	. . .	9.7	15.9
Malaysia	1.5	−0.5	−1.8	−0.8	4.9	2.1	16.9	10.7	6.6	3.7	4.3
Philippines	1.1	−0.2	3.4	−1.9	7.6	7.0	14.6	13.4	7.1	20.6	16.8
Vietnam	0.7	−1.6	0.8	−2.2	6.7	5.0	. . .	. . .	. . .	. . .	10.6
Europe, Middle East, & Africa											
Bulgaria	1.8	−0.9	−1.3	−1.9	6.3	2.1	12.2	10.2	8.9	2.1	5.1
Côte d'Ivoire	17.8	28.3	21.4	0.0	−5.9	−6.3	−20.7	34.8	12.9	20.0	7.1
Egypt	1.9	0.5	−1.9	−0.7	3.8	2.7	18.5	14.4	6.8	3.8	3.8
Hungary	1.7	−1.4	−2.7	−1.2	5.6	2.2	12.3	3.7	1.2	2.8	3.7
Iraq	2.6	−3.8	. . .	1.0	0.6	0.7	. . .	. . .	. . .	. . .	. . .
Lebanon	4.8	0.2	2.6	0.4	−0.9	−0.5	14.1	19.5	9.9	8.7	1.6
Morocco	. . .	. . .	1.1	1.3	1.5	1.0	7.2	10.2	2.4	6.3	5.0
Nigeria	2.4	0.0	0.5	1.2	2.5	0.3	3.3	55.8	11.9	10.7	4.6
Pakistan	0.7	−0.1	1.7	−2.7	6.0	5.2	31.3	−0.2	−33.3	4.5	10.3
Poland	1.8	−1.1	−1.9	−0.7	5.0	1.5	14.2	3.7	7.5	5.0	3.8
Russia	1.6	−1.4	−1.3	−1.5	5.9	2.5	35.9	22.4	11.5	13.3	5.5
Serbia[1]	2.6	1.2	2.2	−7.0	7.7	5.9	. . .	. . .	. . .	. . .	8.3
South Africa	2.6	−0.6	−1.0	−1.8	5.1	1.5	22.9	9.6	8.8	4.3	3.7
Tunisia	2.5	−0.1	−1.7	−1.1	5.3	1.4	. . .	13.3	8.7	3.7	3.8
Turkey	2.0	1.1	1.1	−7.4	8.2	4.7	21.1	30.8	10.0	9.5	6.1
Ukraine	2.9	0.3	−0.9	−1.8	5.2	3.5	21.0	19.8	7.2	7.7	5.9
Latin America	**2.9**	**−2.3**	**2.5**	**−2.0**	**7.0**	**4.2**	**6.8**	**33.0**	**13.4**	**10.9**	**11.9**
Non-Latin America	**1.8**	**−0.4**	**0.1**	**−2.3**	**5.9**	**3.4**	**21.0**	**17.7**	**9.2**	**10.6**	**7.2**

Source: JPMorgan Chase & Co.
[1]Data prior to 2006 refer to Serbia and Montenegro.

Table 13. Emerging Market Bond Index: EMBI Global Yield Spreads

(In basis points)

	2007 End of Period		2007 End of Period				End of Period					12-Month High	12-Month Low	All-Time High	All-Time Low
	Q1	Q2	Q1	Q2	Q3	Q4	2002	2003	2004	2005	2006				
EMBI Global	**170**	**181**	**191**	**218**	**208**	**171**	**725**	**403**	**347**	**237**	**171**	**217**	**151**	**1,631**	**151**
Latin America															
Argentina	204	325	344	385	342	216	6,342	5,485	4,527	504	216	385	185	7,222	185
Brazil	167	160	232	252	232	190	1,460	459	376	308	190	253	138	2,451	138
Chile	85	83	73	83	85	84	176	90	64	80	84	90	77	260	52
Colombia	157	119	174	239	202	161	633	427	332	244	161	251	95	1,076	95
Dominican Republic	189	157	278	299	250	196	499	1,141	824	378	196	299	122	1,750	122
Ecuador	650	711	503	506	608	920	1,801	799	690	661	920	1,048	458	4,764	436
El Salvador	156	127	171	217	201	159	411	284	245	239	159	225	99	434	99
Mexico	116	111	140	154	141	115	329	201	174	143	115	145	89	1,149	89
Panama	152	130	176	212	187	146	446	324	274	239	146	211	114	769	114
Peru	129	117	226	202	169	118	609	325	239	257	118	206	95	1,061	95
Uruguay	184	157	223	307	254	185	1,228	636	388	298	185	306	133	1,982	133
Venezuela	207	354	190	226	233	183	1,131	586	403	313	183	354	181	2,658	161
Asia															
China	53	54	68	65	67	51	84	58	57	68	51	67	48	364	39
Indonesia	171	165	213	220	205	153	. . .	. . .	244	269	153	232	136	433	136
Malaysia	73	75	86	97	89	66	212	100	78	82	66	99	65	1,141	65
Philippines	167	155	233	259	232	155	522	415	457	302	155	263	132	993	132
Vietnam	108	122	149	175	155	95	. . .	. . .	. . .	190	95	182	89	197	89
Europe, Middle East, & Africa															
Bulgaria	67	68	83	105	87	66	291	177	77	90	66	101	42	1,679	42
Côte d'Ivoire	3,050	2,483	2,568	2,713	2,895	3,325	3,195	3,013	3,121	3,070	3,325	3,426	2,292	3,609	582
Egypt	53	51	80	103	101	52	325	131	101	58	52	123	34	646	20
Hungary	63	71	75	90	79	58	52	28	32	74	58	88	55	196	−29
Iraq	537	570	465	444	514	526	. . .	. . .	. . .	. . .	526	575	433	575	376
Lebanon	364	371	172	189	366	395	776	421	334	246	395	419	182	1,082	111
Morocco	. . .	. . .	87	54	90	72	390	160	170	75	72	92	48	1,606	48
Nigeria	16	37	259	253	325	66	1,946	499	457	329	66	377	9	2,937	9
Pakistan	181	214	144	251	240	154	271	0	233	198	154	265	133	2,225	0
Poland	53	61	64	69	61	47	185	76	69	62	47	77	42	410	17
Russia	102	106	105	123	115	99	478	257	213	118	99	125	87	7,063	87
Serbia[1]	183	152	181	266	246	186	. . .	. . .	. . .	238	186	285	134	322	134
South Africa	73	87	85	123	99	84	250	152	102	87	84	120	50	757	50
Tunisia	79	73	92	121	90	83	273	146	91	81	83	122	55	394	48
Turkey	216	189	182	294	256	207	696	309	264	223	207	292	175	1,196	168
Ukraine	164	156	198	257	218	172	671	258	255	184	172	257	125	2,314	125
Latin America	**173**	**196**	**208**	**231**	**218**	**180**	**981**	**518**	**415**	**272**	**180**	**232**	**157**	**1,532**	**157**
Non-Latin America	**166**	**160**	**164**	**198**	**193**	**159**	**444**	**248**	**239**	**179**	**159**	**202**	**142**	**1,812**	**142**

Table 13 *(concluded)*

	2007 End of period		2006 End of period				End of period				
	Q1	Q2	Q1	Q2	Q3	Q4	2002	2003	2004	2005	2006
EMBI Global	**−1**	**11**	**−46**	**27**	**−10**	**−37**	**−3**	**−322**	**−56**	**−110**	**−66**
Latin America											
Argentina	−12	121	−160	41	−43	−126	979	−857	−958	−4,023	−288
Brazil	−23	−7	−76	20	−20	−42	596	−1,001	−83	−68	−118
Chile	1	−2	−7	10	2	−1	1	−86	−26	16	4
Colombia	−4	−38	−70	65	−37	−41	125	−206	−95	−88	−83
Dominican Republic	−7	−32	−100	21	−49	−54	53	642	−317	−446	−182
Ecuador	−270	61	−158	3	102	312	568	−1,002	−109	−29	259
El Salvador	−3	−29	−68	46	−16	−42	. . .	−127	−39	−6	−80
Mexico	1	−5	−3	14	−13	−26	23	−128	−27	−31	−28
Panama	6	−22	−63	36	−25	−41	42	−122	−50	−35	−93
Peru	11	−12	−31	−24	−33	−51	88	−284	−86	18	−139
Uruguay	−1	−27	−75	84	−53	−69	944	−592	−248	−90	−113
Venezuela	24	147	−123	36	7	−50	1	−545	−183	−90	−130
Asia											
China	2	1	0	−3	2	−16	−15	−26	−1	11	−17
Indonesia	18	−6	−56	7	−15	−52	. . .	. . .	. . .	25	−116
Malaysia	7	2	4	11	−8	−23	5	−112	−22	4	−16
Philippines	12	−12	−69	26	−27	−77	56	−107	42	−155	−147
Vietnam	13	14	−41	26	−20	−60	. . .	. . .	. . .	. . .	−95
Europe, Middle East, & Africa											
Bulgaria	1	1	−7	22	−18	−21	−142	−114	−100	13	−24
Côte d'Ivoire	−275	−567	−502	145	182	430	777	−182	108	−51	255
Egypt	1	−2	22	23	−2	−49	−35	−194	−30	−43	−6
Hungary	5	8	1	15	−11	−21	−41	−24	4	42	−16
Iraq	11	33	. . .	−21	70	12	. . .	. . .	. . .	. . .	. . .
Lebanon	−31	7	−74	17	177	29	131	−355	−87	−88	149
Morocco	. . .	. . .	12	−33	36	−18	−128	−230	10	−95	−3
Nigeria	−50	21	−70	−6	72	−259	843	−1,447	−42	−128	−263
Pakistan	27	33	−54	107	−11	−86	−844	−271	233	−35	−44
Poland	6	8	2	5	−8	−14	−10	−109	−7	−7	−15
Russia	3	4	−13	18	−8	−16	−191	−221	−44	−95	−19
Serbia[1]	−3	−31	−57	85	−20	−60	. . .	. . .	. . .	. . .	−52
South Africa	−11	14	−2	38	−24	−15	−69	−98	−50	−15	−3
Tunisia	−4	−6	11	29	−31	−7	. . .	−127	−55	−10	2
Turkey	9	−27	−41	112	−38	−49	−6	−387	−45	−41	−16
Ukraine	−8	−8	14	59	−39	−46	−269	−413	−3	−71	−12
Latin America	**−7**	**23**	**−64**	**23**	**−13**	**−38**	**93**	**−463**	**−103**	**−143**	**−92**
Non-Latin America	**7**	**−6**	**−15**	**34**	**−5**	**−34**	**−79**	**−196**	**−9**	**−60**	**−20**

Source: JPMorgan Chase & Co.
[1]Data prior to 2006 refer to Serbia and Montenegro.

Table 14. Emerging Market External Financing: Total Bonds, Equities, and Loans
(In millions of U.S. dollars)

	2001	2002	2003	2004	2005	2006	2006 Q3	2006 Q4	2007 Q1	2007 Q2
Total	**147,523.6**	**133,509.0**	**195,504.1**	**176,759.6**	**101,699.0**	**112,726.4**	**103,463.9**	**183,063.7**	**134,546.1**	**175,558.4**
Africa	**1,025.3**	**1,833.2**	**10,662.6**	**11,101.2**	**11,601.3**	**13,052.1**	**1,879.3**	**1,827.2**	**1,947.4**	**1,025.0**
Algeria	10.0	150.0	10.0	171.7	112.7	1.0	1.0	—	—	—
Angola	155.0	150.0	1,522.0	1,900.0	1,122.7	18.0	12.1	—	14.6	—
Botswana	12.5	—	—	—	—	—	—	—	—	—
Burkina Faso	—	—	—	—	11.0	—	—	—	14.5	—
Cameroon	13.8	—	100.0	—	—	—	—	—	—	—
Chad	100.0	—	—	—	—	—	—	—	—	—
Côte d'Ivoire	15.0	—	—	100.0	—	—	—	—	—	—
Djibouti	—	—	—	10.0	—	—	—	—	—	—
Ethiopia	—	—	—	10.0	—	—	—	—	—	—
Gabon	—	—	—	12.0	—	14.3	—	—	—	—
Ghana	191.0	120.0	150.0	170.0	162.5	160.0	110.0	—	—	150.0
Guinea	—	—	—	10.0	—	—	—	—	—	—
Kenya	10.2	—	134.0	—	13.5	10.6	—	13.8	—	—
Malawi	—	—	—	1.8	—	—	—	—	—	—
Mali	—	150.4	187.6	188.9	—	—	—	—	149.9	—
Mauritius	—	—	—	—	—	180.0	10.0	—	—	—
Morocco	136.1	—	174.7	—	—	147.6	136.0	—	16.1	170.7
Mozambique	160.0	—	15.5	—	—	—	—	—	—	—
Namibia	—	—	15.0	—	10.0	100.0	10.0	10.0	—	—
Niger	—	—	17.0	—	—	—	—	—	125.0	100.0
Nigeria	15.0	160.0	188.0	125.0	118.8	180.0	100.0	180.0	150.0	127.3
Senegal	—	10.0	—	—	—	—	—	—	—	—
Seychelles	—	150.0	—	10.0	—	—	—	—	—	—
South Africa	1,833.7	1,872.3	1,353.6	1,233.5	1,118.0	1,953.3	1,689.1	155.8	1,717.2	1,626.9
Sudan	—	—	—	11.0	—	—	—	—	—	—
Tunisia	133.0	140.5	185.2	124.4	182.1	173.5	—	—	—	150.0
Uganda	—	—	—	—	—	12.6	—	12.6	—	—
Zambia	—	—	10.0	—	—	105.0	—	105.0	—	—
Zimbabwe	—	—	—	—	—	15.1	—	—	—	—
Asia	**54,185.0**	**52,082.5**	**85,898.3**	**116,344.9**	**146,864.7**	**195,709.4**	**14,610.2**	**17,714.3**	**10,827.0**	**13,227.0**
Bangladesh	—	—	—	176.8	—	12.6	—	—	—	—
Brunei Darussalam	—	129.0	—	—	—	—	—	—	—	—
China	1,254.8	1,256.1	12,842.9	12,634.6	14,632.2	11,771.5	1,745.3	15,486.1	1,305.5	10,090.0
Hong Kong SAR	1,406.4	1,591.9	1,693.4	13,041.2	14,569.5	18,040.2	1,175.7	1,208.4	1,057.1	1,403.0
India	1,340.4	1,443.3	1,775.7	14,447.4	10,229.5	12,492.8	1,105.5	17,082.5	1,659.0	16,066.2
Indonesia	171.9	118.0	1,198.2	1,636.1	1,255.2	1,014.4	195.8	1,995.2	1,108.0	1,388.2
Korea	16,181.2	15,909.3	17,244.1	13,916.0	14,985.6	17,920.9	1,499.1	1,663.1	1,855.1	14,021.1
Lao P.D.R.	—	—	—	110.0	100.0	—	—	—	—	—
Macao SAR	—	—	—	157.0	—	1,980.3	1,180.3	—	1,600.0	—
Malaysia	1,628.3	1,142.1	1,550.1	1,300.9	1,547.9	1,964.5	1,825.5	1,182.7	1,559.2	1,965.0
Marshall Islands	—	14.7	—	—	14.0	170.0	—	—	104.2	—
Mongolia	—	—	—	—	10.0	1.0	1.0	—	—	—
Pakistan	182.5	15.0	—	100.0	191.8	1,251.5	10.0	1,211.7	—	1,472.4
Papua New Guinea	—	—	153.7	—	—	—	—	—	—	—
Philippines	1,263.8	1,384.9	1,727.3	1,897.3	1,681.6	1,185.2	1,698.4	1,960.2	1,039.1	141.8
Singapore	1,503.4	1,976.2	1,816.4	1,907.7	1,693.9	15,192.0	1,471.8	1,609.2	1,024.1	1,515.0
Sri Lanka	105.0	—	186.0	135.0	167.0	129.7	10.0	100.0	—	110.0
Taiwan Province of China	1,662.8	1,198.4	18,337.1	12,986.3	11,221.6	1,385.7	1,077.9	1,581.8	1,029.6	1,990.3
Thailand	184.4	130.1	1,322.4	1,784.6	1,520.8	1,397.3	115.5	1,299.2	—	141.2
Vietnam	—	183.5	11.0	114.0	1,014.0	174.7	13.2	134.2	186.1	123.0
Europe	**11,727.4**	**10,040.0**	**16,459.3**	**12,517.6**	**101,489.8**	**148,721.5**	**17,906.7**	**12,881.4**	**12,533.7**	**11,736.0**
Armenia	—	—	—	—	—	—	—	—	—	19.1
Azerbaijan	16.0	—	—	1,005.0	183.7	1,917.0	1.0	1,130.0	—	164.0
Belarus	—	—	14.0	—	12.0	136.0	123.8	119.3	17.0	15.0
Bulgaria	130.4	1,260.8	122.5	118.1	173.7	1,587.5	188.8	148.2	19.2	135.3
Croatia	1,724.2	1,384.1	1,944.4	1,196.9	137.2	1,268.2	175.6	192.6	—	137.7
Cyprus	133.0	147.9	148.2	1,174.0	1,453.8	1,848.8	1,400.5	128.9	18.0	1,329.1
Czech Republic	185.1	153.4	1,518.8	1,904.1	1,169.5	1,448.4	198.6	1,044.8	119.7	198.0
Estonia	102.1	133.9	157.3	1,187.7	193.5	149.4	—	—	—	123.9

Table 14 *(concluded)*

	2001	2002	2003	2004	2005	2006	2006 Q3	2006 Q4	2007 Q1	2007 Q2
Europe *(continued)*										
Faroe Islands	—	—	—	—	85.3	206.2	—	206.2	206.1	—
Georgia	—	—	6.0	—	—	7.0	7.0	—	—	—
Gibraltar	1,319.6	—	—	—	2,168.9	2,371.7	—	—	94.1	—
Hungary	1,347.2	1,040.2	3,870.4	8,134.5	8,687.5	7,685.9	1,072.6	2,031.9	2,676.7	1,135.6
Kazakhstan	573.5	1,043.5	2,200.0	5,093.2	5,457.9	16,094.7	3,741.9	8,098.3	5,480.4	5,025.3
Kyrgyz Republic	—	95.0	—	—	—	—	—	—	—	—
Latvia	212.1	74.6	70.7	889.3	391.3	1,449.3	656.5	246.8	111.7	897.0
Lithuania	247.3	374.3	431.7	888.2	1,222.0	1,292.1	—	806.6	—	277.2
Macedonia, FYR	—	—	—	17.4	—	—	—	—	—	—
Malta	85.0	—	114.7	392.7	—	256.0	196.0	—	—	—
Moldova	—	—	—	—	1.0	—	—	—	—	—
Poland	3,135.1	5,941.2	8,550.3	4,909.3	14,949.6	7,321.0	327.6	2,903.8	2,847.8	2,259.7
Romania	1,347.2	1,442.2	1,738.8	659.0	2,229.8	665.3	153.0	305.4	193.3	146.2
Russia	2,831.2	8,534.5	12,238.8	22,532.1	37,062.1	63,387.3	21,306.4	20,097.0	21,023.8	25,915.9
Serbia[1]	—	19.4	—	—	—	—	—	—	—	—
Slovak Republic	219.9	143.1	940.6	1,315.7	579.3	1,217.1	—	—	—	1,352.5
Slovenia	827.2	309.3	394.8	1,430.8	1,881.5	1,828.5	—	488.1	2,604.3	431.4
Turkey	6,271.3	6,482.5	9,549.5	14,534.5	17,798.4	25,889.4	6,308.2	6,417.9	5,605.2	5,328.1
Ukraine	15.0	514.0	1,400.0	2,434.9	3,031.8	5,189.7	1,249.2	3,311.0	1,366.4	2,724.9
Uzbekistan	5.0	46.0	37.8	—	—	4.9	—	4.9	—	—
Middle East	**11,247.3**	**10,943.0**	**8,954.3**	**23,253.4**	**56,601.2**	**86,172.8**	**12,350.7**	**29,207.5**	**12,313.2**	**22,010.1**
Bahrain	202.0	922.6	2,326.6	1,767.0	3,070.9	4,487.1	670.0	1,703.0	—	5,106.8
Egypt	2,500.0	670.0	155.0	1,138.7	3,395.1	3,323.2	200.0	87.5	1,691.5	—
Iran, I.R. of	887.0	2,666.4	700.0	1,942.7	1,928.8	134.8	17.7	—	—	—
Iraq	—	—	—	—	107.8	2,877.0	—	—	—	—
Israel	1,897.6	344.4	766.6	3,514.0	3,986.4	4,331.6	339.1	2,134.8	2,073.0	369.3
Jordan	—	80.9	—	199.4	—	60.0	—	60.0	—	—
Kuwait	770.0	750.0	365.0	1,282.5	4,783.0	4,761.3	468.5	200.0	75.0	1,890.5
Lebanon	3,300.0	990.0	160.0	5,083.0	1,780.0	5,818.1	656.6	50.0	1,120.0	400.0
Oman	—	2,332.0	818.3	1,328.6	4,747.1	3,430.2	2,835.9	344.3	—	782.4
Qatar	895.0	1,536.7	880.8	2,042.7	10,418.5	11,426.4	2,242.5	4,135.4	—	650.0
Saudi Arabia	275.0	280.0	839.5	2,214.0	4,981.0	10,132.4	89.5	1,987.2	1,155.1	4,729.0
United Arab Emirates	520.7	370.0	1,942.6	2,741.0	17,402.6	35,390.7	4,830.9	18,505.3	6,198.6	8,082.1
Latin America	**54,338.8**	**33,610.3**	**43,529.5**	**53,542.4**	**85,142.1**	**69,070.6**	**15,717.0**	**21,433.3**	**32,924.8**	**19,560.4**
Argentina	5,017.9	824.2	130.0	1,882.4	22,180.6	2,814.9	325.5	970.0	458.1	3,227.8
Bolivia	10.0	90.0	—	116.0	123.0	—	—	—	—	—
Brazil	19,265.6	11,119.4	12,908.6	15,834.0	24,962.2	28,465.6	7,346.5	6,598.0	14,020.0	11,087.6
Chile	4,335.3	2,959.6	4,631.0	6,439.9	5,956.0	5,968.1	1,152.1	2,007.1	490.0	541.8
Colombia	4,974.8	2,096.0	1,911.3	1,626.8	2,780.9	4,951.6	2,300.1	2,048.4	—	1,456.8
Costa Rica	365.0	250.0	490.0	310.0	117.2	1.7	1.7	—	—	—
Cuba	—	—	—	69.8	1.9	—	—	—	—	—
Dominican Republic	531.1	258.0	650.4	140.5	244.4	762.7	112.0	305.8	458.3	175.0
Ecuador	910.0	10.0	—	—	712.5	19.1	—	19.1	—	—
El Salvador	421.5	1,745.0	381.0	467.0	454.5	1,326.6	721.6	205.0	—	—
Grenada	—	100.0	—	—	—	—	—	—	—	—
Guadeloupe	—	17.4	—	—	—	—	—	—	—	—
Guatemala	325.0	44.0	300.0	439.3	365.0	—	—	—	15.0	—
Haiti	—	—	—	—	—	126.5	—	70.0	—	—
Honduras	—	—	—	169.0	4.6	—	—	—	—	—
Jamaica	946.5	345.0	49.6	903.2	1,466.6	1,268.4	150.0	200.0	1,000.0	125.0
Mexico	12,648.0	10,040.6	16,964.3	18,832.8	16,314.4	16,432.0	1,711.9	6,623.1	5,723.7	1,715.6
Nicaragua	—	—	—	22.0	—	—	—	—	—	—
Paraguay	70.0	—	—	—	—	—	—	—	—	—
Peru	237.5	1,993.0	1,375.0	1,475.7	2,184.2	1,253.8	150.0	696.9	2,120.0	188.5
St. Lucia	—	—	20.0	—	—	—	—	—	—	—
Trinidad and Tobago	70.0	303.0	46.0	415.0	100.0	2,610.4	1,242.3	156.0	—	955.4
Uruguay	1,147.4	400.0	—	—	1,061.3	2,700.0	500.0	1,200.0	1,049.7	87.0
Venezuela	3,063.4	1,015.0	3,672.5	4,399.1	6,112.6	369.3	3.2	334.0	7,590.0	—

Source: Data provided by the Bond, Equity and Loan database of the International Monetary Fund sourced from Dealogic.
[1]Data prior to 2006 refer to Serbia and Montenegro.

Table 15. Emerging Market External Financing: Bond Issuance

(In millions of U.S. dollars)

	2001	2002	2003	2004	2005	2006	2006 Q3	2006 Q4	2007 Q1	2007 Q2
Developing Countries	**80,643.8**	**64,951.9**	**100,497.6**	**135,528.8**	**189,218.9**	**183,039.0**	**34,279.6**	**61,496.7**	**68,748.6**	**77,793.9**
Africa	**1,509.6**	**2,161.1**	**4,357.8**	**2,236.7**	**3,059.2**	**6,287.6**	**1,223.1**	**703.7**	**2,861.4**	**6,458.3**
Morocco	—	—	464.9	—	—	—	—	—	—	670.7
Niger	—	—	—	—	—	—	—	—	525.0	—
South Africa	1,047.7	1,511.1	3,535.9	1,692.2	2,568.3	6,287.6	1,223.1	703.7	2,336.4	5,787.6
Tunisia	462.0	650.0	357.0	544.5	490.9	—	—	—	—	—
Asia	**27,454.2**	**24,207.0**	**37,035.7**	**52,067.4**	**54,001.1**	**54,376.7**	**13,670.6**	**13,896.3**	**17,287.3**	**28,096.7**
China	2,341.9	340.0	2,039.2	4,888.1	3,953.9	3,107.0	745.7	1,528.5	1,230.4	3,015.7
Hong Kong SAR	3,050.3	1,923.3	2,160.6	3,725.3	6,457.9	4,979.6	225.0	1,727.0	1,898.7	4,838.2
India	374.2	153.0	450.0	5,609.1	5,647.7	6,187.5	1,169.5	1,287.0	4,155.9	3,290.0
Indonesia	137.0	275.0	609.0	1,363.5	3,217.7	2,000.0	—	1,500.0	550.0	
Korea	7,279.7	9,071.5	11,880.1	17,529.2	19,426.9	20,422.2	6,391.0	5,093.9	5,059.5	10,770.9
Malaysia	2,566.1	1,280.0	1,142.5	1,414.5	2,303.1	3,510.5	1,910.5	400.0	289.4	1,575.0
Pakistan	—	—	—	500.0	—	1,050.0	—	250.0	—	750.0
Philippines	1,842.4	4,773.8	4,449.6	4,449.1	3,900.0	4,619.0	1,654.2	750.0	1,300.0	—
Singapore	7,431.5	696.5	4,493.6	3,828.9	3,203.2	5,033.0	816.8	1,665.0	1,479.4	2,365.7
Sri Lanka	—	—	—	100.0	—	—	—	—	—	—
Taiwan Province of China	2,152.4	5,645.8	9,511.0	7,259.7	2,898.1	2,289.0	634.0	730.0	374.0	400.0
Thailand	278.6	48.0	300.0	1,400.0	2,242.6	1,179.0	124.0	465.0	—	541.2
Vietnam	—	—	—	—	750.0	—	—	—	—	—
Europe	**10,981.3**	**15,442.0**	**24,173.1**	**36,969.3**	**53,969.0**	**62,026.1**	**8,764.1**	**26,308.7**	**26,632.8**	**24,099.7**
Azerbaijan	—	—	—	—	—	4,001.0	—	4,000.0	—	—
Bulgaria	223.4	1,247.8	62.1	10.0	385.4	221.4	—	221.4	—	—
Croatia	934.0	847.5	983.6	1,651.0	—	383.5	191.8	191.7	—	337.7
Cyprus	480.5	479.8	648.2	1,174.0	1,133.1	1,701.4	500.0	—	—	2,929.1
Czech Republic	50.7	428.4	337.7	2,538.6	1,324.5	908.3	274.9	633.4	—	798.0
Estonia	65.5	292.6	323.3	964.8	427.3	—	—	—	—	—
Gibraltar	1,319.6	—	—	—	—	—	—	—	—	—
Hungary	1,247.8	70.5	2,447.5	5,751.0	7,340.3	7,537.3	1,012.5	2,031.9	2,676.7	680.5
Kazakhstan	250.0	509.0	825.0	3,225.0	2,850.0	6,800.5	1,182.5	2,065.9	5,343.5	3,375.8
Latvia	180.8	—	—	536.1	125.4	261.8	—	—	—	—
Lithuania	222.4	355.6	431.7	815.7	780.6	1,241.7	—	756.2	—	237.0
Poland	1,155.8	2,679.9	5,220.3	3,526.5	11,812.8	4,632.4	—	822.7	1,946.2	1,720.5
Romania	908.6	1,062.2	813.6	—	1,199.0	—	—	—	—	—
Russia	1,073.7	3,430.0	4,455.0	7,129.9	15,436.7	20,794.2	2,652.2	10,343.0	10,093.2	11,418.6
Slovak Republic	219.9	143.1	861.3	1,198.8	—	1,217.1	—	—	—	1,352.5
Slovenia	490.0	30.2	—	66.3	156.7	—	—	—	1,469.9	—
Turkey	2,158.7	3,366.3	5,453.8	6,066.5	8,898.6	9,210.4	2,291.7	3,232.4	3,868.4	150.0
Ukraine	—	499.0	1,310.0	2,315.0	2,098.4	3,115.1	658.5	2,010.0	1,235.0	1,100.0
Middle East	**6,285.7**	**3,964.2**	**2,706.6**	**10,855.0**	**17,907.3**	**29,009.3**	**2,946.8**	**10,780.4**	**4,854.7**	**8,912.9**
Bahrain	—	582.6	1,326.6	292.0	1,299.7	1,620.0	300.0	100.0	—	1,570.8
Egypt	1,500.0	—	—	—	1,250.0	—	—	—	750.0	—
Iran, I.R. of	—	986.3	—	—	—	—	—	—	—	—
Iraq	—	—	—	—	—	2,700.0	—	—	—	—
Israel	1,485.7	344.4	750.0	2,520.0	905.1	2,892.5	—	1,500.0	—	—
Jordan	—	80.9	—	145.0	—	—	—	—	—	—
Kuwait	—	750.0	200.0	500.0	500.0	534.7	—	—	—	100.0
Lebanon	3,300.0	990.0	160.0	5,083.0	1,780.0	5,519.7	656.6	—	1,000.0	400.0
Oman	—	—	—	250.0	—	25.0	—	25.0	—	—
Qatar	—	—	—	665.0	2,250.0	3,040.0	1,550.0	840.0	—	—
Saudi Arabia	—	—	270.0	—	1,300.0	2,913.1	58.5	1,461.2	—	—
United Arab Emirates	—	230.0	—	1,400.0	8,622.4	9,764.4	381.7	6,854.2	3,104.7	6,842.1
Latin America	**34,413.1**	**19,177.6**	**32,224.4**	**33,400.4**	**60,282.3**	**31,339.3**	**7,674.8**	**9,807.6**	**17,112.4**	**10,226.1**
Argentina	3,094.5	—	100.0	1,115.4	19,092.6	1,745.5	325.5	970.0	300.0	2,580.9
Brazil	12,053.4	6,809.5	11,718.8	9,573.2	17,683.2	12,349.7	3,824.2	3,336.3	4,189.2	3,917.8
Chile	1,936.0	1,728.9	2,900.0	2,350.0	900.0	1,100.0	200.0	500.0	250.0	—
Colombia	4,343.1	1,000.0	1,765.0	1,543.8	2,432.1	3,176.6	2,300.1	468.4	—	1,404.4
Costa Rica	250.0	250.0	490.0	310.0	—	—	—	—	—	—
Dominican Republic	500.0	—	600.0	—	196.6	550.0	—	250.0	255.0	175.0
Ecuador	—	—	—	—	650.0	—	—	—	—	—
El Salvador	353.5	1,745.0	348.5	286.5	375.0	625.0	225.0	—	—	—
Grenada	—	100.0	—	—	—	—	—	—	—	—
Guatemala	325.0	—	300.0	380.0	200.0	—	—	—	—	—
Jamaica	940.7	300.0	—	806.9	1,050.0	880.0	150.0	200.0	350.0	125.0
Mexico	8,181.7	4,914.1	9,082.1	11,369.0	8,455.7	7,109.4	150.0	2,762.8	1,894.3	1,036.0
Peru	100.0	1,930.0	1,250.0	1,305.7	2,157.1	220.0	—	120.0	2,120.0	—
Trinidad and Tobago	—	—	—	100.0	100.0	883.1	—	—	—	900.0
Uruguay	1,106.1	400.0	—	—	1,061.3	2,700.0	500.0	1,200.0	254.0	87.0
Venezuela	1,229.1	—	3,670.0	4,260.0	5,928.7	—	—	—	7,500.0	—

Source: Data provided by the Bond, Equity and Loan database of the International Monetary Fund sourced from Dealogic.

Table 16. Emerging Market External Finance: Equity Issuance

(In millions of U.S. dollars)

	2001	2002	2003	2004	2005	2006	2006 Q3	2006 Q4	2007 Q1	2007 Q2
Developing Countries	**10,743.1**	**16,474.3**	**27,625.7**	**45,528.2**	**78,223.7**	**120,731.6**	**20,684.1**	**47,493.5**	**26,100.9**	**53,516.8**
Africa	**6.8**	**159.7**	**720.2**	**1,855.7**	**924.7**	**2,369.7**	**135.4**	**52.1**	**1,507.0**	**550.3**
Algeria	—	—	—	—	—	2.0	2.0	—	—	—
Côte d'Ivoire	—	—	—	100.0	—	—	—	—	—	—
Morocco	6.8	—	—	—	—	133.3	133.3	—	16.1	—
Niger	—	—	—	—	—	—	—	—	—	100.0
South Africa	—	159.7	720.2	1,724.7	924.7	2,159.2	—	52.1	1,490.8	450.3
Sudan	—	—	—	31.0	—	—	—	—	—	—
Zimbabwe	—	—	—	—	—	75.1	—	—	—	—
Asia	**9,127.5**	**12,637.9**	**24,252.5**	**35,458.6**	**58,264.5**	**78,012.8**	**6,537.3**	**34,381.9**	**10,838.9**	**29,177.8**
China	1,570.0	2,475.0	6,415.7	14,191.1	25,721.9	41,809.1	2,282.9	23,419.2	3,798.9	13,842.3
Hong Kong SAR	1,638.0	2,880.6	2,962.2	5,238.8	4,675.3	8,643.4	1,367.3	3,462.0	1,681.4	1,409.3
India	467.2	348.1	1,299.7	4,347.1	6,708.4	8,287.9	286.9	4,081.9	1,863.1	6,677.1
Indonesia	347.2	281.0	1,096.7	535.2	1,283.5	665.9	204.3	409.7	—	380.8
Korea	3,676.4	1,553.7	1,222.6	3,223.3	7,814.9	7,329.8	97.6	69.0	1,246.0	1,471.8
Macao SAR	—	—	—	—	—	0.3	0.3	—	—	—
Malaysia	15.4	888.4	618.2	887.2	735.2	217.3	197.5	19.7	489.2	—
Pakistan	—	—	—	—	—	922.2	—	922.2	—	565.4
Papua New Guinea	—	—	153.7	—	—	—	—	—	—	—
Philippines	—	—	—	114.9	535.8	756.0	—	444.2	248.7	191.8
Singapore	61.4	940.9	1,168.7	2,472.7	2,651.5	3,646.6	637.6	538.9	822.4	1,264.1
Sri Lanka	—	—	—	—	55.5	—	—	—	—	—
Taiwan Province of China	1,126.6	3,213.9	8,276.3	3,350.0	7,602.6	3,644.5	1,374.4	791.8	218.6	3,375.3
Thailand	225.3	56.3	1,038.7	1,098.4	479.7	1,772.4	88.5	223.3	—	—
Vietnam	—	—	—	—	—	317.3	—	—	470.7	—
Europe	**259.4**	**1,681.7**	**1,809.0**	**5,287.3**	**10,276.1**	**24,595.1**	**12,455.9**	**8,166.8**	**6,494.0**	**15,096.9**
Croatia	22.3	—	—	—	—	220.0	—	220.0	—	—
Cyprus	—	—	—	—	320.7	1,181.7	107.7	840.9	—	1,400.0
Czech Republic	—	—	824.6	174.4	295.1	287.3	—	287.3	—	—
Estonia	—	41.3	—	—	266.2	—	—	—	—	123.9
Gibraltar	—	—	—	—	2,168.9	437.5	—	—	94.1	—
Hungary	—	—	13.2	884.7	—	—	—	—	—	—
Kazakhstan	—	—	—	—	—	3,953.8	2,255.4	1,698.4	120.0	50.0
Latvia	—	22.7	—	—	—	—	—	—	—	—
Lithuania	—	—	—	—	51.2	—	—	—	—	—
Poland	—	245.4	602.6	841.4	944.0	712.6	108.0	532.7	240.0	—
Romania	—	—	—	—	—	172.5	—	172.5	—	—
Russia	237.1	1,301.0	368.7	2,480.1	6,210.0	17,598.5	9,959.5	4,409.1	5,821.1	11,735.8
Turkey	—	71.4	—	906.5	—	6.0	—	6.0	218.8	1,682.3
Ukraine	—	—	—	—	19.9	25.3	25.3	—	—	104.9
Middle East	**86.8**	**—**	**16.6**	**868.5**	**2,963.3**	**3,365.6**	**31.5**	**399.5**	**2,147.1**	**451.3**
Bahrain	—	—	—	—	81.2	581.8	—	—	—	—
Egypt	—	—	—	141.0	678.2	257.8	—	—	—	—
Israel	86.8	—	16.6	624.0	1,157.5	342.3	—	159.8	2,073.0	201.3
Jordan	—	—	—	—	—	—	—	—	—	—
Lebanon	—	—	—	—	—	248.4	—	—	—	—
Oman	—	—	—	23.6	148.4	—	—	—	—	—
Qatar	—	—	—	—	—	1,133.2	—	—	—	—
Saudi Arabia	—	—	—	80.0	—	457.7	—	—	74.1	250.0
United Arab Emirates	—	—	—	—	898.0	344.3	31.5	239.6	—	—
Latin America	**1,262.5**	**1,995.0**	**827.4**	**2,058.2**	**5,795.2**	**12,388.3**	**1,524.0**	**4,493.3**	**5,113.9**	**8,240.5**
Argentina	34.4	—	—	—	—	769.4	—	—	158.1	306.9
Brazil	1,228.1	1,148.5	287.4	1,651.0	3,433.1	9,142.7	1,524.0	3,023.3	4,830.8	6,916.4
Chile	—	—	—	266.4	522.7	677.1	—	677.1	—	126.8
Colombia	—	—	—	—	—	—	—	—	—	52.4
Dominican Republic	—	—	—	—	—	—	—	—	—	—
Mexico	—	846.6	540.0	140.8	1,839.3	1,222.3	—	216.1	125.0	649.6
Peru	—	—	—	—	—	576.9	—	576.9	—	188.5

Source: Data provided by the Bond, Equity and Loan database of the International Monetary Fund sourced from Dealogic.

Table 17. Emerging Market External Financing: Loan Syndication
(In millions of U.S. dollars)

	2001	2002	2003	2004	2005	2006	2006 Q3	2006 Q4	2007 Q1	2007 Q2
Total	**56,136.7**	**52,082.8**	**67,380.8**	**95,702.7**	**134,256.5**	**208,955.8**	**48,500.2**	**74,073.5**	**39,696.6**	**44,247.7**
Africa	**4,508.8**	**4,512.4**	**5,584.6**	**7,008.9**	**7,617.4**	**4,394.8**	**1,520.8**	**1,071.4**	**1,579.0**	**2,016.3**
Algeria	50.0	150.0	40.0	271.7	412.7	—	—	—	—	—
Angola	455.0	350.0	1,522.0	2,900.0	3,122.7	88.0	12.1	—	74.6	—
Botswana	22.5	—	—	—	—	—	—	—	—	—
Burkina Faso	—	—	—	—	11.0	—	—	—	14.5	—
Cameroon	53.8	—	100.0	—	—	—	—	—	—	—
Chad	300.0	—	—	—	—	—	—	—	—	—
Côte d'Ivoire	15.0	—	—	—	—	—	—	—	—	—
Djibouti	—	—	—	40.0	—	—	—	—	—	—
Ethiopia	—	—	—	40.0	—	—	—	—	—	—
Gabon	—	—	—	22.0	—	34.3	—	—	—	—
Ghana	291.0	420.0	650.0	870.0	662.5	860.0	810.0	—	—	150.0
Guinea	—	—	—	70.0	—	—	—	—	—	—
Kenya	80.2	—	134.0	—	23.5	40.6	—	23.8	—	—
Malawi	—	—	—	4.8	—	—	—	—	—	—
Mali	—	150.4	287.6	288.9	—	—	—	—	149.9	—
Mauritius	—	—	—	—	—	180.0	80.0	—	—	—
Morocco	129.3	—	9.8	—	—	14.2	2.7	—	—	—
Mozambique	160.0	—	35.5	—	—	—	—	—	—	—
Namibia	—	—	35.0	—	50.0	100.0	50.0	50.0	—	—
Niger	—	—	27.0	—	—	—	—	—	—	—
Nigeria	95.0	960.0	488.0	225.0	618.8	580.0	100.0	480.0	450.0	327.3
Senegal	—	40.0	—	—	—	—	—	—	—	—
Seychelles	—	150.0	—	80.0	—	—	—	—	—	—
South Africa	2,786.0	2,201.5	2,097.5	1,816.6	2,625.0	1,506.5	466.0	—	890.0	1,389.0
Tunisia	71.0	90.5	128.2	379.9	91.2	473.5	—	—	—	150.0
Uganda	—	—	—	—	—	12.6	—	12.6	—	—
Zambia	—	—	30.0	—	—	505.0	—	505.0	—	—
Asia	**17,603.3**	**15,237.7**	**24,610.2**	**28,818.9**	**34,599.1**	**63,319.8**	**14,402.3**	**29,436.0**	**12,700.8**	**15,952.4**
Bangladesh	—	—	—	176.8	—	32.6	—	—	—	—
Brunei Darussalam	—	129.0	—	—	—	—	—	—	—	—
China	343.0	1,441.2	4,388.1	3,555.3	4,956.3	6,855.4	2,716.8	538.5	2,276.2	3,232.0
Hong Kong SAR	4,718.1	1,788.0	2,570.6	4,077.2	3,436.3	4,417.2	1,583.4	1,019.4	477.0	155.5
India	1,499.0	942.2	2,025.9	4,491.2	7,873.4	18,017.4	2,649.1	11,713.6	1,640.0	6,099.1
Indonesia	487.6	62.0	3,492.5	1,737.4	754.0	6,348.5	191.5	5,585.5	608.0	457.4
Korea	5,225.1	5,284.2	4,141.3	3,163.4	7,743.8	10,168.9	2,010.4	3,500.2	2,549.6	1,778.5
Lao P.D.R.	—	—	—	210.0	500.0	—	—	—	—	—
Macao SAR	—	—	—	357.0	—	1,980.0	1,180.0	—	1,600.0	—
Malaysia	2,046.7	1,973.6	3,789.4	3,999.2	2,509.7	4,236.7	717.5	1,762.9	780.6	1,390.0
Marshall Islands	—	34.7	—	—	24.0	170.0	—	—	804.2	—
Mongolia	—	—	—	—	30.0	6.0	6.0	—	—	—
Pakistan	182.5	85.0	—	300.0	591.8	1,279.3	20.0	1,039.5	—	157.0
Philippines	1,421.4	611.1	1,277.7	1,333.4	1,245.8	810.2	44.2	766.0	490.4	150.0
Singapore	1,010.6	1,338.8	1,154.1	1,606.1	1,839.2	6,512.4	3,017.5	2,405.3	722.4	1,885.1
Sri Lanka	105.0	—	186.0	35.0	311.5	129.7	20.0	100.0	—	210.0
Taiwan Province of China	383.7	338.7	549.8	2,376.6	720.8	452.2	69.5	60.0	437.0	214.9
Thailand	180.5	825.7	983.7	1,286.2	1,798.6	1,445.9	103.0	610.9	—	100.0
Vietnam	—	383.5	51.0	114.0	264.0	457.4	73.2	334.2	315.5	123.0
Europe	**10,486.7**	**12,916.3**	**20,477.2**	**30,261.1**	**37,244.8**	**62,100.3**	**16,686.7**	**18,406.0**	**9,406.9**	**12,539.4**
Armenia	—	—	—	—	—	—	—	—	—	19.1
Azerbaijan	16.0	—	—	1,005.0	383.7	916.0	1.0	130.0	—	164.0
Belarus	—	—	24.0	—	32.0	336.0	123.8	119.3	27.0	35.0
Bulgaria	7.0	13.0	260.4	808.1	188.2	1,366.1	588.8	726.8	49.2	435.3
Croatia	768.0	536.6	960.8	545.9	637.2	664.8	283.8	380.9	—	—
Cyprus	152.5	68.1	—	—	—	965.7	792.8	87.9	28.0	—
Czech Republic	434.4	25.0	356.5	191.1	549.9	252.8	23.7	124.1	219.7	—
Estonia	136.6	—	133.9	222.9	—	449.4	—	—	—	—

162

Table 17 *(concluded)*

	2001	2002	2003	2004	2005	2006	2006 Q3	2006 Q4	2007 Q1	2007 Q2
Faroe Islands	—	—	—	—	85.3	206.2	—	206.2	206.1	—
Georgia	—	—	6.0	—	—	7.0	7.0	—	—	—
Gibraltar	—	—	—	—	—	1,934.2	—	—	—	—
Hungary	99.4	969.7	1,409.7	1,498.8	1,347.3	148.6	60.1	—	—	455.1
Kazakhstan	323.5	534.5	1,375.0	1,868.2	2,607.9	5,340.4	304.0	4,334.0	16.9	1,599.5
Kyrgyz Republic	—	95.0	—	—	—	—	—	—	—	—
Latvia	31.3	51.9	70.7	353.2	265.8	1,187.5	656.5	246.8	111.7	897.0
Lithuania	24.9	18.8	—	72.5	390.2	50.4	—	50.4	—	40.2
Macedonia, FYR	—	—	—	17.4	—	—	—	—	—	—
Malta	85.0	—	114.7	392.7	—	256.0	196.0	—	—	—
Moldova	—	—	—	—	1.0	—	—	—	—	—
Poland	1,979.3	3,016.0	2,727.4	541.4	2,192.8	1,975.9	219.6	1,548.4	661.7	539.2
Romania	438.6	380.0	925.2	659.0	1,030.8	492.8	153.0	132.9	193.3	146.2
Russia	1,520.4	3,803.5	7,415.1	12,922.0	15,415.3	24,994.6	8,694.6	5,344.9	5,109.5	2,761.5
Serbia[1]	—	19.4	—	—	—	—	—	—	—	—
Slovak Republic	—	—	79.3	117.0	579.3	—	—	—	—	—
Slovenia	337.2	279.0	394.8	1,364.5	1,724.8	1,828.5	—	488.1	1,134.4	431.4
Turkey	4,112.6	3,044.8	4,095.7	7,561.5	8,899.7	16,673.1	4,016.5	3,179.4	1,517.9	3,495.8
Ukraine	15.0	15.0	90.0	119.9	913.6	2,049.3	565.5	1,301.0	131.4	1,520.0
Uzbekistan	5.0	46.0	37.8	—	—	4.9	—	4.9	—	—
Middle East	**4,874.7**	**6,978.8**	**6,231.2**	**11,530.0**	**35,730.6**	**53,797.9**	**9,372.3**	**18,027.7**	**5,311.4**	**12,645.9**
Bahrain	202.0	340.0	1,000.0	1,475.0	1,690.0	2,285.2	370.0	1,603.0	—	3,536.0
Egypt	1,000.0	670.0	155.0	997.7	1,466.8	3,065.4	200.0	87.5	941.5	—
Iran, I.R. of	887.0	1,680.1	700.0	1,942.7	1,928.8	134.8	17.7	—	—	—
Iraq	—	—	—	—	107.8	177.0	—	—	—	—
Israel	325.0	—	—	370.0	1,923.8	1,096.8	339.1	475.0	—	168.0
Jordan	—	—	—	54.4	—	60.0	—	60.0	—	—
Kuwait	770.0	—	165.0	782.5	4,283.0	4,226.7	468.5	200.0	75.0	1,790.5
Lebanon	—	—	—	—	—	50.0	—	50.0	120.0	—
Oman	—	2,332.0	818.3	1,055.0	4,598.7	3,405.2	2,835.9	319.3	—	782.4
Qatar	895.0	1,536.7	880.8	1,377.7	8,168.5	7,253.1	692.5	3,295.4	—	650.0
Saudi Arabia	275.0	280.0	569.5	2,134.0	3,681.0	6,761.7	31.0	526.0	1,081.0	4,479.0
United Arab Emirates	520.7	140.0	1,942.6	1,341.0	7,882.3	25,282.0	4,417.6	11,411.5	3,093.9	1,240.0
Latin America	**18,663.2**	**12,437.6**	**10,477.7**	**18,083.9**	**19,064.6**	**25,343.0**	**6,518.2**	**7,132.5**	**10,698.4**	**1,093.7**
Argentina	1,889.0	824.2	30.0	767.0	3,088.0	300.0	—	—	—	340.0
Bolivia	10.0	90.0	—	116.0	123.0	—	—	—	—	—
Brazil	5,984.0	3,161.4	902.4	4,609.8	3,845.9	6,973.2	1,998.3	238.5	5,000.0	253.4
Chile	2,399.3	1,230.7	1,731.0	3,823.5	4,533.3	4,191.0	952.1	830.0	240.0	415.0
Colombia	631.7	1,096.0	146.3	83.0	348.8	1,775.0	—	1,580.0	—	—
Costa Rica	115.0	—	—	—	117.2	1.7	1.7	—	—	—
Cuba	—	—	—	69.8	1.9	—	—	—	—	—
Dominican Republic	31.1	258.0	50.4	140.5	47.8	212.7	112.0	55.8	203.3	—
Ecuador	910.0	10.0	—	—	62.5	19.1	—	19.1	—	—
El Salvador	68.0	—	32.5	180.5	79.5	701.6	496.6	205.0	—	—
Guadeloupe	—	17.4	—	—	—	—	—	—	—	—
Guatemala	—	44.0	—	59.3	165.0	—	—	—	15.0	—
Haiti	—	—	—	—	—	126.5	—	70.0	—	—
Honduras	—	—	—	169.0	4.6	—	—	—	—	—
Jamaica	5.8	45.0	49.6	96.3	416.6	388.4	—	—	650.0	—
Mexico	4,466.3	4,280.0	7,342.2	7,323.0	6,019.3	8,100.3	1,561.9	3,644.2	3,704.4	30.0
Nicaragua	—	—	—	22.0	—	—	—	—	—	—
Paraguay	70.0	—	—	—	—	—	—	—	—	—
Peru	137.5	63.0	125.0	170.0	27.1	456.9	150.0	—	—	—
St. Lucia	—	—	20.0	—	—	—	—	—	—	—
Trinidad and Tobago	70.0	303.0	46.0	315.0	—	1,727.3	1,242.3	156.0	—	55.4
Uruguay	41.3	—	—	—	—	—	—	—	795.7	—
Venezuela	1,834.3	1,015.0	2.5	139.1	184.0	369.3	3.2	334.0	90.0	—

Source: Data provided by the Bond, Equity and Loan database of the International Monetary Fund sourced from Dealogic.

[1] Data prior to 2006 refer to Serbia and Montenegro.

Table 18. Equity Valuation Measures: Dividend-Yield Ratios

	2001	2002	2003	2004	2005	2006	2006 Q3	2006 Q4	2007 Q1	2007 Q2
Composite	**2.81**	**2.27**	**2.28**	**2.29**	**2.28**	**2.14**	**2.53**	**2.14**	**2.14**	**1.93**
Asia	**1.68**	**1.76**	**1.97**	**2.20**	**2.42**	**1.88**	**2.34**	**1.88**	**1.91**	**1.70**
Europe/Middle East/Africa	**3.61**	**2.69**	**2.41**	**2.00**	**1.76**	**2.36**	**2.61**	**2.36**	**2.42**	**2.27**
Latin America	**5.57**	**3.63**	**3.26**	**3.24**	**3.07**	**2.56**	**2.99**	**2.56**	**2.30**	**2.09**
Argentina	7.83	0.51	1.37	0.98	1.20	1.21	1.37	1.21	1.12	1.39
Bahrain	7.19	5.24	2.27	1.19	1.77	4.16	4.01	4.16	2.82	2.41
Brazil	6.61	4.36	4.23	4.24	3.98	3.38	3.86	3.38	3.13	2.75
Chile	8.23	2.97	2.95	4.62	2.99	2.07	2.51	2.07	1.80	2.15
China	1.35	1.43	2.31	1.82	2.56	1.29	2.07	1.29	1.16	1.07
Colombia	5.22	4.70	5.89	5.44	1.38	1.96	2.00	1.96	2.03	2.04
Czech Republic	10.48	1.82	5.04	4.19	1.42	3.71	4.03	3.71	3.55	2.78
Egypt	7.72	10.30	4.94	1.45	1.54	2.29	2.20	2.29	2.16	2.38
Hungary	1.63	1.65	0.91	1.73	2.05	1.83	2.00	1.83	2.54	2.41
India	2.39	2.96	1.74	1.70	1.25	1.07	1.21	1.07	1.29	1.05
Indonesia	2.68	3.14	3.42	3.35	2.74	2.18	2.26	2.18	2.21	2.30
Israel	1.32	0.72	1.20	1.83	1.58	2.55	2.40	2.55	2.00	1.65
Jordan	2.75	2.79	2.40	1.49	2.19	1.06	0.91	1.06	1.02	1.91
Korea	1.77	1.61	2.08	2.25	1.70	1.49	1.57	1.49	1.81	1.53
Kuwait	—	—	—	—	—	2.97	3.48	2.97	2.94	2.46
Malaysia	3.27	3.15	3.02	3.50	4.33	3.72	4.21	3.72	3.18	3.56
Mexico	3.04	1.76	2.12	1.85	2.18	1.24	1.67	1.24	1.08	1.15
Morocco	4.54	5.27	4.65	2.71	3.61	2.22	2.90	2.22	1.79	1.84
Nigeria	5.27	5.41	4.11	3.70	3.14	2.29	2.67	2.29	1.73	1.68
Oman	9.21	3.04	5.38	3.32	2.15	4.64	5.33	4.64	5.76	4.22
Pakistan	12.50	9.20	7.47	6.98	2.50	3.96	3.76	3.96	3.39	2.64
Peru	4.25	2.37	2.83	3.10	3.45	3.83	4.56	3.83	2.84	2.56
Philippines	1.37	2.34	2.12	1.79	2.63	2.00	2.42	2.00	2.15	2.03
Poland	2.56	1.42	1.43	1.20	2.48	3.36	4.33	3.36	2.99	3.99
Qatar	—	—	—	—	—	1.69	2.40	1.69	3.22	2.86
Russia	1.04	2.43	1.78	1.21	1.07	1.83	2.16	1.83	1.90	1.50
Saudi Arabia	3.94	3.94	2.58	2.05	1.25	2.65	1.86	2.65	2.88	2.98
South Africa	5.08	3.61	3.96	3.09	3.09	2.77	3.37	2.77	2.80	2.75
Sri Lanka	6.22	3.09	3.64	4.67	2.47	1.77	2.36	1.77	1.78	1.90
Taiwan Province of China	1.14	1.21	1.47	2.67	3.39	3.06	3.72	3.06	3.11	2.85
Thailand	2.56	2.21	1.64	2.24	3.05	4.51	4.63	4.51	3.51	3.55
Turkey	1.06	0.73	1.15	2.97	1.81	2.19	2.47	2.19	2.10	2.43
United Arab Emirates	—	—	—	—	—	2.12	1.99	2.12	2.39	2.05
Venezuela	10.75	8.39	9.86	12.28	6.27	5.71	7.31	5.71	0.00	0.00

Source: Standard & Poor's Emerging Market Database.

Table 19. Equity Valuation Measures: Price-to-Book Ratios

	2001	2002	2003	2004	2005	2006	2006 Q3	2006 Q4	2007 Q1	2007 Q2
Composite	**1.62**	**1.42**	**1.96**	**1.86**	**2.65**	**2.73**	**2.44**	**2.73**	**2.83**	**3.13**
Asia	**1.69**	**1.42**	**2.06**	**1.78**	**2.11**	**2.43**	**2.10**	**2.43**	**2.53**	**3.01**
Europe/Middle East/Africa	**1.76**	**1.51**	**1.86**	**2.21**	**3.91**	**3.26**	**3.20**	**3.26**	**3.34**	**3.46**
Latin America	**1.30**	**1.29**	**1.83**	**1.58**	**2.30**	**2.91**	**2.40**	**2.91**	**3.06**	**3.00**
Argentina	0.60	0.76	1.99	2.16	2.50	4.09	3.08	4.09	4.03	3.43
Bahrain	0.97	1.19	2.02	2.02	2.73	2.23	1.99	2.23	2.19	2.55
Brazil	1.24	1.25	1.79	1.93	2.16	2.68	2.17	2.68	2.74	2.71
Chile	1.40	1.31	1.87	0.55	1.93	2.43	2.07	2.43	2.64	2.74
China	2.33	1.87	2.55	2.03	1.81	3.12	2.24	3.12	3.41	4.39
Colombia	0.64	0.78	0.94	1.58	2.41	1.78	1.51	1.78	1.68	1.69
Czech Republic	0.75	0.77	0.99	1.58	2.35	2.39	2.15	2.39	2.50	2.81
Egypt	1.02	1.01	2.08	4.38	9.08	5.85	6.10	5.85	6.01	6.57
Hungary	1.76	1.83	2.00	2.78	3.08	3.08	2.46	3.08	2.93	3.60
India	1.92	2.00	3.50	3.31	5.15	4.89	4.78	4.89	4.50	5.26
Indonesia	1.70	0.95	1.62	2.75	2.50	3.35	2.76	3.35	3.31	3.92
Israel	2.08	1.80	2.61	2.58	3.00	3.48	3.35	3.48	3.76	4.18
Jordan	1.46	1.31	2.08	2.99	6.24	3.30	3.60	3.30	3.71	3.32
Korea	1.24	1.12	1.57	1.25	1.95	1.74	1.66	1.74	1.78	2.09
Kuwait	—	—	—	—	4.64	4.52	4.31	4.52	5.12	6.27
Malaysia	1.21	1.32	1.71	1.93	1.67	2.08	1.74	2.08	2.45	2.38
Mexico	1.67	1.54	2.02	2.51	2.88	3.84	3.25	3.84	4.25	4.00
Morocco	1.95	1.61	1.70	2.06	2.92	3.11	2.97	3.11	3.99	4.08
Nigeria	3.67	3.96	2.52	3.19	5.36	5.22	5.45	5.22	7.15	8.84
Oman	0.78	1.13	1.50	1.80	2.28	2.19	2.15	2.19	2.21	2.54
Pakistan	0.93	1.90	2.25	2.63	3.51	3.17	3.39	3.17	3.60	4.61
Peru	1.36	1.16	1.80	1.56	2.17	3.47	3.49	3.47	4.55	6.22
Philippines	0.92	0.77	1.06	1.35	1.73	1.92	1.67	1.92	2.05	2.69
Poland	1.39	1.28	1.76	2.04	2.53	2.52	2.21	2.52	2.76	3.03
Qatar	—	—	—	—	8.80	2.73	3.42	2.73	2.36	2.84
Russia	1.12	0.86	1.18	1.18	2.19	2.53	2.16	2.53	2.44	2.44
Saudi Arabia	2.42	2.75	3.56	6.50	14.54	7.57	10.33	7.57	7.45	6.50
South Africa	2.06	1.90	2.06	2.52	2.98	3.80	3.28	3.80	4.18	4.16
Sri Lanka	0.87	1.08	1.63	1.93	2.56	2.41	1.84	2.41	2.60	1.79
Taiwan Province of China	2.08	1.63	2.18	1.94	1.93	2.36	2.02	2.36	2.37	2.69
Thailand	1.27	1.49	2.84	2.03	2.06	1.85	1.86	1.85	1.86	2.15
Turkey	3.81	2.77	2.64	1.74	2.13	1.95	1.83	1.95	2.14	2.30
United Arab Emirates	—	—	—	—	9.98	3.07	3.73	3.07	2.89	3.55
Venezuela	0.48	0.53	1.10	1.18	0.72	2.59	1.10	2.59	0.00	0.00

Source: Standard & Poor's Emerging Market Database.

Table 20. Equity Valuation Measures: Price/Earnings Ratios

	2001	2002	2003	2004	2005	2006	2006 Q3	2006 Q4	2007 Q1	2007 Q2
Composite	**17.8**	**17.9**	**21.7**	**16.5**	**18.9**	**17.7**	**16.1**	**17.7**	**18.2**	**19.8**
Asia	**26.8**	**20.0**	**30.3**	**16.8**	**17.9**	**18.0**	**16.1**	**18.0**	**18.3**	**21.4**
Europe/Middle East/ Africa	**12.6**	**14.5**	**18.0**	**18.6**	**25.2**	**18.7**	**18.6**	**18.7**	**19.2**	**19.9**
Latin America	**11.8**	**19.2**	**13.3**	**12.8**	**12.2**	**15.2**	**12.3**	**15.2**	**16.0**	**16.0**
Argentina	32.6	−1.4	21.1	27.7	11.1	18.0	13.7	18.0	17.8	14.5
Bahrain	34.5	20.5	21.3	21.5	31.7	14.3	13.9	14.3	14.0	16.3
Brazil	8.8	13.5	10.0	10.6	10.7	12.7	10.1	12.7	13.0	13.6
Chile	16.2	16.3	24.8	17.2	15.7	24.2	20.5	24.2	26.2	24.2
China	22.2	21.6	28.6	19.1	13.9	24.6	18.1	24.6	26.9	34.6
Colombia	20.9	−44.8	13.0	19.2	28.8	21.9	18.6	21.9	20.8	20.7
Czech Republic	5.8	11.2	10.8	25.0	21.1	20.0	17.8	20.0	20.9	23.6
Egypt	6.5	5.6	11.7	21.8	30.9	20.2	19.3	20.2	20.7	22.7
Hungary	13.4	14.6	12.3	16.6	13.5	13.4	10.9	13.4	12.7	15.6
India	12.8	15.0	20.9	18.1	19.4	20.1	20.9	20.1	17.8	20.9
Indonesia	−7.7	22.0	39.5	13.3	12.6	20.1	17.8	20.1	19.9	23.0
Israel	−81.5	80.0	75.6	39.7	20.0	25.3	26.2	25.3	27.3	30.5
Jordan	18.8	11.4	20.7	30.4	57.1	20.8	23.7	20.8	23.4	21.0
Korea	28.7	21.6	30.2	13.5	20.8	12.8	12.2	12.8	13.1	15.2
Kuwait	. . .	. . .	. . .	. . .	21.5	21.1	20.0	21.1	23.9	29.3
Malaysia	50.6	21.3	30.1	22.4	15.0	21.7	17.8	21.7	25.5	21.0
Mexico	13.7	15.4	17.6	15.9	14.2	18.6	15.6	18.6	21.4	20.2
Morocco	11.7	9.5	25.2	24.6	22.4	22.5	20.7	22.5	28.8	29.5
Nigeria	12.6	16.4	18.5	23.5	20.7	24.1	24.2	24.1	32.9	40.7
Oman	24.4	52.7	15.2	14.2	15.8	13.1	12.8	13.1	13.2	15.1
Pakistan	7.5	10.0	9.5	9.9	13.1	10.8	11.9	10.8	12.3	15.7
Peru	21.3	12.8	13.7	10.7	12.0	15.7	16.1	15.7	20.7	21.3
Philippines	45.9	21.8	21.1	14.6	15.7	14.4	13.8	14.4	15.5	17.7
Poland	6.1	88.6	−353.0	39.9	11.7	13.9	12.2	13.9	15.3	16.7
Qatar	. . .	. . .	. . .	. . .	48.7	15.9	19.8	15.9	13.6	16.5
Russia	5.6	12.4	19.9	10.8	24.1	16.6	13.9	16.6	16.0	16.0
Saudi Arabia	22.2	23.4	27.2	50.6	104.8	52.0	74.4	52.0	51.2	44.7
South Africa	11.7	10.1	11.5	16.2	12.8	16.6	14.1	16.6	18.2	18.2
Sri Lanka	14.4	15.6	15.0	18.1	23.6	15.4	12.4	15.4	16.6	11.9
Taiwan Province of China	29.4	20.0	55.7	21.2	21.9	25.6	22.8	25.6	25.4	28.6
Thailand	163.8	16.4	16.6	12.8	10.0	8.7	9.5	8.7	8.7	10.1
Turkey	72.5	37.9	14.9	12.5	16.2	17.2	19.1	17.2	19.8	21.3
United Arab Emirates	. . .	. . .	. . .	. . .	54.7	13.4	17.6	13.4	12.6	15.5
Venezuela	−347.6	−11.9	14.4	6.0	5.1	13.1	7.8	13.1	. . .	. . .

Source: Standard & Poor's Emerging Market Database.

Table 21. Emerging Markets: Mutual Fund Flows
(In millions of U.S. dollars)

| | 2001 | 2002 | 2003 | 2004 | 2005 | 2006 | 2006 | | | | 2007 | |
							Q1	Q2	Q3	Q4	Q1	Q2
Bonds	−444	606	3,153	1,947	5,729	6,233	4,209	−1,240	32	3,232	2,534	2,003
Equities	−1,781	−1,512	8,500	2,784	21,706	22,441	23,257	−6,279	−1,813	7,276	−1,674	3,815
Global	−67	−2,082	2,119	−5,348	3,148	4,209	8,056	−1,523	−2,702	377	−758	1,454
Asia	−768	817	5,148	5,609	6,952	16,790	9,193	980	252	6,366	1,159	−2,487
Latin America	−619	−312	376	338	4,020	3,319	3,004	−1,465	651	1,130	−239	5,174
Europe/Middle East/Africa	−327	65	857	2,185	7,587	−1,877	3,004	−4,272	−14	−596	−1,836	−326

Source: Emerging Portfolio Fund Research, Inc.

Table 22. Bank Regulatory Capital to Risk-Weighted Assets
(In percent)

	2002	2003	2004	2005	2006	2007	Latest
Latin America							
Argentina	...	...	...	...	...	...	...
Bolivia	16.1	15.3	14.9	14.7	13.3	13.5	March
Brazil	16.6	18.8	18.6	17.9	18.9	18.5	March
Chile	14.0	14.1	13.6	13.0	12.5	12.8	April
Colombia	12.6	13.1	13.8	13.2	12.2	12.9	May
Costa Rica[1]	15.8	16.5	18.1	15.9	15.3	15.3	May
Dominican Republic	12.0	8.8	14.0	12.5	12.4	13.1	March
Ecuador	14.4	14.9	14.5	14.4	14.8	15.6	May
El Salvador	12.2	12.8	13.4	13.5	13.6	...	December
Guatemala	14.9	15.6	14.5	13.7	13.6	13.8	March
Mexico	15.7	14.4	14.1	14.5	16.3	16.1	March
Panama	18.5	18.1	17.6	16.8	17.2	...	December
Paraguay	17.9	20.9	20.5	20.4	20.1	19.9	January
Peru	12.5	13.3	14.0	12.0	12.5	12.5	March
Uruguay[1,2]	−20.1	18.1	21.7	22.7	16.9	19.1	May
Venezuela	20.5	25.1	19.2	15.5	14.3	13.7	April
Emerging Europe							
Albania	...	28.5	21.6	18.6	18.1	...	December
Belarus	24.2	26.0	25.2	26.7	24.4	...	December
Bosnia and Herzegovina	20.5	20.3	18.7	17.8	17.7	...	December
Bulgaria	25.2	22.0	16.1	15.2	14.5	...	December
Croatia	17.4	16.5	16.0	15.2	13.6	15.9	March
Czech Republic	14.3	14.5	12.6	11.9	11.4	11.8	March
Estonia	15.3	14.5	13.4	11.7	13.2	13.7	March
Hungary	13.0	11.8	12.4	11.6	11.3	...	December
Israel	9.9	10.3	10.8	10.7	10.8	11.0	March
Latvia	13.1	11.7	11.7	10.1	10.2	10.4	March
Lithuania[3]	14.8	13.3	12.4	10.3	10.8	...	December
Macedonia, FYR	28.1	25.8	23.0	21.3	18.3	17.9	March
Montenegro	...	...	31.3	27.8	21.3	18.5	March
Poland	13.8	13.7	15.5	14.5	14.0	...	June
Romania[4]	25.0	20.0	18.8	20.2	17.8	...	September
Russia	19.1	19.1	17.0	16.0	14.9	16.2	April
Serbia[5]	25.6	31.1	27.9	26.0	24.7	25.9	June
Slovak Republic	21.3	22.4	18.7	14.8	13.0	...	December
Turkey[6]	24.4	29.5	27.4	22.8	21.1	...	December
Ukraine	18.0	15.2	16.8	15.0	14.2	14.0	March
Western Europe							
Austria[7]	13.3	14.5	12.4	11.8	12.8	...	September
Belgium	13.2	12.9	12.9	11.5	12.0	...	June
Denmark	13.5	13.9	13.4	13.2	13.8	...	December
Finland[8]	11.7	18.7	19.1	17.2	15.0	...	June
France	11.5	11.9	11.5	11.4	...	...	December
Germany	12.7	13.4	13.2	12.2	...	...	December
Greece	10.5	12.0	12.8	13.2	12.3	...	June
Iceland	12.2	12.3	12.8	12.8	15.1	...	December
Ireland[9]	14.4	15.0	14.6	13.6	...	...	December
Italy[10]	11.2	11.4	11.6	10.6	10.7	...	December
Luxembourg	15.0	17.1	17.5	16.3	14.8	...	December
Malta	...	...	21.4	20.4	22.0	...	December
Netherlands	12.0	12.3	12.3	12.6	11.7	...	September
Norway	12.2	12.4	12.2	11.9	11.2	...	December
Portugal[11]	9.8	10.0	10.4	11.3	10.9	...	December
Spain	12.5	12.6	12.3	12.2	11.9	...	December
Sweden[12]	7.1	7.3	7.6	7.0	7.1	7.6	July
Switzerland	12.6	12.4	12.6	12.4	13.4	...	December
United Kingdom	13.1	13.0	12.7	12.8	12.9	...	December

Table 22 *(concluded)*

	2002	2003	2004	2005	2006	2007	Latest
Asia							
Bangladesh	7.5	8.4	8.8	7.3	8.3	...	December
China	...	...	...	...	...	...	...
Hong Kong SAR	15.8	15.3	15.4	15.3	15.0	...	December
India	12.0	12.7	12.9	12.8	12.4	...	June
Indonesia	20.1	22.3	19.4	19.3	21.3	22.1	March
Korea	11.2	11.1	12.1	13.0	12.8	13.0	March
Malaysia	13.2	13.8	14.3	13.7	13.5	13.1	June
Philippines[13]	16.9	17.4	18.4	17.6	...	...	December
Singapore	16.9	17.9	16.2	15.8	15.4	14.9	March
Thailand	13.0	13.4	12.4	13.2	13.8	14.1	March
Middle East and Central Asia							
Armenia	30.5	33.8	32.3	33.7	34.9	32.7	June
Egypt	11.0	11.1	13.8	14.5	16.3	...	December
Georgia	21.9	20.3	18.8	17.5	20.6	18.5	May
Jordan	16.6	15.9	17.8	17.6	21.4	...	December
Kazakhstan	17.2	16.9	15.9	15.1	14.9	14.8	February
Kuwait	19.7	18.4	17.3	21.3	22.0	...	September
Lebanon	19.4	22.3	22.2	22.9	24.7	...	December
Morocco	12.2	9.3	10.2	11.5	12.3	...	December
Oman	17.1	17.6	17.6	18.1	17.2	...	June
Pakistan	8.8	8.5	10.5	11.3	12.7	...	September
Saudi Arabia	21.3	19.4	17.8	17.8	21.9	21.8	March
Tunisia	9.8	9.3	11.6	12.4	11.8	...	December
United Arab Emirates	19.0	18.6	16.9	17.4	16.6	...	December
Sub-Saharan Africa							
Gabon	17.6	19.9	17.8	24.0	32.0	...	December
Ghana	13.4	9.3	13.7	16.2	15.8	...	December
Kenya	13.9	11.7	11.8	13.4	...	...	December
Lesotho	...	...	22.0	22.0	25.0	...	March
Mozambique	14.0	17.0	18.7	16.0	13.1	...	June
Namibia	14.1	14.8	15.4	14.6	14.8	...	June
Nigeria	18.1	17.8	14.6	14.3	25.8	...	December
Rwanda	12.5	14.6	18.3	14.7	...	...	December
Senegal	15.5	11.7	11.5	10.8	14.1	...	August
Sierra Leone	32.5	27.3	25.1	26.4	...	...	December
South Africa	12.6	12.4	14.0	12.7	12.3	12.7	March
Swaziland	...	14.0	14.0	15.0	19.0	...	September
Uganda	20.7	16.9	20.5	18.3	18.3	...	June
Other							
Australia	9.6	10.0	10.4	10.4	10.4	10.4	March
Canada	12.4	13.4	13.3	12.9	12.5	12.4	March
Japan[14]	9.4	11.1	11.6	12.2	13.1	...	March
United States	13.0	13.0	13.2	12.9	13.0	13.0	March

Sources: National authorities; and IMF staff estimates.

Note: Due to differences in national accounting, taxation, and supervisory regimes, FSI data are not strictly comparable across countries.

[1]Banking sector excludes offshore banks in Costa Rica, and the state mortgage bank in Uruguay.

[2]In 2006, the Uruguay Central Bank changed the methodology for calculating the regulatory capital ratio, changing the weights and adding a factor to the denominator to account for market risk. Regulatory capital ratios are smaller in 2006 and 2007, compared to previous years, due to this calculation.

[3]Without foreign bank branches.

[4]Statistical break starting in 2003.

[5]Data prior to 2006 refer to Serbia and Montenegro.

[6]Statistical break starting in 2002.

[7]Starting in 2004 data reported on a consolidated basis.

[8]Statistical break starting in 2003.

[9]All banks.

[10]Consolidated reports for banking groups and individual reports for banks not belonging to groups.

[11]For 2005 and 2006, the figures are for the sample of institutions that are already complying with IAS, accounting as of December 2004 for about 87 percent of the usual aggregate considered.

[12]Tier 1 ratio; not comparable with the other indicators in the table. Data for the four large banking groups.

[13]On a consolidated basis.

[14]For the end of the fiscal year, i.e., March of the following calendar year; for major banks.

Table 23. Bank Capital to Assets
(In percent)

	2002	2003	2004	2005	2006	2007	Latest
Latin America							
Argentina	. . .	11.9	11.8	13.0	13.6	13.7	March
Bolivia	11.9	12.1	11.5	11.3	10.0	9.0	March
Brazil	9.2	9.6	10.1	9.8	9.9	9.4	March
Chile	7.2	7.3	7.0	6.9	6.8	6.8	May
Colombia	9.3	9.7	10.3	11.3	10.8	11.1	May
Costa Rica[1]	10.1	10.4	9.2	9.5	10.2	10.7	May
Dominican Republic	10.7	7.9	9.0	9.4	10.0	9.7	March
Ecuador	. . .	14.7	13.9	13.3	13.7	13.7	May
El Salvador	. . .	10.2	10.7	11.1	11.8	11.6	March
Guatemala	8.9	9.0	8.9	8.5	8.2	9.1	March
Mexico	9.6	10.0	10.2	11.5	13.2	. . .	December
Panama	10.2	12.2	13.2	12.8	11.3	. . .	November
Paraguay	10.9	9.5	10.5	11.0	12.5	12.2	January
Peru	10.1	9.3	9.8	7.7	9.5	8.6	March
Uruguay[1]	−10.0	7.2	8.3	8.6	9.8	10.2	May
Venezuela	15.9	14.3	12.5	11.1	9.8	9.7	April
Emerging Europe							
Albania	. . .	4.7	4.8	5.6	6.2	. . .	December
Belarus	18.7	20.4	20.1	19.8	17.8	. . .	December
Bosnia and Herzegovina	19.1	17.0	15.7	14.4	13.8	. . .	October
Bulgaria	13.3	13.1	11.0	10.5	10.4	. . .	September
Croatia	9.5	8.9	8.6	9.0	10.3	11.6	March
Czech Republic	5.2	5.7	5.6	5.7	6.2	6.3	March
Estonia	12.1	11.3	9.8	8.6	8.4	8.4	March
Hungary	8.7	8.3	8.5	8.2	8.7	. . .	December
Israel	4.9	5.3	5.5	5.6	5.9	6.0	March
Latvia	8.7	8.4	8.0	7.6	7.6	7.4	March
Lithuania[2]	10.5	9.8	8.7	7.2	7.1	. . .	December
Macedonia, FYR	. . .	. . .	. . .	. . .	. . .	. . .	. . .
Montenegro	. . .	. . .	20.4	15.3	10.4	10.4	March
Poland	8.7	8.3	8.0	7.8	7.9	. . .	March
Romania[3]	11.6	10.1	8.5	8.8	8.9	. . .	September
Russia	14.4	14.8	14.0	13.2	12.5	. . .	September
Serbia[4]	18.3	22.5	18.8	16.0	15.6	15.9	June
Slovak Republic	7.7	8.9	7.7	9.7	8.0	. . .	December
Turkey[5]	11.5	13.7	14.4	12.9	11.3	. . .	June
Ukraine	14.7	12.3	13.1	11.5	12.1	12.9	March
Western Europe							
Austria	4.7	4.9	4.9	4.8	5.2	. . .	September
Belgium	3.0	3.1	3.1	2.7	3.7	. . .	June
Denmark[6]	5.7	5.9	5.7	5.7	6.2	. . .	December
Finland	5.6	9.7	8.7	8.8	9.2	. . .	December
France	6.8	6.9	6.6	5.8	5.8	. . .	December
Germany	4.6	4.6	4.4	4.4	4.7	. . .	December
Greece[7]	6.9	6.9	5.0	5.8	5.2	. . .	June
Iceland[8]	7.2	7.1	7.1	7.4	7.8	. . .	December
Ireland	5.5	5.2	4.9	4.7	4.3	. . .	December
Italy[9]	7.0	7.0	6.9	6.8	7.1	. . .	December
Luxembourg	4.6	4.8	4.8	4.5	4.6	. . .	December
Malta	. . .	. . .	7.9	6.8	8.6	. . .	December
Netherlands	4.7	4.3	3.9	4.2	4.0	. . .	December
Norway	6.2	5.9	5.9	5.2	5.0	. . .	September
Portugal[10,11]	5.6	5.8	6.2	5.8	6.4	. . .	December
Spain	8.2	7.8	8.3	7.6	7.2	. . .	December
Sweden[12]	5.2	5.0	4.8	4.8	4.9	4.6	July
Switzerland	5.5	5.7	5.3	5.1	4.9	. . .	December
United Kingdom	9.9	9.8	9.6	9.1	8.9	. . .	December
Asia							
Bangladesh	4.1	3.2	2.7	2.6	4.0	. . .	September
China[13]	. . .	4.9	4.9	5.5	6.1	. . .	June
Hong Kong SAR	10.1	10.6	10.8	11.8	11.8	. . .	December

Table 23 *(concluded)*

	2002	2003	2004	2005	2006	2007	Latest
Asia *(continued)*							
India	5.5	5.7	5.9	6.4	6.6	. . .	March
Indonesia	8.8	9.6	10.8	10.2	10.7	11.1	May
Korea[14]	7.2	7.0	8.0	9.3	9.2	9.5	March
Malaysia	8.7	8.5	8.2	7.7	7.6	. . .	November
Philippines	13.4	13.1	12.6	11.8	11.7	11.5	March
Singapore	10.7	10.7	9.6	9.6	9.6	9.6	March
Thailand	6.1	7.4	8.0	9.6	9.2	. . .	May
Middle East and Central Asia							
Armenia	18.4	18.1	17.8	21.5	22.9	23.9	June
Egypt	. . .	4.9	4.8	5.0	5.5	. . .	September
Georgia	28.3	26.2	21.9	18.8	. . .	. . .	December
Jordan	6.2	6.4	7.2	8.2	10.7	. . .	December
Kazakhstan[15]	9.0	9.0	8.0	8.0	8.9	9.5	February
Kuwait	10.3	10.7	12.1	12.7	12.0	. . .	July
Lebanon	6.3	6.9	6.8	7.5	8.4	9.4	February
Morocco	8.5	7.6	7.6	7.7	7.4	. . .	December
Oman[16]	12.8	12.6	12.9	13.7	13.2	. . .	June
Pakistan	4.8	5.5	6.7	7.9	8.8	. . .	September
Saudi Arabia	9.3	8.8	8.0	8.8	9.3	. . .	December
Tunisia	7.7	7.6	7.5	7.7	. . .	. . .	December
United Arab Emirates	11.8	11.4	11.1	11.9	12.6	. . .	December
Sub-Saharan Africa							
Gabon	. . .	. . .	. . .	. . .	. . .	. . .	. . .
Ghana	12.0	12.0	12.5	13.0	12.4	. . .	August
Kenya	. . .	. . .	. . .	. . .	. . .	. . .	. . .
Lesotho	. . .	. . .	. . .	. . .	. . .	. . .	. . .
Mozambique	18.4	14.9	10.0	7.9	6.4	. . .	June
Namibia	7.5	8.3	8.8	7.8	8.3	. . .	June
Nigeria	10.7	9.6	9.3	13.1	14.7	. . .	September
Rwanda	8.1	8.9	10.1	9.4	9.2	. . .	April
Senegal	10.3	7.8	7.7	7.6	8.1	. . .	August
Sierra Leone	21.4	21.1	22.5	20.0	19.0	. . .	November
South Africa	9.3	8.0	8.2	7.9	7.8	. . .	May
Swaziland	. . .	. . .	. . .	. . .	. . .	. . .	. . .
Uganda	9.6	9.0	10.5	8.4	9.7	. . .	November
Other							
Australia[15]	5.3	5.2	5.1	5.2	4.9	4.9	March
Canada	4.6	4.7	4.4	4.4	5.7	5.6	March
Japan[17]	3.3	3.9	4.2	4.9	5.3	. . .	March
United States	9.2	9.2	10.3	10.3	10.5	10.6	March

Sources: National authorities; and IMF staff estimates.

Note: Due to differences in national accounting, taxation, and supervisory regimes, FSI data are not strictly comparable across countries.

[1]Banking sector excludes offshore banks in Costa Rica, and the state mortgage bank in Uruguay.

[2]Capital is defined as bank shareholders' equity and foreign bank branches funds received from the head office.

[3]Statistical break starting in 2003.

[4]Data prior to 2006 refer to Serbia and Montenegro.

[5]Statistical break starting in 2002.

[6]Shareholders' equity to total assets.

[7]Data on a nonconsolidated basis. From 2004 in accordance with IFRS.

[8]Commercial banks and six largest savings banks (five largest savings banks from 2006 due to a merger of two banks).

[9]Calculated on period average data.

[10]For 2005 and 2006, the figures are for the sample of institutions that are already complying with IAS, accounting as of December 2004 for about 87 percent of the usual aggregate considered.

[11]On accounting basis, consolidated.

[12]Data for the four large banking groups.

[13]Data for six of the large banks.

[14]Core capital ratio.

[15]Tier 1 capital to total assets.

[16]Tier 1 and Tier 2 capital to total assets.

[17]For the end of the fiscal year, i.e., March of the following calendar year; all banks.

Table 24. Bank Nonperforming Loans to Total Loans
(In percent)

	2002	2003	2004	2005	2006	2007	Latest
Latin America							
Argentina	18.1	17.7	10.7	5.2	3.4	3.2	May
Bolivia	17.7	16.7	14.0	11.3	8.7	8.8	March
Brazil	4.5	4.9	3.5	4.2	4.1	4.0	March
Chile	1.8	1.6	1.2	0.9	0.8	0.8	May
Colombia	8.7	6.8	3.3	3.2	2.6	2.9	May
Costa Rica[1]	3.2	1.7	2.0	1.5	1.5	1.6	May
Dominican Republic	4.9	9.0	7.4	5.9	4.5	5.0	March
Ecuador	8.4	7.9	6.4	4.9	3.3	3.6	May
El Salvador	15.8	12.3	2.3	1.9	1.9	2.1	March
Guatemala	7.9	6.5	7.1	4.2	4.6	5.6	March
Mexico	3.7	2.8	2.2	1.8	2.1	2.2	March
Panama	3.5	2.5	1.8	1.8	1.5	1.4	March
Paraguay	19.7	20.6	10.8	6.6	3.3	3.4	January
Peru	7.6	5.8	3.7	2.1	1.6	1.6	March
Uruguay[1]	33.9	14.3	4.7	3.6	1.9	2.1	May
Venezuela	9.2	7.7	2.8	1.2	1.1	1.1	April
Emerging Europe							
Albania	...	4.6	4.2	2.3	3.1	...	December
Belarus	9.0	3.7	2.8	1.9	1.2	...	December
Bosnia and Herzegovina	11.0	8.4	6.1	5.3	4.0	...	December
Bulgaria	2.6	3.2	2.0	2.2	2.2	...	December
Croatia	10.2	8.9	7.5	6.2	5.2	4.9	March
Czech Republic	8.1	4.9	4.1	4.3	4.1	...	September
Estonia	0.8	0.4	0.3	0.2	0.2	0.2	March
Hungary	2.9	2.6	2.7	2.5	2.5	...	December
Israel	2.4	2.6	2.5	2.3	1.9	1.9	March
Latvia	2.0	1.4	1.1	0.7	0.4	0.4	March
Lithuania[2]	5.3	2.4	2.2	0.6	1.0	...	December
Macedonia, FYR[3]	23.1	22.1	17.0	15.0	11.2	10.3	March
Montenegro	...	...	5.2	5.3	2.9	2.0	March
Poland	21.1	21.2	14.9	11.0	9.4	...	June
Romania	...	8.3	8.1	8.3	8.4	...	September
Russia	5.6	5.0	3.8	3.2	2.6	2.4	April
Serbia[4]	21.6	24.1	22.8	23.2	21.4	...	September
Slovak Republic	7.9	3.7	2.6	5.0	3.7	3.2	December
Turkey[5]	12.7	8.9	5.0	3.9	3.2	...	December
Ukraine[6]	21.9	28.3	30.0	19.6	17.8	17.6	March
Western Europe							
Austria	3.0	3.0	2.7	2.6	...	...	December
Belgium	3.0	2.6	2.3	2.0	1.8	...	June
Denmark	0.9	0.8	0.7	0.4	...	...	December
Finland[7]	0.5	0.5	0.4	0.3	0.3	...	June
France[8]	4.2	4.0	3.7	3.3	3.2	...	June
Germany[9]	5.0	5.3	5.1	4.1	4.0	...	June
Greece	5.5	5.1	5.4	5.5	5.5	...	June
Iceland[10]	2.6	2.1	0.9	...	...	...	December
Ireland	1.0	0.9	0.8	0.7	0.7	...	December
Italy[11,12]	6.5	6.7	6.6	6.2	5.3	...	December
Luxembourg	0.4	0.3	0.3	0.2	0.2	...	June
Malta	...	...	6.5	3.9	2.8	...	December
Netherlands[13]	2.4	2.0	1.5	1.2	1.0	...	June
Norway	1.8	1.6	1.0	0.7	0.6	...	September
Portugal[14,15]	2.3	2.4	2.0	1.5	1.3	...	December
Spain	1.1	1.0	0.8	0.8	0.6	...	December
Sweden[16]	1.2	1.0	0.8	0.6	0.5	0.4	July
Switzerland	1.8	1.3	0.9	0.5	0.3	...	December
United Kingdom	2.6	2.5	1.9	1.0	0.9	...	December
Asia							
Bangladesh	28.1	22.1	17.6	13.6	13.2	...	December
China	26.0	20.4	12.8	9.8	7.5	7.0	March
Hong Kong SAR	5.0	3.9	2.3	1.4	1.1	1.0	March
India	10.4	8.8	7.2	5.2	3.5	...	June
Indonesia[17]	24.0	19.4	14.2	14.8	13.1	13.5	March
Korea[18]	2.4	2.6	1.9	1.2	0.8	0.8	March
Malaysia	15.9	13.9	11.7	9.5	8.5	8.2	March
Philippines[19]	26.5	26.1	24.7	19.7	18.6	...	June

Table 24 (concluded)

	2002	2003	2004	2005	2006	2007	Latest
Asia (continued)							
Singapore[20]	7.7	6.7	5.0	3.8	2.8	2.5	March
Thailand[21]	15.7	12.9	10.9	8.3	7.5	. . .	December
Middle East and Central Asia							
Armenia	9.9	5.4	2.1	1.9	2.5	2.8	June
Egypt	20.2	24.2	26.4	24.8	24.7	. . .	December
Georgia	7.9	7.5	6.2	3.8	2.5	2.3	May
Jordan[22]	17.1	15.5	10.3	6.6	4.3	. . .	December
Kazakhstan	. . .	8.4	5.7	5.3	4.8	6.3	February
Kuwait	7.8	6.1	5.3	5.0	3.9	. . .	September
Lebanon	12.4	12.8	17.7	16.1	13.5	13.3	February
Morocco	17.2	18.1	19.4	15.7	10.9	. . .	December
Oman	11.3	15.5	13.5	9.1	7.8	. . .	June
Pakistan	21.8	17.0	11.6	8.3	7.7	. . .	September
Saudi Arabia	8.8	5.4	2.8	1.9	2.0	. . .	December
Tunisia	21.4	24.2	23.6	20.9	19.2	. . .	December
United Arab Emirates	15.3	14.3	12.5	8.3	6.3	. . .	December
Sub-Saharan Africa							
Gabon	11.4	13.8	15.8	14.3	11.1	. . .	December
Ghana	22.7	18.3	16.1	13.0	7.9	. . .	December
Kenya	18.1	17.7	10.7	5.2	. . .	. . .	December
Lesotho	. . .	. . .	1.0	2.0	1.0	. . .	March
Mozambique	20.8	26.8	6.4	3.8	3.7	. . .	June
Namibia	3.5	3.9	2.4	2.3	2.9	. . .	June
Nigeria	21.4	19.8	21.6	21.9	. . .	. . .	June
Rwanda	57.0	52.0	27.0	27.2	. . .	. . .	December
Senegal	18.5	13.3	12.6	11.9	16.0	. . .	August
Sierra Leone	11.0	7.4	12.1	20.9	. . .	. . .	December
South Africa	2.8	2.4	1.8	1.5	1.2	1.1	March
Swaziland	. . .	2.0	3.0	2.0	2.0	. . .	September
Uganda	3.0	7.2	2.2	2.3	2.8	. . .	June
Other							
Australia[23]	0.4	0.3	0.2	0.2	0.2	0.2	March
Canada	1.6	1.2	0.7	0.5	0.4	. . .	September
Japan[24]	7.4	5.8	4.0	2.9	2.5	. . .	March
United States	1.4	1.1	0.8	0.7	0.8	0.8	March

Sources: National authorities; and IMF staff estimates.

Note: Due to differences in national accounting, taxation, and supervisory regimes, FSI data are not strictly comparable across countries.

[1]Banking sector excludes offshore banks in Costa Rica, and the state mortgage bank in Uruguay.

[2]From end-2005 nonperforming loans are loans with payments overdue more than 60 days. Until 2004 they are defined as loans in "substandard," "doubtful," and "loss" loan categories.

[3]Includes only loans to nonfinancial sector.

[4]Data prior to 2006 refer to Serbia and Montenegro. The numbers represent share of assets in the three lowest risk categories (C,D,E).

[5]Statistical break starting in 2002.

[6]The increase in nonperforming loans in 2003 reflects a revision in the official definition.

[7]Net of provisions. Loans are defined as the sum of claims on credit institutions, the public, and public sector entities.

[8]Gross doubtful debts.

[9]2006 figure is preliminary; for large banks and not strictly comparable with previous years.

[10]Commercial banks and six largest savings banks (five largest savings banks from 2006 due to a merger of two banks).

[11]Banking groups.

[12]For the 2001–04 period, nonperforming loans include only substandard loans and bad debts. For the 2005–06 period, the aggregate includes also loans overdue for more than 180 days.

[13]2006 data cover two of the large banks only; not strictly comparable with previous years.

[14]For 2005 and 2006, the figures are for the sample of institutions that are already complying with IAS, accounting as of December 2004 for about 87 percent of the usual aggregate considered.

[15]On a consolidated basis. Nonperforming loans are defined as credit to customers overdue.

[16]Data for the four large banking groups.

[17]Compromised assets ratio; includes reported nonperforming loans, restructured loans and foreclosed assets for the 16 largest banks. Not directly comparable to the other indicators in the table. Starting from 2005 the ratio is based on financial information for the 15 largest banks as of December 2005.

[18]Refers to loans classified "substandard" and below.

[19]Nonperforming assets ratio; includes nonperforming loans plus real and other properties owned or acquired. Not directly comparable to the other indicators in the table.

[20]Nonperforming loans to nonbank loans.

[21]All commercial banks (includes foreign branches).

[22]Classified loans excluding interest in suspense.

[23]Figures exclude loans in arrears that are covered by collateral.

[24]For the end of the fiscal year, i.e., March of the following calendar year; for all banks.

Table 25. Bank Provisions to Nonperforming Loans
(In percent)

	2002	2003	2004	2005	2006	2007	Latest
Latin America							
Argentina	73.8	79.2	102.9	125.1	130.2	132.3	March
Bolivia	63.7	74.0	84.3	81.1	90.7	88.4	March
Brazil	155.9	144.7	177.5	151.8	152.8	153.0	March
Chile	128.1	130.9	165.5	177.6	198.5	191.1	May
Colombia	86.5	98.5	149.2	167.3	153.6	140.9	May
Costa Rica[1]	102.6	145.9	122.6	153.0	162.2	145.9	May
Dominican Republic	68.2	65.6	102.4	127.6	144.7	131.7	March
Ecuador	131.4	127.3	119.0	143.7	182.7	174.6	May
El Salvador	115.1	129.8	129.8	130.0	116.4	129.8	March
Guatemala	. . .	. . .	. . .	43.2	39.6	38.0	March
Mexico	138.1	167.1	201.8	232.1	207.4	194.7	March
Panama	132.1	150.3	149.4	116.2	127.9	. . .	September
Paraguay	46.6	54.8	54.6	57.7	59.1	59.6	January
Peru	69.1	67.1	68.7	80.3	100.3	104.3	March
Uruguay[1]	58.3	91.4	106.8	118.8	218.6	296.2	May
Venezuela	97.9	103.7	130.2	196.3	229.1	194.5	April
Emerging Europe							
Albania	. . .	. . .	. . .	. . .	. . .	. . .	. . .
Belarus	15.8	29.9	32.4	48.4	51.3	. . .	December
Bosnia and Herzegovina	. . .	. . .	. . .	. . .	. . .	. . .	. . .
Bulgaria[2]	59.6	50.0	48.5	45.3	47.6	. . .	September
Croatia	68.0	60.6	62.3	60.0	61.5	62.5	March
Czech Republic	77.5	76.7	69.4	63.2	62.2	. . .	September
Estonia	130.6	214.5	276.9	215.0	153.6	. . .	November
Hungary	50.8	47.3	51.3	54.4	53.5	. . .	December
Israel	. . .	. . .	. . .	. . .	. . .	. . .	. . .
Latvia	78.3	89.4	99.1	98.8	116.6	122.8	March
Lithuania	. . .	. . .	. . .	. . .	. . .	. . .	. . .
Macedonia, FYR	. . .	. . .	. . .	. . .	. . .	. . .	. . .
Montenegro	. . .	. . .	77.3	67.4	78.8	99.0	March
Poland	56.3	53.4	61.3	61.6	57.8	. . .	September
Romania[3]	. . .	33.5	34.3	31.4	32.0	. . .	September
Russia[4]	112.5	118.0	139.5	156.3	159.3	. . .	September
Serbia[5]	. . .	54.0	58.9	47.8	. . .	. . .	September
Slovak Republic	82.5	85.8	86.4	85.1	99.0	. . .	September
Turkey[6]	64.2	88.6	88.1	89.8	90.8	. . .	December
Ukraine	37.0	22.3	21.1	25.0	23.1	20.8	March
Western Europe							
Austria[7]	65.8	68.0	70.8	71.5	64.1	. . .	December
Belgium	51.8	52.8	54.2	51.6	52.4	. . .	June
Denmark	66.5	63.0	66.0	75.7	. . .	. . .	December
Finland	66.8	77.7	78.5	85.8	. . .	. . .	December
France	58.4	57.7	57.6	59.7	58.7	. . .	June
Germany	. . .	. . .	. . .	. . .	. . .	. . .	. . .
Greece	46.9	49.9	51.4	61.9	60.9	. . .	June
Iceland[8]	66.8	77.5	80.9	112.9	. . .	. . .	December
Ireland	105.0	90.0	70.0	50.0	. . .	. . .	December
Italy[9]	. . .	. . .	. . .	. . .	46.0	. . .	December
Luxembourg	. . .	. . .	. . .	. . .	. . .	. . .	. . .
Malta	. . .	. . .	. . .	. . .	. . .	. . .	. . .
Netherlands[8]	65.2	74.1	69.6	65.4	. . .	. . .	December
Norway[8]	63.1	59.1	65.1	51.5	. . .	. . .	December
Portugal[10,11]	62.8	73.0	83.4	79.0	80.0	. . .	December
Spain	197.2	245.4	219.6	251.8	. . .	. . .	December
Sweden[12]	71.5	73.9	78.9	84.7	78.5	79.9	July
Switzerland	89.4	89.9	90.9	116.0	122.6	. . .	December
United Kingdom[8]	75.0	71.2	64.5	56.1	. . .	. . .	December

Table 25 *(concluded)*

	2002	2003	2004	2005	2006	2007	Latest
Asia							
Bangladesh	...	18.3	18.9	25.3	26.3	...	June
China	...	...	...	...	...	...	...
Hong Kong SAR	...	...	...	...	...	...	...
India	...	46.4	56.6	60.3	58.9	...	March
Indonesia	130.0	146.5	158.7	82.2	99.7	105.6	March
Korea	89.6	84.0	104.5	131.4	175.2	177.7	March
Malaysia	38.1	38.9	41.0	45.4	50.7	55.9	June
Philippines	30.1	30.9	33.2	38.3	37.4	36.2	March
Singapore	61.2	64.9	76.0	80.9	89.5	94.4	March
Thailand	62.9	72.8	79.8	83.7	79.4	...	September
Middle East and Central Asia							
Armenia	32.1	34.3	77.0	70.7	64.3	54.4	June
Egypt	62.3	57.0	60.2	61.5	68.2	...	December
Georgia	...	...	...	...	...	...	...
Jordan[13]	50.6	51.9	63.8	78.4	80.0	...	December
Kazakhstan	...	...	...	...	...	...	...
Kuwait	64.3	77.7	82.5	107.2	100.6	...	September
Lebanon	...	...	57.3	63.3	72.0	73.0	February
Morocco	54.7	54.9	59.3	67.1	71.2	...	December
Oman	75.6	59.8	75.3	72.7	77.6	...	June
Pakistan	60.6	63.9	70.4	76.7	77.8	...	September
Saudi Arabia	110.4	136.0	164.0	178.0	...	...	December
Tunisia	43.9	43.1	45.8	46.4	49.2	...	December
United Arab Emirates	87.5	88.5	94.6	95.7	98.2	...	December
Sub-Saharan Africa							
Gabon	66.5	78.8	78.4	80.7	84.5	...	December
Ghana	...	...	...	...	...	...	...
Kenya	73.8	79.2	102.9	115.6	115.6	...	September
Lesotho	...	...	...	...	...	...	...
Mozambique	...	...	...	...	...	...	...
Namibia	...	...	...	...	...	...	...
Nigeria	...	...	...	...	...	...	...
Rwanda	...	58.4	60.2	56.7	...	...	December
Senegal	70.5	75.3	75.7	75.4	56.4	...	August
Sierra Leone	84.2	65.0	56.6	44.2	...	...	December
South Africa	46.0	54.2	61.3	64.3	...	...	December
Swaziland	...	...	...	...	...	...	...
Uganda	81.5	76.5	97.8	103.8	93.7	...	June
Other							
Australia	106.2	131.8	182.9	203.0	204.5	...	September
Canada	41.1	43.5	47.7	49.3	55.3	...	September
Japan[14]	...	23.9	26.8	31.4	30.3	...	March
United States	123.7	140.4	168.1	155.0	137.2	129.9	March

Sources: National authorities; and IMF staff estimates.

Note: Due to differences in national accounting, taxation, and supervisory regimes, FSI data are not strictly comparable across countries.

[1]Banking sector excludes offshore banks in Costa Rica, and the state mortgage bank in Uruguay.

[2]Provisions to nonstandard loans.

[3]Nonperforming loans reflect unadjusted exposure to loans classified as "loss," "doubtful," and "substandard." The steady level of nonperforming loans in the face of growing credit partly reflects Romania's relatively conservative classification and provisioning requirements. Provisioning requirements, net of collateral, are 100 percent for loss, 50 percent for doubtful.

[4]Change in definition in 2004; not strictly comparable with previous years.

[5]Data prior to 2006 refer to Serbia and Montenegro.

[6]Statistical break starting in 2002.

[7]2006 data cover two of the large banks only; not strictly comparable with previous years.

[8]Large banks.

[9]Banking groups.

[10]For 2005 and 2006, the figures are for the sample of institutions that are already complying with IAS, accounting as of December 2004 for about 87 percent of the usual aggregate considered.

[11]On a consolidated basis. Nonperforming loans are defined as credit to customers overdue.

[12]Data for the four large banking groups.

[13]Provisions to classified loans net of interest in suspense.

[14]For the end of the fiscal year, i.e., March of the following calendar year; coverage of nonperforming loans by provisions for all banks.

Table 26. Bank Return on Assets
(In percent)

	2002	2003	2004	2005	2006	2007	Latest
Latin America							
Argentina	−8.9	−3.0	−0.5	0.9	2.0	2.1	March
Bolivia	0.1	0.3	−0.1	0.7	1.3	1.1	March
Brazil[1]	2.1	1.5	1.9	2.5	2.5	2.1	March
Chile	1.1	1.3	1.2	1.3	1.3	1.2	May
Colombia	1.1	1.9	2.8	2.8	3.0	2.2	May
Costa Rica[1,2]	1.8	2.1	2.0	2.5	2.5	2.6	May
Dominican Republic	2.5	−0.1	1.9	1.8	1.9	2.5	March
Ecuador	1.5	1.4	1.5	1.6	2.0	2.6	May
El Salvador	1.1	1.1	1.0	1.2	1.5	1.5	March
Guatemala	0.8	1.1	1.3	1.6	1.2	1.5	March
Mexico[1]	0.7	1.6	1.8	2.7	3.1	3.2	March
Panama[1]	0.5	2.1	2.3	2.1	1.7	1.8	March
Paraguay[1]	1.0	0.4	1.7	2.1	3.0	4.0	January
Peru	0.8	1.1	1.2	2.2	2.2	2.4	March
Uruguay[2]	−25.3	−1.1	−0.1	0.7	1.2	1.7	May
Venezuela	5.3	6.2	5.9	3.7	3.0	2.4	April
Emerging Europe							
Albania	. . .	1.2	1.3	1.4	1.4	. . .	December
Belarus	1.0	1.5	1.5	1.3	1.7	. . .	December
Bosnia and Herzegovina	−0.3	0.4	0.7	0.7	0.9	. . .	December
Bulgaria	2.1	2.4	2.1	2.1	2.2	. . .	December
Croatia	1.6	1.6	1.7	1.6	1.5	1.6	March
Czech Republic	1.2	1.2	1.3	1.4	1.2	1.3	March
Estonia[1]	1.6	1.7	2.1	2.0	1.7	1.3	March
Hungary	1.4	1.5	2.0	2.0	1.9	. . .	December
Israel	0.3	0.7	1.0	1.1	1.0	1.2	March
Latvia	1.5	1.4	1.7	2.1	2.1	2.1	March
Lithuania[3]	0.9	1.2	1.3	1.1	1.5	. . .	December
Macedonia, FYR[4]	0.4	0.5	0.6	1.2	1.8	1.7	March
Montenegro	. . .	. . .	−0.3	0.8	1.1	1.5	March
Poland	0.5	0.5	1.4	1.7	2.1	. . .	June
Romania[5]	2.7	2.7	2.5	1.9	1.7	. . .	September
Russia	2.6	2.6	2.9	3.2	3.2	0.8	April
Serbia[6]	−8.4	−0.3	−1.2	1.1	1.7	2.1	June
Slovak Republic	1.2	1.2	1.2	1.2	1.3	. . .	December
Turkey[7]	1.2	2.4	2.3	1.6	2.4	. . .	December
Ukraine	1.2	1.0	1.1	1.3	1.6	1.6	March
Western Europe							
Austria[8]	0.2	0.3	0.6	0.6	0.7	. . .	September
Belgium[9]	0.5	0.5	0.6	0.7	1.1	. . .	June
Denmark	0.7	0.9	0.9	1.0	1.0	. . .	December
Finland[10]	0.6	0.7	0.8	0.9	1.0	. . .	December
France	0.5	0.4	0.5	0.6	. . .	. . .	December
Germany[11]	0.1	−0.1	0.1	0.3	0.5	. . .	June
Greece	0.5	0.6	0.3	0.9	1.2	. . .	June
Iceland	1.1	1.3	1.8	2.3	2.6	. . .	December
Ireland	1.0	0.9	1.0	1.4	. . .	. . .	December
Italy	0.5	0.5	0.6	0.7	0.8	. . .	December
Luxembourg	0.7	0.6	0.7	0.7	0.9	. . .	December
Malta	. . .	. . .	1.3	1.4	1.1	. . .	December
Netherlands	0.5	0.5	0.4	0.4	0.4	. . .	September
Norway	0.4	0.6	0.9	0.9	0.8	. . .	December
Portugal[12]	0.7	0.8	0.8	0.8	1.0	. . .	December
Spain	0.9	0.9	0.9	0.9	1.0	. . .	December
Sweden[13]	0.7	0.7	0.9	1.0	1.0	1.0	July
Switzerland[9]	0.5	0.7	0.8	0.9	0.9	. . .	December
United Kingdom[1]	0.4	0.6	0.7	0.8	0.5	. . .	December

Table 26 *(concluded)*

	2002	2003	2004	2005	2006	2007	Latest
Asia							
Bangladesh	0.5	0.5	0.7	0.6	0.8	...	December
China[14]	...	...	0.8	0.8	0.9	...	December
Hong Kong SAR[15]	2.1	1.9	1.7	1.7	1.8	1.8	March
India	0.8	1.0	1.1	0.9	0.9	...	June
Indonesia[1]	1.4	2.6	3.5	2.6	2.6	2.7	March
Korea	0.6	0.2	0.9	1.3	1.1	1.1	March
Malaysia[1]	1.3	1.3	1.4	1.4	1.3	...	September
Philippines	0.8	1.1	0.9	1.1	1.3	1.0	March
Singapore	0.8	1.0	1.2	1.2	1.4	1.4	March
Thailand[1]	...	...	1.7	1.9	2.3	...	September
Middle East and Central Asia							
Armenia	−6.4	2.7	3.2	3.1	3.6	3.6	June
Egypt	0.5	0.5	0.6	0.5	0.9	...	September
Georgia	4.3	3.9	1.9	3.0	2.5	...	June
Jordan	0.6	0.7	1.1	2.0	1.7	...	December
Kazakhstan[1]	2.0	2.0	1.4	1.8	1.4	...	December
Kuwait	1.8	2.0	2.5	3.0	2.6	...	September
Lebanon	0.6	0.7	0.7	0.7	0.9	0.9	February
Morocco	0.3	−0.2	0.8	0.5	1.3	...	December
Oman	1.5	0.3	1.9	2.7	1.5	...	June
Pakistan[1]	0.9	1.8	1.9	2.8	3.1	...	September
Saudi Arabia	2.3	2.3	2.5	3.7	4.3	...	December
Tunisia	0.7	0.6	0.4	0.6	0.2	...	June
United Arab Emirates	2.2	2.3	2.1	2.7	2.3	...	December
Sub-Saharan Africa							
Gabon	1.8	0.7	2.7	...	...	...	December
Ghana	6.8	6.2	5.8	4.6	4.3	...	December
Kenya[1]	−8.9	−2.9	−0.5	1.0	...	...	December
Lesotho	...	...	3.0	2.0	1.0	...	March
Mozambique	1.6	1.2	1.4	1.8	2.3	...	June
Namibia	4.5	3.6	2.1	3.5	2.9	...	June
Nigeria	2.4	1.7	3.1	0.5	0.3	...	December
Rwanda	−5.0	1.4	2.2	1.5	...	...	December
Senegal	1.8	1.8	1.8	...	...	...	December
Sierra Leone	10.0	10.5	9.7	7.9	...	...	December
South Africa	0.4	0.8	1.3	1.2	1.4	1.4	March
Swaziland	...	4.0	3.0	3.0	4.0	...	September
Uganda	2.7	4.5	4.3	3.6	3.5	...	June
Other							
Australia[9]	1.4	1.6	1.5	1.8	...	...	December
Canada	0.4	0.7	0.8	0.7	1.0	...	October
Japan[16]	−0.7	−0.1	0.2	0.5	0.4	...	March
United States	1.3	1.4	1.3	1.3	1.3	1.2	March

Sources: National authorities; and IMF staff estimates.
Note: Due to differences in national accounting, taxation, and supervisory regimes, FSI data are not strictly comparable across countries.
[1] Before tax.
[2] Banking sector excludes offshore banks in Costa Rica, and the state mortgage bank in Uruguay.
[3] Net income before extraordinary items and taxes to average total assets.
[4] Adjusted for unallocated provisions for potential loan losses.
[5] Statistical break starting in 2003.
[6] Data prior to 2006 refer to Serbia and Montenegro.
[7] Statistical break starting in 2002.
[8] Starting in 2004 data reported on a consolidated basis.
[9] Gross profits.
[10] 2001 adjusted for large intra-financial conglomerate transactions.
[11] Simple average for large banks in 2006; not strictly comparable with previous years.
[12] For 2005 and 2006 the figures are for the sample of institutions that are already complying with IAS, accounting as of December 2004 for about 87 percent of the usual aggregate considered.
[13] Data for the four large banking groups.
[14] Simple average for the reformed state-owned commercial banks (two banks in 2004, three banks in 2005 and 2006). Aggregate data not available.
[15] Net interest margin, not comparable with the other indicators in the table.
[16] For the end of the fiscal year, i.e., March of the following calendar year; all banks.

Table 27. Bank Return on Equity
(In percent)

	2002	2003	2004	2005	2006	2007	Latest
Latin America							
Argentina	−59.2	−22.7	−3.8	7.2	15.0	15.7	March
Bolivia	0.7	2.8	−1.2	6.4	13.3	12.7	March
Brazil[1]	22.1	16.3	19.3	25.2	25.2	21.6	March
Chile	14.4	16.7	16.7	17.9	18.6	17.4	May
Colombia	9.6	16.9	23.2	22.5	25.9	19.4	May
Costa Rica[1,2]	17.1	19.5	20.7	25.0	24.4	24.3	May
Dominican Republic	23.7	−1.2	22.1	19.3	19.7	26.2	March
Ecuador	15.4	14.7	16.5	18.5	23.1	24.7	May
El Salvador	12.2	11.5	10.9	11.8	14.6	14.6	March
Guatemala	8.5	12.2	14.0	19.1	15.1	17.1	March
Mexico[1]	7.9	16.1	17.2	24.4	26.2	23.5	March
Panama	. . .	16.9	16.7	15.7	18.5	. . .	March
Paraguay[1]	9.0	4.5	18.3	22.6	31.7	33.7	January
Peru	8.3	10.7	11.6	22.2	23.9	25.8	March
Uruguay[2]	−70.0	−15.3	−0.9	7.6	12.7	18.6	May
Venezuela	35.6	44.0	45.2	32.2	31.6	29.9	April
Emerging Europe							
Albania	. . .	19.5	21.1	22.2	20.2	. . .	December
Belarus	6.5	8.4	7.8	6.8	9.6	. . .	December
Bosnia and Herzegovina	2.5	3.4	5.8	6.2	8.5	. . .	December
Bulgaria	14.9	22.7	20.6	22.1	24.4	. . .	December
Croatia	13.7	14.1	16.1	15.1	13.0	12.3	March
Czech Republic	27.4	21.2	22.5	23.4	19.4	19.5	September
Estonia	14.7	14.1	20.0	21.0	19.8	21.2	March
Hungary	16.2	19.3	25.3	24.7	24.3	. . .	December
Israel	6.1	14.1	17.9	19.4	17.6	19.7	March
Latvia	16.4	16.7	21.4	27.1	26.3	28.5	March
Lithuania[3]	9.1	11.8	13.5	13.8	21.3	. . .	December
Macedonia, FYR[4]	2.0	2.3	3.1	7.5	12.3	12.7	March
Montenegro	. . .	. . .	−1.4	5.3	6.8	12.5	March
Poland	5.2	5.4	17.1	21.9	21.0	25.6	June
Romania	. . .	20.0	19.3	15.4	13.9	. . .	September
Russia	18.0	17.8	20.3	24.2	26.3	6.6	April
Serbia[5]	−60.6	−1.2	−5.3	6.7	10.0	12.8	June
Slovak Republic	11.5	10.8	11.9	16.9	16.6	. . .	December
Turkey[6]	10.6	18.8	16.7	11.9	21.5	. . .	December
Ukraine	8.0	7.6	8.4	10.4	13.5	12.7	March
Western Europe							
Austria[7]	5.2	7.0	14.8	14.8	13.6	. . .	September
Belgium[8]	17.1	17.1	21.1	23.8	17.7	. . .	June
Denmark	12.1	15.4	13.7	16.3	17.1	. . .	December
Finland[9]	10.7	11.3	12.4	10.5	10.6	. . .	June
France	9.1	8.5	10.6	11.9	. . .	. . .	December
Germany	2.9	−1.5	1.9	9.0	. . .	. . .	December
Greece	6.8	8.9	5.6	16.2	21.7	. . .	June
Iceland[10]	18.1	22.1	30.9	41.7	39.1	. . .	December
Ireland	18.0	17.8	20.7	21.8	. . .	. . .	December
Italy	7.1	7.4	9.3	9.7	11.5	. . .	December
Luxembourg	36.4	34.9	39.8	37.8	55.6	. . .	December
Malta	. . .	. . .	16.6	20.8	12.6	. . .	December
Netherlands	10.9	14.0	16.0	16.0	15.9	. . .	September
Norway	6.2	9.6	14.6	18.0	15.7	. . .	December
Portugal[11]	11.7	13.9	12.8	14.5	15.6	. . .	December
Spain	12.1	13.2	14.1	16.9	19.9	. . .	December
Sweden[12]	10.0	12.3	14.6	17.4	18.6	18.2	July
Switzerland[8]	8.9	11.7	14.3	18.0	17.7	. . .	December
United Kingdom[1]	6.1	8.6	10.9	11.8	8.9	. . .	December

Table 27 *(concluded)*

	2002	2003	2004	2005	2006	2007	Latest
Asia							
Bangladesh	11.6	9.8	13.0	12.4	14.1	. . .	December
China[13]	. . .	. . .	13.7	15.1	14.8	. . .	December
Hong Kong SAR[14]	17.2	17.8	20.3	19.1	. . .	. . .	December
India	15.3	18.8	20.8	13.3	12.7	. . .	March
Indonesia[15]	. . .	25.3	37.1	32.3	33.2	35.5	March
Korea	10.9	3.4	15.2	18.4	14.6	. . .	December
Malaysia[14]	16.7	17.1	16.6	14.1	. . .	. . .	December
Philippines	5.8	8.5	7.1	8.8	10.6	8.3	March
Singapore	7.6	8.7	11.6	11.2	13.7	13.8	March
Thailand	4.2	10.5	16.8	14.2	15.1	. . .	September
Middle East and Central Asia							
Armenia	−113.4	14.4	18.4	15.5	15.9	15.6	June
Egypt	8.9	9.8	10.6	9.6	17.4	. . .	September
Georgia	15.3	15.0	7.9	15.0	15.2	. . .	June
Jordan	9.7	10.9	15.2	24.3	15.9	. . .	December
Kazakhstan[1]	13.8	14.2	11.2	14.1	10.9	. . .	December
Kuwait	17.4	18.6	20.9	22.9	21.6	. . .	September
Lebanon	9.4	10.9	9.3	11.0	10.6	9.8	February
Morocco	1.9	−2.1	10.9	6.3	17.4	. . .	December
Oman	11.0	1.7	12.9	16.6	. . .	. . .	June
Pakistan[1]	21.1	35.4	30.5	38.2	38.2	. . .	September
Saudi Arabia	21.0	22.7	24.3	28.5	30.5	. . .	December
Tunisia	7.6	7.3	5.1	6.9	9.1	. . .	June
United Arab Emirates	15.6	16.4	18.6	22.5	18.0	. . .	December
Sub-Saharan Africa							
Gabon	11.8	14.4	17.1	. . .	. . .	. . .	December
Ghana	36.9	32.7	33.7	23.6	24.2	. . .	December
Kenya	−59.2	−22.7	−4.2	3.1	. . .	. . .	September
Lesotho	. . .	. . .	27.0	15.0	7.0	. . .	March
Mozambique	22.1	16.3	18.7	27.4	32.8	. . .	June
Namibia	59.8	43.2	24.2	45.6	34.9	. . .	June
Nigeria	28.1	19.8	27.4	7.2	1.9	. . .	December
Rwanda	−125.3	31.1	21.6	16.5	. . .	. . .	December
Senegal	21.1	22.1	17.6	. . .	. . .	. . .	December
Sierra Leone	. . .	67.1	73.2	52.5	. . .	. . .	December
South Africa	5.2	11.6	16.2	15.2	18.3	18.6	March
Swaziland	. . .	29.0	20.0	20.0	20.0	. . .	September
Uganda	24.6	33.1	32.9	. . .	. . .	. . .	December
Other							
Australia[8]	20.2	24.2	22.8	25.3	. . .	. . .	December
Canada	9.3	14.7	16.7	14.9	20.9	. . .	October
Japan[16]	−19.5	−2.7	4.1	11.3	18.5	. . .	March
United States	14.1	15.0	13.2	12.7	12.3	11.4	March

Sources: National authorities; and IMF staff estimates.

Note: Due to differences in national accounting, taxation, and supervisory regimes, FSI data are not strictly comparable across countries.

[1]Before tax.

[2]Banking sector excludes offshore banks in Costa Rica, and the state mortgage bank in Uruguay.

[3]Capital is defined as bank shareholders' equity and foreign bank branches funds received from the head office. Net income before extraordinary items and taxes.

[4]Adjusted for unallocated provisions for potential loan losses.

[5]Data prior to 2006 refer to Serbia and Montenegro.

[6]Statistical break starting in 2002.

[7]Starting in 2004 data reported on a consolidated basis.

[8]Gross profits.

[9]2001 adjusted for large intra-financial conglomerate transactions.

[10]Commercial banks and six largest savings banks (five largest savings banks from 2006 due to a merger of two banks).

[11]For 2005 and 2006, the figures are for the sample of institutions that are already complying with IAS, accounting as of December 2004 for about 87 percent of the usual aggregate considered.

[12]Data for the four large banking groups.

[13]Simple average for the reformed state-owned commercial banks (two banks in 2004, three banks in 2005 and 2006). Aggregate data are not available.

[14]2005 figure on a domestic consolidation basis; not strictly comparable with previous years.

[15]Financial sector.

[16]For the end of the fiscal year, i.e., March of the following calendar year; all banks.

World Economic and Financial Surveys

This series (ISSN 0258-7440) contains biannual, annual, and periodic studies covering monetary and financial issues of importance to the global economy. The core elements of the series are the *World Economic Outlook* report, usually published in April and September, the semiannual *Global Financial Stability Report,* and the semiannual Regional Economic Outlooks published by the IMF's area departments. Occasionally, studies assess international trade policy, private market and official financing for developing countries, exchange and payments systems, export credit policies, and issues discussed in the *World Economic Outlook.* Please consult the IMF *Publications Catalog* for a complete listing of currently available World Economic and Financial Surveys.

World Economic Outlook: A Survey by the Staff of the International Monetary Fund

The *World Economic Outlook,* published twice a year in English, French, Spanish, and Arabic, presents IMF staff economists' analyses of global economic developments during the near and medium term. Chapters give an overview of the world economy; consider issues affecting industrial countries, developing countries, and economies in transition to the market; and address topics of pressing current interest.

Annual subscription: $94.00
Published twice yearly. Paperback.
ISSN: 0256-6877. **Stock# WEOSEA**
Available in English, French, Spanish, and Arabic.

Global Financial Stability Report

The *Global Financial Stability Report,* published twice a year, examines trends and issues that influence world financial markets. It focuses on current market conditions, highlighting issues of financial imbalances, and of a structural nature, that could pose risks to financial market stability and sustained market access by emerging market borrowers. The report is designed to deepen understanding of international capital flows, which play a critical role as an engine of world economic growth.

Annual subscription: $94.00
Published twice yearly. Paperback. **Stock# GFSREA**

Regional Economic Outlooks

These in-depth studies of the Asia and Pacific, Europe, Middle East and Central Asia, sub-Saharan Africa, and Western Hemisphere regions drill down to specific regional economic and financial developments and trends—bringing the unique resources, experience, and perspective of the IMF to bear. While near-term responses to exogenous shocks, policies for growth, and the effectiveness of financial policies get center-stage examination, the reports also consider vulnerabilities and opportunities developing in the wings.

Individual copies of the Regional Economic Outlooks are available at $31.00 (academic rate: $26.00). Please visit www.imfbookstore.org/REOs or contact publications@imf.org for further information on all REO subscription packages.

Emerging Local Securities and Derivatives Markets

by Donald Mathieson, Jorge E. Roldos, Ramana Ramaswamy, and Anna Ilyina

The volatility of capital flows since the mid-1990s has sparked an interest in the development of local securities and derivatives markets. This report examines the growth of these markets in emerging market countries and the key policy issues that have arisen as a result.

$42.00 (academic rate: $35.00); paper.
2004. ISBN 1-58906-291-4. **Stock# WEOEA0202004.**

Official Financing: Recent Developments and Selected Issues

by a staff team in the Policy Development and Review Department led by Martin G. Gilman and Jian-Ye Wang

This study provides information on official financing for developing countries, with the focus on low-income countries. It updates the 2001 edition and reviews developments in direct financing by official and multilateral sources.

$42.00 (academic rate: $35.00); paper.
2003. ISBN 1-58906-228-0. **Stock# WEOEA0132003.**
2001. ISBN 1-58906-038-5. **Stock# WEOEA0132001.**

Exchange Arrangements and Foreign Exchange Markets: Developments and Issues
by a staff team led by Shogo Ishii

This study updates developments in exchange arrangements during 1998–2001. It also discusses the evolution of exchange rate regimes based on de facto policies since 1990, reviews foreign exchange market organization and regulations in a number of countries, and examines factors affecting exchange rate volatility.

ISSN 0258-7440
$42.00 (academic rate: $35.00)
March 2003. ISBN 1-58906-177-2. **Stock# WEOEA0192003.**

Available by series subscription or single title (including back issues); academic rate available only to full-time university faculty and students. For earlier editions please inquire about prices.

The IMF *Catalog of Publications* is available on-line at the Internet address listed below.

Please send orders and inquiries to:
International Monetary Fund, Publication Services, 700 19th Street, N.W.
Washington, D.C. 20431, U.S.A.
Tel.: (202) 623-7430   Telefax: (202) 623-7201
E-mail: publications@imf.org
Internet: http://www.imf.org/external/pubind.htm